Looking West

Contemporary Ethnography

Series Editors
Dan Rose
Paul Stoller

A complete list of books in the series
is available from the publisher.

Looking West

John D. Dorst

PENN

University of Pennsylvania Press

Philadelphia

10 9 8 7 6 5 4 3 2 1

Published by
University of Pennsylvania Press
Philadelphia, Pennsylvania 19104-4011

Library of Congress Cataloging-in-Publication Data

Dorst, John Darwin.
Looking West / John D. Dorst.
    p.   cm. — (Contemporary ethnography)
Includes bibliographical references (p.   ) and index.
ISBN 0-8122-3173-2 (cloth : alk. paper). — ISBN 0-8122-1440-4 (pbk. : alk. paper)
1. Human geography—West (U.S.)   2. Ethnology—West (U.S.)   3. Folklore—West (U.S.)
4. West (U.S.)—Social life and customs.   I. Title.   II. Series.
GF504.W35D67   1999
978—dc21   98-37212
                                                                CIP

GF
504
.W35
D67
1999

For
Holly, who agreed to come along
and
Jesse and Emma, who arrived later

Contents

Figures

Introduction

I think we took around two thousand yearling steers. And wilder than hell, long yearlings. And we drove them through the Indian Reservation up there, the Beatty Reservation, over to, what's the name of that cockeyed town up there . . . Klamath Falls. We trailed 'em from Beatty Reservation to Klamath Falls. That's about two hundred miles. They had an old rider from Nevada . . . . He was a pretty witty old guy. There's this big car come down there across the prairie there out on the prairie, big Lincoln or somethin', all flashy, and drove right up in front of them wild yearling steers, and it throwed 'em in a mill . . . . What the hell's his name, Billy, Bill Reed. Bill Reed rode over to him [in the car] and said, "You hadn't oughta ride in front of this cattle here." And they said, "We're kinda wondering how many cattle you had in that bunch." And he said, "Well, we had about four miles of 'em 'fore you run in front of 'em, now we got six acres."

—George Gearhart,
recorded for the Albany Co., Wyoming,
Social History Project,
Nov. 2, 1982 (lightly edited)

I own up freely that what follows is more of a six-acre than a four-mile proposition. Rather than taking an orderly line of march, its elements circle, jostle, and head off in multiple directions. Furthermore, the reader should be prepared to encounter here a textual herd much more heterogeneous than Bill Reed's two thousand yearlings. To keep the metaphor consistent, imagine those steers mixed with some buffalo and elk, and maybe even a few camels. Narratives and material culture, ethnographic details and some abstract theory, official institutions and folk environments, vernacular anecdotes and popular fiction, Lego blocks and Devils Tower National Monument—all these, among other things, amble their way through this study.

I must add immediately that I do not consider this heterogeneity a defect. In fact, it follows appropriately, even inevitably, from the approach I am taking. What has brought the disparate elements of this book together and "throwed 'em in a mill," the big Lincoln of this text, is the foundational premise that "discourse practices" inhabit all spheres of our lives and constitute for us—and through us—the operative regimes of truth in our historical moment. It is hardly news to say that a central mission of cultural studies is to track such discourses and their effects, especially as they bear upon the distribution of power. As Martin Jay reminds us, the Latin root of discourse, *discurrere*, means "running around in all directions." Discourses typically register as "often unsystematic, sometimes internally contradictory texture[s] of statements, associations, and metaphors that never fully cohere in a rigorous way" (Jay 1993:16). It should not be surprising, then, that the task of following a discursive trail requires one to ignore many of the fencelines that serve to organize academic research and writing in the traditional disciplines. Genres, modes, neatly bounded historical periods, cultural hierarchies, and those very academic disciplines themselves are all discursive practices. What keeps the textual herd of this study, spread out though it may be, at least within the confines of a single conceptual watershed is that I am attempting to follow one fairly distinct trail—the discourse of vision and display—as it meanders through the textual landscape of the modern American West, becoming especially visible at particular sites and historical moments. As will quickly be apparent, it is a path with many branchings.

With this Western "visuality" (Foster 1988: ix–x) as the topic on which I claim coherence for this book, it may be worth a little space here to identify a few recurring features of my own discursive practice in what follows. Students and practitioners of cultural studies methods will find these qualities familiar. Other readers, however, may find the nature of the arguments and the selection of evidence idiosyncratic at some points. In particular, I make some leaps of historical connection across normally accepted boundaries, such as those between conventional historical periods and between cultural domains within a single period. My justification is that the straightforward cause-and-effect logic that informs our commonsense notions of historical explanation does not always apply in the tracing of discourses. They require that we adopt a more dialectical way of thinking, one in which texts are not simply isolated as the products of a separate and prior human agency. We need the concept of a general "textuality" to guide our analysis, a concept according to which the institutions, agents, and material processes of history are recognized not only as the producers of discourse, the sources of texts, but also as fully discursive themselves, as textual effects (see Mowitt 1992 on the idea of textuality). While it may be difficult to hold both these positions in mind simultaneously, we can at least cultivate the ability to move easily between them and, more important, to recognize that thinking from one position in the dialectic does not annul the other, but only holds it in temporary suspension for the purpose of local analysis.

The personal anecdote I quote at the head of this Introduction is useful not just as a source of regionally appropriate metaphors. It also anticipates a recurring feature of my method. I will have recourse throughout to an unashamed reliance on local examples, apparent trivialities, vernacular expression, and marginal locales as important sources of evidence. In fact, the only extended analysis I offer of a widely known text is my discussion in Chapter 2 of that most classic of western novels, *The Virginian*, a book some no doubt consider quite marginal enough. Just about everything else I examine in detail will likely be unfamiliar to the majority of readers. My focus on discourse authorizes this predilection. Because discourses operate not just within the confines of bounded "works," but across whole fields of culture, the canonical text (in the narrow sense) loses its privilege as the object of analysis. The subtleties of discourse might sometimes play out more vividly, more complexly, or just plain more interestingly in out-of-the-way locales. It has long been a procedure of cultural studies to seek out marginal spaces, and this book hews to that tradition.

The authorization to reverse hierarchies, to make the trivial central, connects for me personally to another important feature of the broad agenda guiding me here, the insistence on thorough reflexivity. A good deal of this book concerns itself with material that might loosely be characterized as folkloric. That is to say, vernacular productions, unofficial expressions, traditional narratives, and so on figure prominently. I freely confess my bias toward such material and claim it on the basis of my professional training as a folklorist. What a cultural studies approach allows me to say is that my focus on this material does not need special justification. From here on I will simply take it for granted that the evanescent joke, the homemade yard display, or the gruesome migratory legend of swimming rattlesnakes, all of which figure in what follows, might be just as revealing as the canonical novel, the museum gallery, or the career of the famous historical figure, some of which also show up.

One corollary to this promotion of marginality deserves brief mention, since it is reflected frequently in what follows. It is simply that I make rather common use of small folk things as parables for large issues. It is a source of endless amazement to me how folk expression often compresses into very small spaces the most exquisite embodiments of whole domains of discourse. There are numerous occasions here where seemingly evanescent moments of vernacular production bear the weight of extensive analysis. The joke with which I begin Chapter 1, for example, seems to me a graceful expression in miniature of elements central to the whole visual array that occupies me throughout this study. I will be treating such small and obscure things with the seriousness and the assumption of significance normally afforded to "big" books, "important" people, and "historic" events.

*   *   *

Having begun to locate myself in relation to this study by acknowledging my professional inclinations as a folklorist, let me continue a little more concretely by considering the stool on which I am perched as I write these words. It stands fifty-six centimeters at its highest point and is supported by a quadripodal base, each leg terminating in a hexagonal foot formed of two welded-together teeth from a sickle bar, a now rather archaic type of mechanized hay cutting device. The seat of this stool, formed of a single piece of metal and lacking arms or back support, is painted in lime-green exterior enamel. Molded to conform to the curves of the human posterior and upper thigh, it is perforated with twenty-six ventilation holes of slightly variable dimension. These holes display a pleasing variety of minor deviations from precise circularity. This seat is taken from a long-outmoded haymaking device known as a "dump rake," a companion piece to the sickle bar from which the stool's feet are made. For $25.00 I purchased a pair of these items from Mr. Jake Dellos, who thought of them as "lawn furniture." Mr. Dellos lives near Worland, Wyoming, in a region known as the Big Horn Basin. He and his productions make their appearance in Chapter 5.

I am tempted to go on at some length about this stool as itself a parable of modes of production. The history of its manipulations and reframings spans a considerable spectrum of material life, from industrialized but pre-corporate agriculture, to leisure recreation (by way of folk art *bricolage*), and then to advanced capitalist reincarnation as an element in the apparatus of academic information technology, deployed in a self-consciously ironic mode as a chair at a computer terminal. Suffice it to say at this point that my writing stool provides not just a site of immediate textual production, but also a convenient datum point from which I can map a number of the connections through which I am personally implicated in the text that follows, implicated, that is, not just as author/producer, but equally as a textual product.

The stool sits in a northwest corner office of the building that houses the American Studies Program at the University of Wyoming. The campus is situated in the center of the town of Laramie, which sits in the southeast corner of the state and at the western base of the first mountain range one comes to when driving west on U.S. Interstate 80. A straight line running for about two hundred yards roughly northwest from the site of my writing stool intersects the building that houses the university's graduate school. As an academic sideline, the Graduate School Dean has conducted numerous living history exercises at Fort Laramie, a National Historic Site located on the North Platte River near the eastern border of the state. A dozen years ago I participated in one of these exercises. It sought to recreate life on a frontier military post in the 1870s, Fort Laramie having been an important way station on the Oregon Trail, a supply point during the "Indian Wars" period, and the site of important treaty negotiations. It was as a participant observer in this living history exercise that I began thinking about the construction of visual experience in the context of the contemporary American West, especially in relation to advanced capitalist mechanisms of display. That experience, of which there is an account in Chapter 3, constitutes one point of origin for this study.

Following the same northwestern trajectory through the university campus and out into the adjacent residential area of Laramie, one passes near the intersection of 7th and Gibbon Streets. The trim house on the northeast corner is surrounded on three sides by a visually arresting open-work fence constructed from a remarkable variety of tools and utensils, most with distinctly western associations, all welded into intricately designed panels set end to end around the property. The work of Mr. and Mrs. Floyd Young, this fence provides me a comparative example of folk display to set against Mr. Dellos's productions. It was in fact the first western "display environment" to attract my attention when I moved to Wyoming. As such, it constitutes another kind of remote starting point for this study.

Moving once again along our imaginary vector, and following it out some fifty miles across the Laramie Plains, we come to the little town of Medicine Bow, Wyoming. The welcome sign by the road bears the inscription, "When you call me that, *smile!*" This sign sits on the grounds of the Medicine Bow Museum, which consists of the old train depot and the so-called "Owen Wister Cabin." Directly across the road stands the impressive, multi-story, rusticated stone edifice of the Virginian Hotel. A town of only 389 residents, Medicine Bow nevertheless looms large in the mythological landscape of the American West. It is the site of the inaugural appearance of that national icon, the cowboy hero, at least in the modern romantic incarnation by which the world has come to know him in the twentieth century. This figure, the 1902 romance in which he makes his debut, and his principal designer, Owen Wister, are the focus of Chapter 2. It is my argument there that certain distinctive qualities of a Western discourse of looking are pervasive in Wister's work, and perhaps culturally emergent about the time of his writing. Housed in the archives of the University of Wyoming's American Heritage Center are the extensive journals Wister kept and the photographs he took on his western excursions, which began in 1885. One can discern in these documents the emergence of a modern "way of seeing" that anticipates the discourses embodied in late twentieth-century display sites.

Another fifty miles or so along our imaginary path through Wyoming brings us to the shores of the Alcova Reservoir, one of several holding bodies on the North Platte River system, and one among the numerous man-made reservoirs that constitute the only substantial bodies of water in the state. I pause here briefly because Alcova is the first site I heard associated with a grotesque migratory legend of aquatic rattlesnakes. I discuss this narrative in Chapter 1. Since encountering that first version, students in my folklore classes have reported the tale in association with several other reservoirs around the state. I spend some time on this story because it is a good example of how tendrils of a discourse may reach into obscure crannies or go underground, only to emerge in unexpected and not overtly connected places. This contemporary narrative, probably not "indigenous" to the American West, has no tangible connection to Owen Wister, much less to the display environments that occupy later chapters. Nevertheless, I will claim that its imagery resonates with the discursive practices of these other texts.

Following our northwest trajectory another hundred miles, bisecting the state diagonally, brings us into the Big Horn Basin and finally to within a few miles of Mr. Dellos's modest retirement property. And this site is itself not too far from the ranch on Gooseberry Creek where the Delloses spent some forty years in a hard-won existence not at all uncommon in the agricultural history of the American West. In his retirement Mr. Dellos has transformed the few acres around his house into a fantastic folk sculpture garden. This, rather than his "lawn furniture" and other money making productions, is Mr. Dellos's truly significant work, at least for my purposes here. As the embodiment of a Western discourse of display, this folk environment comes in for analysis in Chapter 5. And that brings me to the point of origin for my writing stool.

These selected stops along an imaginary vector through Wyoming convey something of the range of particular texts and sites that come in for analysis in what follows, but this brief journey also illustrates a general feature of the study I have embarked upon here. It might strain credulity that a line laid diagonally across the map of Wyoming, dividing it rather neatly into two roughly equal pieces, just happens to connect a series of discursively related sites. Isn't the selection artificial? Why privilege these places? Could not others do just as well?

The answer to all these questions of course is "yes." It is precisely the point that in looking at the operations of a whole discourse the possible locations where one might tap in are infinite. In the sense that I am using the term, discourses pervade the cultures that reproduce them (or are reproduced through them). We need to imagine such discourses as informing the whole textual landscape. To eyes positioned in a certain way, the operations of a discourse will be more visible at some points than others, like intermittent rock outcrops that indicate a connecting geological formation running beneath vast stretches of territory. If a discursive formation is truly significant to a given historical moment, one *should* expect to find its manifestations in all directions. This I believe to be the case with the discourse of looking that occupies me here. It states the obvious to say that the sites I subject to extended analysis are ones that seem to me deeply invested in this discursive formation, but it is also true that their selection *is* contingent, in the sense that they are things that have accreted over the last decade or so around my own position. They are the outcrops I have noticed, given my vantage point.

To illustrate how the position from which this book proceeds is inextricably bound up with the sites it purports to examine, I will mention here one other location we will visit. Falling along a vector different from the one I have traced above, it is the site that constitutes perhaps the most complete realization of the discourse that is my main concern. Were the intervening trees and buildings removed, I would be able to look west from my office window several miles across town to the Union Pacific Railroad yard, beyond which lies the Laramie River and then the Interstate. Sitting between the river and the highway is the Wyoming Territorial Prison and Old West Park, the newest of Wyoming's state historic sites. Its centerpiece is the expensively restored, rather handsome sandstone structure that served from 1872 until 1890 as the Wyoming territorial penitentiary, and thereafter for some years as the state prison. The avowed mission of the Territorial Park is to interpret the nineteenth-century history of Wyoming. My examination in Chapter 6 of this heritage theme park constitutes a kind of culmination to this study, since the WTP accommodates a remarkably dense intersection of the pathways forming the trail of Western visuality. When a nineteenth-century prison is reframed as a museum, we can be sure that a complex layering of this discourse is operating.

But the Wyoming Territorial Park is also important to this study because it is the place where I am myself most completely implicated in the larger textual processes I have been talking about. It is the place where I have the hardest time maintaining the fiction of detached observation. Several years ago I was asked to serve as the university representative, a mandated position, on the operating board of the non-profit corporation that governs the Park. While serving in this capacity I participated very directly in the ongoing construction of the discourse at this site. When I undertook the assignment as university representative, I had already been planning to make the Territorial Park part of my research, a fact which I attempted to make clear both to the university and to the president of the WTP board. It is impossible for me at this point to distinguish easily among the various roles and viewing positions I have occupied with regard to this site. And I confess here a certain ambivalence about the rhetorical stance I take in writing about it. It should be kept in mind that it is in my discussion of the Territorial Park that I come closest to realizing the cultural studies dictum that one should keep constantly aware of one's own implication in the discourse/practices under analysis. Or, to put it another way, this is the place where the arbitrary line between my own subject position and my textual construction of a site "out there" is most nearly erased. I find it, in terms of cultural studies theory, the ideal position to occupy, and in practice, the most difficult position from which to write.

To complete this preliminary inventory of the excursions we will be taking, I need to mention one other. Devils Tower National Monument is located some two-hundred-thirty-five miles on a direct line north and slightly east from the point where I currently sit. Lying on the western edge of the Black Hills, which spill over from South Dakota into the extreme northeastern corner of Wyoming, Devils Tower is a massive stump of striated, volcanic rock, perhaps most familiar as the landing site for those childlike aliens who descend from heaven in the techno-sublime mother ship of Stephen Spielberg's *Close Encounters of the Third Kind*. Designated in 1906 as the first National Monument, Devils Tower has recently been the site of controversy over landscape definition, control, and use. One aspect of this controversy has to do with how the Tower is viewed, quite literally. The visual order I am mainly concerned with in this study is a regionally coded manifestation of a much larger, even epochal system with nineteenth-century roots and twentieth-century florescence. It is a First World, initially Euro-American discursive practice. As we will see, in deploying the iconography of the America West this mode of visuality depicts non-Euro-Americans in various ways. But it does so for its own discursive purposes, not to acknowledge alternative ways of seeing. In the current controversies over Devils Tower we encounter one example of a post-colonial challenge to the dominant visuality, although the way this controversy plays out through institutional structures and pre-given terms of debate make for a much more complicated situation than can be captured through the simple dichotomies of dominant vs. marginalized or colonizer vs. subaltern.

*   *   *

All the excursions we are about to take, with the exception of a very brief, long-distance detour at the end, are confined to the boundaries of a geographically artificial entity, the almost square box of the state of Wyoming. Given that my focus in this study is on the textual construction of a visual practice, it seems quite fitting that this obviously constructed geographical unit should serve as my laboratory. In acknowledging the contingency and artifice of my geographical limits, in fact embracing these qualities as necessary conditions for a study of this sort, I also mean to make it clear that this is emphatically *not* a book about Wyoming—its culture, its people, its history, its landscape, and so forth. It is a book about a certain discursive practice that reveals itself at sites within the artificially imposed borders of this state. By the same token, this is not in any straightforward sense a book about the West as a region. As I will suggest in Chapter 1, the discourse that concerns me deploys the conventional iconography of the western landscape, the western atmosphere, western character types, and a whole host of other western paraphernalia to construct an apparatus of looking that is not itself inherently bound to an ethnographically definable place. It is a discourse that is western in its accouterments, in its dialect, perhaps in its historical emergence, but not in any simple geographic sense. The phenomena I will be giving accounts of are assimilable to much larger cultural systems that transcend all regional specificity. They are, in fact, concrete enactments of the now vast and pervasive consumer culture of the late twentieth century. Thus the ambiguity of the designation "Western," applying both to a distinct American region and to the world-historical concept of advanced capitalist civilization, is a useful confusion that I want to leave in place.

Nevertheless, it is also my contention that the ways of looking that characterize this "First World" of advanced consumer culture take on a heightened visibility *in* the American West as they are enacted in its regional display sites and institutions. The American far West is a region, perhaps more than any other in the United States, conceived precisely in visual terms. Both literally and metaphorically the open vistas and lucid, magnifying air of this West have made the act of looking a defining feature of how we experience it as an actual place. The optical discourse that stands at the heart of our advanced consumer social order is itself brought up close for inspection, sometimes in funny or offhand ways, in the vast text of the West.

Part I

Chapter One
Short Excursions
Some Moments of Western Looking

Two easterners (or tenderfeet, or tourists) are on a trip out West. They decide one day to head for a mountain range they see looming before them. Expecting a short drive, they find themselves traveling for hours without seeming to draw any nearer their goal. Finally, they spy up ahead an old man, an Indian it turns out, sitting on a fence beside the road. He's just perched there staring off into the distance. They pull over and the passenger leans out his window. "Excuse me," he says, "do you know how far it is to those mountains?" The old man says not a word. "I beg your pardon," the traveler shouts, "can you tell us how long it will take to get to those mountains over there?" Again, silence. His third try, issued at the top of his voice, still gets no response. "Well," says the passenger, turning to his companion, "I guess that Indian is farther away than we thought."[1]

As is so often the case among the seeming trivialities of folk humor, there lies packed into this little joke a rich collection of themes, images, stereotypes, and subtle implications. In fact, it can serve here as an expression in small of the issues that will concern me through the rest of this study. Combining it with a few other specimens that have come within my range of vision since settling in Wyoming, things largely drawn from the domains of folk and popular culture, I intend to offer in this chapter a kind of "home-grown" framework for thinking about my main topic: discourses of looking and display in the contemporary American West, especially discourses enacted in material form.

Our deluded travelers occupy a well-established and important role in this discursive or textual West. Their abstract function is to serve as *new viewers*, possessors of innocent eyes. As such, they are stymied by the unprecedented visual conditions of a West that seems both eminently visible and at the same time maddeningly beyond reach. In our conventional inventory of imaginary landscapes, the American far West is virtually defined by the quality of being open to view. It has no equal in its vastness of horizon or its dearth of those human obstructions that thwart the eye in other (especially eastern) places. How paradoxical it seems, then, that this very visibility becomes a source of visual misprision.

The perplexed tourists of this joke occupy the position of eternally unconsummated visual desire. They see vividly their object of desire and simultaneously misrecognize it. In fact, they misperceive it *because* of its vividness. And this object, the distant mountain range, is virtually the landscape emblem of the West. In following their distorted gaze, the travelers are doomed never to grasp the thing itself. Though elaborated in a great variety of different directions, as we shall see, these elements are at the core of the pattern of Western looking I am after here.

The joke depends, of course, on our awareness of a "real" optical illusion commonly encountered in the West: the atmospheric magnification of distant objects in the landscape so that they temporarily appear much closer than they actually are. Anyone who has spent time in the West is likely to have experienced a morning when the mountains do suddenly seem close enough to touch, or perhaps seen a preternaturally enlarged full moon hovering just above the horizon. These are tricks of vision accountable to empirical factors of atmospheric optics and the physiology and psychology of human perception. As material realities of "vision" they are amenable to scientific explanation. But when taken up into a narrative, the phenomenon described in this joke exists as a component of "visuality," a textual thing to be read rather than a simple fact to be verified (Bryson 1988: 91–92).

We will need a fuller analysis of this atmospheric distortion in terms of its textual properties, but first I want to complete a quick tour of the structure of visuality staged by our joke. Another of its components is a second viewing position, counterpart to and inversion of that represented by the frustrated easterners. For the purpose of abstract exposition, let us call it the position of the "eye that knows."[2] It is the position occupied of course by the silent Indian as he sits staring off into the distance, presumably toward those same mountains sought by the travelers. The economy of visual exchange played out among these positions is remarkably complex. Most important, there is a geometry of double vision at work here. The travelers see and misperceive the mountains, and they also see and misperceive the old man on the fence, or rather they misperceive the spaces these objects occupy. And these misperceptions are neatly symmetrical. They think the mountains are closer than they really are, and they conclude that the old Indian is farther away than *he* really is.

The mirror reflection of this naive, mystified looking is the old man's gaze, which is also double. He too sees the distant landscape, but in a very different way from the travelers. As the source of knowing vision, it

could be said that his sightline does not match theirs. And of course he
also "sees" them, or rather he sees their act of faulty seeing. An important element of the joke, both for its humor and for its relevance here,
is that the old man does not openly exchange looks with the tourists.
This is true in both the literal sense of not looking directly at them and
the figurative sense of not granting them the "line of sight" that would
allow access to the position he occupies, the position of the knowing eye
from which authoritative vision proceeds. He does not "put them in his
place" by demystifying the landscape for them.

To put this another way, the location of his gaze falls within the general domain of covert surveillance, and the object of his observation is
the fully exposed act of naive, deluded looking. At least in a metaphorical sense, he sees their eyes but they do not see his. Their mistake about
his location, source of the joke's punchline, is the folk narrative's literalization of the deeper fact that the naive gaze not only mistakes the
object of its desire, it also misperceives the gaze of an Other, taking it for
neutral, benign, and, most of all, directed at something remote rather
than at their own act of faulty looking.

One other feature of this narrative will complete my initial survey of
its visual elements. It is simply that the two viewing positions I have
identified—naive, occluded spectatorship and knowing, occulted surveillance—differ in their temporal arrangements. The former is motivated, that is, it moves in time. The latter does not. The tourists, impelled
by optical desire, drive through the landscape; the old Indian sits motionless. The difference symbolically represented in these motifs is an
important one, because it suggests that the two viewing positions are of
radically different orders, two fundamentally distinct *kinds* of eyes. It is a
bit misleading to describe the static gaze of the knowing, surveillant eye
as following a "line of sight." In fact, it has as its definitive property the
ability to survey the entire optical field in a timeless gaze. The old Indian
on the fence represents the unblinking Eye that sees uniformly in all
directions. It perceives in a perpetual, static glance the distant mountains, their optical distortion, the movement of the tourists, and, most
important, their mistaken seeing. In other words, the old Indian's visual
gesture represents the gaze of plenitude, of completion and fulfillment;
hence its stasis.

The travelers, on the other hand, occupy the fallen world of partial
vision in which the operations of mirage are omnipresent. Evanescence
is its fundamental condition and the constantly replenished sources of
desire are its motive force. What this leads us to, finally, in our reading of
the folk narrative is the recognition that, in coming upon the Indian, the
travelers have in fact reached their goal without knowing it. In the general iconography of the West, manifest through countless mass cultural

examples, the image of distant mountains carries with it a number of associations relevant here. The western mountains are the source of waters, the place of abundant game, and the repository of mineral wealth. They are also a place of refuge, where one may escape the terrible exposure of desert or prairie. Then, too, they are the locus of mystery, where hidden, perhaps uncanny forces are at play. All these associations are consistent with the symbolic identification of the distant mountains with the site of plenitude—fulfillment, mastery, the end of desire.

And in one other feature this symbolic connection is also at work. Mountains are the place of visual mastery. From their peaks the surrounding world may be surveyed—and surveilled. Although I will invoke it more directly below, it is worth mentioning here that what one art historian refers to as "the magisterial gaze," that is, the overview of the world from the elevated prospect of a mountaintop, is a trope deeply rooted in the iconography of American art (Boime 1991). What the uncannily vivid but unattainable mountains represent is precisely the completion of the ability to see everything, the achievement of *visual* plenitude.

With the elegant parsimony so often found in folk expression, this seemingly distant position is in fact the very one occupied by the old Indian on the fence. His is the position of the static, knowing eye, the visual plenum that the travelers desire but cannot see accurately. We know at the end of the joke that they will inevitably be moving on. All these confusions, literal and symbolic, of the faraway and the nearby, the delusions inherent in the desire for the location that is the end of visual desire, make this "trivial" folk text a small masterpiece in the discourse of Western looking.

*   *   *

Although remarkably efficient as a symbolic expression and a paradigm for what follows, this joke does not cover all the complexities of the visual discourse in question. The elements it displays, though basic, are only a starting point for examining the full range of discursive operations. It is not merely incidental, for example, that the iconic figure of the American Indian occupies the position of the knowing eye in this folk narrative. We will encounter this figure again at other sites in the landscape of Western looking. And it is also meaningful that this position can be occupied by other figures, such substitutions resulting in the rich textual variations inherently characteristic of active discourses.

In the interest of demonstrating some of these possibilities for variation, we might consider a second story. Not long after settling in Wyoming I encountered a localized comic anecdote that has stayed with me, perhaps as a ceremonial marker of my own arrival in the West. Appropriately enough, it begins with the appearance of the tenderfoot in Laramie:

On his first morning in town a visitor from the East looks out across the Laramie Basin to the Medicine Bow Mountains, a range commonly known as the Snowies. In the sparkling air of the new day they appear to stand but a few miles west of town. Inspired by this sight, the easterner announces to a number of locals gathered nearby that he has decided to take a morning stroll out to inspect these mountains. Strictly observing the western etiquette that one never stands between a tenderfoot and his folly, the locals smile and wave the newcomer on his way, never mentioning that in fact he has a hike of over thirty miles in front of him. The hours roll by and finally some of the more sentimentally inclined of the townspeople decide they had better go find the new arrival before he has to spend a night on the prairie. When they finally come upon him he is sitting down beside a small stream, easily stepped over, removing his shoes and rolling his pants as high as they will go. "Well," he says, in response to his rescuer's perplexity, "if those mountains are any indication, this little trickle is really a damn big river and I want to keep my clothes dry."[3]

The surface similarities between this anecdote and the previous joke are obvious: looking West to the vivid, shining mountains, the "natural" deceptiveness of the western landscape, the eastern tenderfoot who falls for it, the representatives of the West who are in on the joke and keep still. Even such minimal evidence as this single set of redundancies goes some way toward confirming that the joke is not an entirely isolated event, that there are in fact discursive forces at work in these stories.[4] But it is not just in these obvious correspondences that we may trace the patterns of a discourse. Rather it is through the combination of such continuities with subtle shifts, substitutions, and variations that discursive pathways are most visible. As I have emphasized in my Introduction, discourses are not just given, nor are they simply the result of some prior agency. They are themselves apparatuses of production. They are generative, adaptive, one might even say exploratory and experimental. The apparent stabilities and visible trends within a discourse are always local, inflected by immediate circumstances, in short, historically situated.

When we compare the two comic narratives, the most obvious difference is in who occupies the role of the knowing viewer. In the second story it is filled by "the townsfolk" instead of the old Indian. This difference is not trivial. It represents a diminution in the distance between the two viewing positions. For one thing, the townsfolk directly engage the new arrival. The tale sets them up explicitly as bemused spectators of the tenderfoot's delusion, even if he is not aware of being the object of this superior gaze. Whereas the stereotypic Indian often serves as the virtual embodiment of Otherness, underscored in the joke by the impenetrable covertness of his gaze, the townsfolk differ from the tenderfoot only in degree. In fact, one can imagine that many of them were once new arrivals themselves, and thus former possessors of the naive gaze. There is introduced, then, at least the shadow of initiation. One gets a sense from this tale, unlike the first one, that the newcomer is learning a lesson, implying that he may move toward the position of authoritative looking. The solicitude of the townsfolk in going to find the wanderer marks them as potential mentors.

This narrative suggests, perhaps, that the two viewing positions are not entirely inaccessible to one another. Whereas in the joke the utter difference between the two was marked by the contrast of motion and stasis, here the possessors of the authoritative gaze become mobilized themselves. In fact, they could be said to enact a second form of desire in their pursuit of the tenderfoot. They are concerned for the welfare of and go after the representative of unfulfilled desire, the possessor of the innocent eye. In symbolic terms, this action could fairly be considered the enactment of desire for their own former desire, a nostalgic impulse that is the inverse counterpart to the anticipated initiation of the tenderfoot into the wisdom of visual mastery over the western landscape.

What this story expresses, then, besides the basic elements it shares with the joke, is a recognition of the possibility for movement between positions within the structure of Western visuality. It thereby acknowledges a greater complexity in the relationships of desire than the first text would suggest. As we will see in a number of other places, the movement or change of places by participants in this economy of optical desire is an important feature of Western visuality. In particular, the complex interplay among the positions of surveillance, spectatorship, and spectacle is of greatest importance for our understanding of the display environments I will be examining in later chapters.

This second tale adds one further element to the mix. It introduces the western town as the place where the comic visual drama begins. The town functions here as a kind of viewing platform, which is to say, an element in an optical apparatus. In considering visual discourses, the material conditions that enable and constrain acts of looking are as important as the subjects and objects of the gaze and the narrative frameworks into which they are placed. As we shall see, various technologies of looking figure prominently in the mode of visuality under consideration here.

As a visual apparatus, then, the town is the analogue to the tourist's automobile and the Indian's fence. And here again we see a kind of merging of the two viewing positions. In the joke the contrast between the moving car from which the travelers see the mountains and the fixed fence that is the Indian's vantage underscore the contrast between the naive and the knowing gaze. The moving frame of the automobile windshield materially embodies the partial, distorted view, whereas the static, unframed prospect from the fence realizes a universality of vision. This difference is in some measure collapsed in the second narrative, where the town is the physical locus of both gazes, underscoring the lessening distance between viewing positions that we have seen in other aspects of the story. One might say the town is the frame or the stage that enables the spectatorship of both the greenhorn and the locals. However, there remains a fundamental difference between the objects seen by these two spectators. The tenderfoot sees "through the frame" of the town the uncannily vivid mountains. The townsfolk see "through the proscenium" of the town the comic spectacle of the tenderfoot's folly. This basic structure, one act of looking laid on top of another, is the most important continuity between the two stories and lies at the heart of the culturally rooted visual practice that concerns me.

*   *   *

Given the general approach I am taking in this study, determinations of simple before-and-after temporal relationships between particular texts are secondary to the global examination of discursive relationships. That the two narratives I have so far invoked are probably not genetically related in any direct way is rather beside the point. That they seem to draw on the same discursive gene pool is what matters. And if simple temporal sequence is relatively unimportant, by the same token, boundaries between genres or between modes of textual production may be temporarily bracketed as well. Discourses may well show themselves in the most disparate of cultural locations, creating connections between otherwise unlikely partners. In fact, the wider the range of manifestations, the more we can be sure of a given discourse's cultural force. It would be especially useful for my argument, then, to locate a text with obvious connections to the two folk narratives I have examined so far, but in quite a different cultural arena. And even better if this example were less evanescent and "marginal" than the pair of comic anecdotes I have more or less chanced to gather in as they happened to flit by.

Happily, such a text is close to hand, and in a place that many would agree is about as central to the larger, twentieth-century text of the West as one can get. We need only turn to the book widely identified as the premier inaugural document in the modern tradition of the popular western novel. I have already invoked *The Virginian* as the place where that supreme icon of the West, the cowboy hero, first makes his definitive appearance. I will return to this book in the next chapter for a more thorough examination of its complex deployment of Western visuality. But for immediate purposes I only want to point out that some elements I have identified as redundancies in our two vernacular tales are already in place in an early episode of this most classic of westerns. More than that, the context in which these elements occur make them stand out as truly archetypal.

Owen Wister's novel, published in 1902 under the full title *The Virginian: A Horseman of the Plains*, has usually been discussed in terms of its overt thematics, for example the struggle between the values of a civilized but increasingly decadent East and a virile but sometimes savage West, the passing away of the far western frontier, where there had briefly flowered, according to Wister's mythopoesis, the race virtues of Anglo-Saxon manhood in the person of the open range cowboy, or the variations on the Social Darwinist principle that quality will out and that the self-evident superiority of certain types and classes of people gives them the right to define the just society and to act on the basis of this definition. Frequently, and admirably, these and other thematic strands are placed in the context of Wister's own history and class position as a member of the turn-of-century ruling elite, or in the context of more general social and political developments of that time, such as the growing unease about "alien" elements in the body politic or a concern about the seeming lack of those outlets for manly endeavor perceived as crucial to the preservation of the moral health of the nation (Slotkin 1992; Tompkins 1992).

Generally absent from the literature on *The Virginian* is a recognition that behind its explicit thematics and its consolidation of most of the genre conventions that will be endlessly repeated in the twentieth-century western, there are more subtle discourses tucked away in corners that may seem individually insignificant, but that collectively are of great relevance to the modern text of the West. One of these corners is the novel's early acknowledgment that the West is a space of visual deceptiveness, a landscape viewed through the lens of, in the Virginian's own words, "a mos' deceivin' atmospheah."

As in the two folk narratives, *The Virginian* begins with the arrival of the eastern tenderfoot. But this is not just any arrival, it is one of the symbolically *premier* arrivals. In the person of the tenderfoot the general cultural consciousness of the nation encounters[5] the imaginary West, the twentieth-century textual West that is very quickly to become a collective iconography, perhaps even the quintessentially American iconography. There are a great many instances of first encounter with the West in the historical record and many other paradigmatic moments.

The longitude of these moments and encounters moves all the way to the East Coast, if we go back far enough in time. And of course the American far West had been a part of national consciousness for a good half century prior to Wister. But it seems to me hard to deny that it is only in the century since *The Virginian* that the truly emblematic West, the definitive textual West has been permanently established as that remote region where Wister's tenderfoot narrator descends from the train.

Although notoriously loose in its management of narrative voice, Wister's romantic novel firmly establishes the stock figure of the eastern sojourner who observes and, over time, adapts to the ways of the West. He is the outsider to whom everything seems new and strange, and, cast in the role of narrator, he serves as the ideal guide for the readers of Wister's day. The novel has as one organizational thread the process of the tenderfoot's initiation and acceptance. He is, then, the prototype for characters like the auto tourists and the befuddled wanderer in our first two narratives. The salient point here is that this figure in the novel, like his folk brethren, also finds that his first physical entry into the western landscape is marked by visual confusion.

Delayed overnight in the railhead town of Medicine Bow, Wyoming Territory, the narrator gets his first taste of western types and social mores. This is the episode in which the Virginian issues his famous challenge to the villain Trampas, the phrase now wryly commemorated on Medicine Bow's welcome sign. The wagon ride out of town next day, beginning the two-hundred-sixty-three mile journey to Judge Henry's ranch, is presented in two scenes, each organized around explicitly optical imagery. The contrast between these scenes illustrates very nicely that the discourse of Western looking I am trying to identify here differs from other modes of visuality.

During their night in town the Virginian has, according to the conventions of manly virtue subscribed to in the novel, made an apparently easy conquest of an attractive boarding house keeper who to that point had spurned the advances of numerous suitors. The next day, as the Virginian handles the reins of the departing wagon, the greenhorn narrator sits beside him and participates in a subtle exchange of glances:

As we drove by the eating-house, the shade of a side window was raised, and the landlady looked her last upon the Virginian. Her lips were faintly parted, and no woman's eyes ever said more plainly, "I am one of your possessions." She had forgotten that it might be seen. Her glance caught mine, and she backed into the dimness of the room. What look she may have received from him, if he gave her any at this too public moment, I could not tell. His eyes seemed to be upon the horses, and he drove with the same mastering ease that had roped the wild pony yesterday. (Wister 1988 [1902]:37–38)[6]

Such subtle exchanges of glance and gesture, the genteel calculation of propriety, and above all the narrator's complete understanding of what is going on behind these exchanges makes this little scene a rather direct transposition of drawing room romance to a western setting. The only thing the narrator does not "see" is any response from his wagon-mate, and it is exactly in this absence that the Virginian communicates his full comprehension of the situation. In short, everyone involved knows what is going on, namely, the hero's mastery and his conquest's complete submission. Throughout the novel the Virginian's facility with horses is the correlative of his dominance in other spheres (cf. Tompkins 1992:101).

As the educated, over-refined product of those eastern drawing rooms, the narrator is better equipped than anyone else to appreciate this delicate communication carried on entirely through visual gestures. What we witness in this passage is a language of looks that belongs to the town, and so by extension to the East, since in Wister's worldview the western town is the sordid outpost of eastern civilization. It is also a discourse one expects to find in nineteenth-century sentimental fiction, and thus is a product of the eastern culture industry of which Wister himself was very much a part. Although in its immediate context the Virginian's dalliance with the landlady is meant to enhance his prestige and reflect the vital force of his youth, in the larger framework of the novel it suffers severely in comparison with the pure love that must inevitably blossom, in another defining moment for the modern western, between the cowboy hero and the schoolmarm.

Much of *The Virginian* "belongs," conceptually, to the East. But standing in contrast to these elements are things that bespeak the Western visuality I have been talking about. Immediately after the passage just quoted, the travelers pass beyond the "ramparts" of the town, marked by the "thick heaps and fringes of tin cans, and shelving mounds of bottles cast out of saloons" (38), detritus of the decadent civilization Wister deplored. Immediately they find themselves "in the clean plains," where the air is "pure as water and strong as wine" and "sunlight flooded the world" (38). But as soon as they enter this charmed realm its capacity to mystify is revealed:

It must have been five miles that we traveled in silence, losing and seeing the horizon among the ceaseless waves of the earth. Then I looked back, and there was Medicine Bow, seemingly a stone's throw behind us. It was a full half-hour before I looked back again, and there sure enough was always Medicine Bow. A size or two smaller, I will admit, but visible in every feature, like something seen through the wrong end of a field glass. The East-bound express was approaching the town, and I noticed the white steam from its whistle; but when the sound reached us, the train had almost stopped. And in reply to my comment upon this, the Virginian deigned to remark that it was more so in Arizona. (38)

Again we encounter that paradoxical property of a western landscape whereby it seems to open up a "vast horizon" and simultaneously collapse distance. Note, though, that this basic motif is deployed here in a narrative situation virtually the opposite of the previous two tales. Now we have the tenderfoot moving away from and looking back at the town rather than gazing ahead toward and departing for the mountains. Rather than finding himself unable to get closer to a desired goal, he appears to have difficulty getting away from an object of loathing.

In this scene the distortion of vision thwarts, temporarily at least, the desire to escape the town, emblem of social life itself. Wister presents Medicine Bow as a place of deceptions, hidden motives, and conflict. The tenderfoot's whole time there has been filled with social disruptions of one sort or another: practical jokes, charivari play, secret liaisons, and emerging rivalries, though these are by no means all depicted negatively.

The formal difference between this passage from *The Virginian* and the narrative setup in the folk texts illustrates a property of discursive formations I have referred to in passing, namely, their generative nature. We may legitimately view the Wister passage as enacting a common form of discourse permutation—structural inversion. Note that this transformation is not a contradiction of the situation in the folk narratives, but rather its mirror image and completion. The discursive relationship between these two scenes of visual distortion is something like the shot/reverse shot structure so central to the syntax of mainstream films. It is by taking the discourse perspective, in which it makes sense to speak of a general text of the West, that we may legitimately think of these two scenes of looking as occupying a common space and being structural transforms of one another, even though there is no direct relationship between the particular texts in which they appear. Between the two scenes of looking, then, we have represented both sides of the coin of optical desire: in the folk narratives the desire to occupy the position of visual plenitude and in the Wister passage the desire to escape the limitations of partial vision, which is to say, our "fallen" condition as social beings. In both cases the desire is thwarted, as concretely expressed by the atmospheric distortion of space.

As we might expect from the more "sophisticated" genre of the novel, the interplay between the two viewing positions I have identified above, the knowing and the naive eye, is more complicated in Wister's text than in either of the folk narratives. Just as Wister's narrator is not so much the deluded buffoon as his fellow easterners in those tales, so we may not simply equate the Virginian with the old Indian on the fence, though both are possessors of the authoritative gaze. What the tenderfoot most actively desires is not so much to occupy the position of visual plenitude itself, to own the knowing eye and "become" the Virginian, but rather to be recognized as the fully revealed object *of* that look, the completed spectacle worthy of attention from the authoritative spectator. He desires, in other words, to be seen himself as an ideal display. This tenderfoot is acutely aware at the beginning of the novel of being only partially visible, known only in terms of his mode of dress and manner of speech. He lacks something that would make him fully present to the gaze he desires, and his progress toward achieving this presence is one of the narrative frames for the novel, though not a very successfully sustained one.

We cannot so clearly identify this character as the unknowing victim of covert surveillance, an important element in the first text I examined. Here the emphasis is on the relationships of spectatorship. As we shall see in the next chapter, Wister's novel is dense with visual themes and images that weave together the relationships of spectacle and surveillance. For example, the Virginian himself moves among the positions of supreme spectator, ideal spectacle, and object of a hidden, hostile gaze. In the immediate context, however, the narrator's desire to become an acceptable object for the Virginian's look is the prevailing arrangement.

Regardless of the way these elements of visuality are organized, given certain emphases, and particularized in specific narrative settings, it seems evident that we have before us an identifiable family of tropes and motifs where the image of atmospheric deception in the western landscape serves rather neatly as the compressed material embodiment of a very complex economy of visual desire. At the heart of this economy is the recurring symbolic acknowledgment that the fulfillment of desire is always elsewhere in space and deferred in time. The town that seems to stay right there on his heels is the reminder to the tenderfoot that the place of accomplished desire is in fact far off, like the appallingly remote ranch of his host.

Two other images from this passage are worth mentioning, since they relate to the issue of viewing apparatus that I have raised briefly above. One is the description of the town becoming somewhat reduced in size, but remaining uncannily vivid in detail, as if "seen through the wrong end of a field glass." Here we encounter for the first time an artifact designed explicitly for the manipulation of vision. Through this simile the "natural" atmospheric effects that distort space are likened to the application, or rather misapplication, of a fabricated viewing device.

I would propose that we take this simple image as an unwitting acknowledgment of another important feature of the Western discourse of looking, namely, the hiding of cultural apparatuses behind the screen of nature. The atmospheric distortion of space is like the application of a viewing device because it *is* a viewing device. It is, as I have been arguing, part of the discursive mechanism through which the West is seen. It serves, thus, both as a metaphor for the artifactual quality of the western landscape and as a particular narrative instance of that artifactuality. It is really the perfect metaphor, since it would seem to be a "natural" phenomenon that makes the landscape look unnatural.

And the image of looking through reversed field glasses has another noteworthy feature. This misapplication of a magnifying device both miniaturizes and sharpens the object so viewed. Saving a fuller discussion of the issue for later, I will only suggest here that these are qualities conceptually associated with a certain type of artifact, namely, the commodity, especially the commodity in the advanced consumer order. I have just finished arguing that the town our narrator looks back upon constitutes the rejected object, is in fact the embodiment of that decadent cultural artifice against which the natural environment of cattle land is counterposed. But in the trope of reversed field glasses the town also takes on the quality of a gem-like miniature, "visible in every feature." While in one respect the town may seem like the undesirable artifact one cannot get away from, it also has a hint of being the hyper-vivid, seemingly graspable object one cannot in fact fully capture. It is as if what the narrator sees is not the town but a representation of the town or, perhaps better, an advertisement for the town. Though evoked only lightly, some elements of the commodity artifact lurk within Wister's fieldglasses image. As we will see, the operation of the commodity form is endemic to the discourse of looking and display in the modern text of the West.

The last notable element from this passage is the narrator's mention of the train. When we examine Wister's own historical place in relation to visual practices, train travel will be an important consideration. I have already referred to the automobile as a viewing apparatus, but in this it is really only a further development of the technology of seeing first established in the mechanized movement of trains (Schivel-busch 1986 [1977]). In looking back to view the distant train pulling into town, the narrator is seeing an apparatus of seeing, and he is viewing it through the optical device of the distorting atmosphere. As I have already pointed out, the act of looking at a prior act of looking is a re-curring scenario in Western visuality. A variation on it is the way optical devices of various sorts become themselves objects of display. In this re-gard, the train and the town constitute a homologous pair. If it is true that the western town may function as a viewing platform and thereby be part of a visual apparatus, then the narrator's glance back at the town is also an act of spectatorship in which the spectacle is itself an optical device. This arrangement will, not surprisingly, figure prominently in my later consideration of actual display environments.

The image of the train seen across an expanse of landscape, itself something of a western icon, provides Wister with a bridge between the narrator's astonished encounter with the West's atmospheric distortion and another kind of distorting effect associated with this region, or at least with the context of the frontier. The narrator's remark about the strange visual effect evokes from the Virginian a brief performance of tall tales built around the motif of the West's "deceivin' atmospheah." Wister in fact makes the Virginian a master of this genre, and in an important later episode his skill as a performer of such tales helps establish his authority among his fellow "sons of the sagebrush."

What we have in the passage at hand, then, is a brief literary representation of the comic folk genre perhaps most characteristic of the American frontier. Unlike the straightforward joke, where both the teller and the audience maintain a distance from the tale and a punchline is anticipated, the tall tale depends on a fundamental difference between performer intentions and audience awareness. In fact, the tall tale performance is only working when the audience is unaware, or at least uncertain, that a performance is going on at all. The whole point is for the audience be "taken in" by a deadpan report of seemingly empirical fact that turns out to be ludicrous exaggeration. In some tall tale performances, as would seem to be the case in Wister's literary examples, the goal is to embarrass the audience, leading it slowly to realize that it has been duped into believing a preposterous lie. Perhaps the even more classic context of this genre is the presence of a dual audience, one composed of both insiders who know what is going on and outsiders who remain oblivious and go away believing the earnest report that, for example, it gets so hot in these parts that the chickens need to be fed ice chips so they won't lay hard-boiled eggs (Toelken 1979:112). In either case, the tall tale is a genre that only works if it succeeds in hiding its true nature, mystifying its operation as a narrative apparatus.

The tall tale is thus a subtly aggressive, obfuscating form that depends on separating insiders from outsiders. It is also a genre that turns upon a distortion—the exaggeration of reality. In both these respects, it makes perfect sense that the tall tale should turn up as a vehicle for the discourse I have been tracking. What we have in the Virginian's first "stretcher" is a kind of double landscape distortion in that it ludicrously exaggerates the visual phenomenon of landscape exaggeration. Referring to his recent trip to Arizona, he supports his claim that the magnifying property of the air is even more pronounced there than in Wyoming by offering an account of his own supposed optical deception:

A man come to Arizona . . . with one of them telescopes to study the heavenly bodies. He was a Yankee, seh, and a right smart one, too. And one night we was watchin' for some little old fallin' stars that he said was due, and I saw some lights movin' along acrost the mesa pretty lively, an' I sang out. But he told me it was just the train. And I told him I didn't know yu' could see the cyars that plain from his place. "Yu' can see them," he said to me, "but it is las' night's cyars you're lookin' at." (38–39)

Here the Virginian casts himself in the role of the naive spectator, but only fictively and with the intention of confirming the tenderfoot's status as the outsider. In fact, he emphasizes this difference with a comic reversal of their positions. The role of the knowledgeable viewer is occupied by a Yankee astronomer—the educated eastern dude. This characterization points up the most relevant aspect of this tale: its elaboration of the theme of optical apparatuses. The "protagonist" of the narrative is someone who looks at remote things for a living and who is an expert in the handling of optical devices. His telescope is an echo of the reversed field glasses in the earlier passage. He is in the West to make scientific observations of a meteor shower, which, we might note in passing, is a noteworthy natural phenomenon partly because it appears unnatural— stars falling from the sky. The Virginian depicts himself as having made the visual error of mistaking the distant train lights for these stars. The train's headlamp is in fact a rather explicit metonymy for the railroad as an apparatus of looking. As before, the viewing device itself is made the *object* of viewing.

Up to this point the Virginian's tale is plausible. The kicker comes when the knowledgeable astronomer informs the Virginian that he has made an even greater error in not realizing it is the previous night's train he is seeing. The already disconcerting phenomenon of uncanny atmospheric magnification is here further magnified, indeed to the point of absurdity, through the apparatus of the tall tale. In fact the multiple distortions of space become so outrageous as to undergo an absurdist transformation into impossible distortions of time.

What I intend to accomplish in looking at these brief passages from Wister is to begin building a stack of, I hope, convincing redundancies drawn from the broad text of the West, redundancies that cluster around (and constitute) a distinctive order of visuality. And along with this, I hope to demonstrate that fully active discourses are not static sets of images, themes, or narratives, but dynamic resources of cultural production, and thus subject to variations, inversions, even inconsistency and contradiction—but above all virtually infinite in the forms and locations where they may become manifest. As we will see in the next chapter, Wister's classic novel is much more profoundly bound up with a Western discourse of looking than these few passages suggest. In fact, I will be making the case that the "phenomenon" of Wister occupies an important position in the emergence of this distinctive visual mode. Before leaving him to his fate in that chapter, however, there is one final motif in the tall tale passage that deserves a brief comment.

The standard procedure of the tall tale is to pile ever more ridiculous notions on top of one another until the structure collapses in the comic discomfiture of the gullible listener. In this case, having hooked the tenderfoot with his story of the distant train, the Virginian confirms his "mastery" with some further nonsense about the clarity of Arizona air: "Another man told me," he comments dryly, "he had seen a lady close one eye at him when he was two minutes hard run from her" (39). An explicitly erotic dimension of visual desire is here lightly touched upon. We have encountered just prior to the tall tale episode a scene in which a romantic, genteel exchange of glances is presented as "real." This "fictive" account by the Virginian is a second screening of that previous scenario, but now entirely transformed by the discursive lens I am trying to bring into focus here. The woman's wink, in this context the most explicitly erotic of ocular gestures, is comically enlarged to preposterous dimensions, as if to confirm the point through caricature that this discourse of looking is motivated by an economy of gendered desire. The uncannily magnified wink, and its reception at an impossibly remote location, could serve as a nigh perfect metaphor for the whole system of visuality under consideration here. Those conversant with the rich theoretical literature pertaining to matters of gender, looking, and desire (e.g., Stacey 1994; Gamman and Marshment 1989; Mulvey 1989: 14–26, 29–38) will not be surprised to find an enactment of gendered vision turning up. This issue becomes vitally important to my consideration of some of the other texts and sites I examine in what follows.

*   *   *

Beginning with his first western story, "Hank's Woman," which Wister wrote in 1891, and reaching its high point in the watershed classic of 1902, Wister's fiction was one of the most important forces in the early production of the modern textual West, the West as it became fixed in the national consciousness and as it continues to operate today. Another early site of cultural production with a claim to comparable, if not greater influence was the Wild West extravaganza, the arena shows that near the end of the nineteenth century began to present live action spectacles of the most picturesque aspects of western life.

The national and then international tours of such shows contributed at least as significantly as Wister's fiction to the establishment of the basic lexicon of the modern discourse of the West. The premier example of this fairly short-lived form of entertainment was, of course, Buffalo Bill's

Wild West, which operated between 1883 and 1916, with spectacular success for many of those years. The basic iconography of western types and activities was given definitive expression in William F. Cody's shows, which he insisted were slices of the "real" West transported wholesale to the arenas of the East and of Europe. This iconography, combined with the narrative motifs, characterizations, and dramatic devices brought together by Wister, formed the foundation for the first truly mass mediator of the textual West, the film western.

Buffalo Bill's Wild West might well be positioned as the first clear moment where the textual West becomes self-aware through the specifically visual mechanisms of staged spectacle. However, it is not my intention here to give an account of Wild West shows themselves as obviously important embodiments of Western visual discourse. Instead, I propose to look at one small textual moment from the Wild West phenomenon. Another instance that might seem marginal, this text has elements of visuality related to ones we have encountered above. And it is like the jokes and tall tales in being a single, densely packed expression, a kind of paradigm for the widely distributed discourse of Western looking. In this case we shift not only from one genre to another, or from a vernacular mode to the formally literary, but from verbal media to a visual one, photography.

In its 1885 season the cast of Buffalo Bill's Wild West was joined by no less a personage than the Sioux chief and medicine man, Sitting Bull. He was of course well known to the American public as one of the main architects of Custer's defeat at the Little Bighorn. In the wake of the Indian Wars period one theme of the Wild West show had come to be the reconciliation between "the red man and the white" (Slotkin 1992:78–79). Sitting Bull's presence must have seemed a major endorsement of this ideology. During the Canadian tour of that year Buffalo Bill and Sitting Bull went into a Montreal photography studio to sit (or rather, stand) for a publicity shot. The resulting image (Figure 1) is quite remarkable as an icon of Western visuality.

Posed incongruously against a backdrop of what appears to be an eastern deciduous forest, Cody and Sitting Bull stand in close proximity to one another—so close that their upper arms touch. If we take the burst of light behind their heads as indication of a rising sun, then this is quite literally a scene of looking West. We could, of course, imagine various scenarios by which to interpret the image. It would be plausible, for example, to imagine these two men out on a hunting trip. Cody has spotted the quarry and is about to take the rifle for a shot, which would effectively cast Sitting Bull in the role of gun bearer. In such a reading one recognizes a familiar, nineteenth-century colonialist relationship.[7] Or alternatively, the white man might be seen as handing the rifle over

Figure 1. Sitting Bull and Buffalo Bill Cody. 1885 promotional photo taken during the Canadian tour of Buffalo Bill's Wild West. Photo courtesy of the Buffalo Bill Historical Center, Cody, Wyoming.

to the Indian, casting Cody in the role of hunting guide, an office he in fact performed for eastern visitors and European nobility, though it would seem immensely ironic in the present context.

The fact is that as soon as we go beyond the mere content of this image it opens to interpretations more relevant to present concerns. I want to suggest that we may detect in some subtle gestures of this photograph a discourse that cannot be understood in terms of straightforward intentionality or narrative coherence. From the perspective I have been taking in this chapter I would claim that active discourses will "find a way out," showing themselves through the cracks in texts that seem to have entirely different agendas. It is often precisely in those subtle gestures that seem hardly worth mentioning that a discourse operates most effectively.

Take the seemingly superficial evidence of costume, for example. Cody is dressed not in his trademark buckskins and fringed gloves but rather in a show costume that appears inspired mainly by Hispanic tradition. Shiny, thigh-high leather boots over light corduroy pants; a wide belt with heavy buckle; a satin shirt elaborately embroidered with floral designs; knotted kerchief around his neck; and a circular, broad brimmed hat topping it all off and framing his face. Spurs are at his heels; the grips of a pistol are visible in silhouette beneath his right arm; and a hunting knife hangs on his left side. Taken all together, these elements constitute the show version of *vaquero* dress, the costume of the Mexican cowboy, precursor of the Anglo cowpuncher epitomized by the Virginian.

Sitting Bull is in full ceremonial regalia, as marked especially by his eagle feather headdress. The elaborate decoration of his parfleche, its strap running diagonally across his chest, is another indication that this is not everyday wear. As widely acknowledged, the mounted warrior of the Plains tribes has come to be the popular culture image par excellence of the Native American as noble savage (Berkhofer 1978:89). The feathered headdress and fringed buckskin shirt are his trademarks. Of course Buffalo Bill's Wild West played no small part in investing this image with its iconic status.

What we have in this publicity photo, then, is that now-automatic pairing enshrined in our common parlance—cowboys and Indians. Of course as fixed in the popular mind, the link between these terms is conflict, not the apparent concord represented in the photo. The dime novel tradition had already established this agonistic convention, and, as we will see, Wister carries it forward into the twentieth century, as do countless other practitioners of western fiction. In one respect, then, the photograph is a departure from cultural expectations. But in other ways it fits comfortably within the boundaries of the Western visuality under consideration here.

The first, and perhaps most obvious thing to notice about the image is that looking is its subject. Cody and Sitting Bull are looking at something that seems to lie outside the frame. If the wink is one kind of optical gesture, another is to point with the index finger, as Cody is doing.

It is the definitive gesture by which we, at least in European-derived cultures, direct the eye. As such, Cody's use of it puts him implicitly in charge of the scene. He controls Sitting Bull's gaze. His own line of sight would suggest he is pointing out something at a distance and at some elevation above his viewing position, and the clarity with which his own eyes are visible confirms his visually coded authority.

This is conveyed through other elements as well, the arrangement of dark and light values, for example. Cody is a study in alternations of dark and light that articulate his form and clarify it. The sharp boundaries between his dark boots and light pants, between pants and belt, between face and hat, and between hat brim and the burst of light behind his head all serve to define the conventional segments of the body according to which the human form "makes sense." This clarity of forms renders Cody not just visible but emphatically "viewable."

And then there is that visual effect where the eye tends to follow sharply highlighted elements in the composition. In this case Cody's hands, one on the barrel of the rifle and one in the directive gesture, serve as compositional foci that echo his face. Furthermore, the line of the rifle, that of Cody's left leg, and the diagonal formed by the train of the headdress, the ornamented strap, and Cody's right forearm all converge roughly in the area of his raised hand and his head. This hand, with its directive finger, and Cody's face, seen almost full on and set off dramatically by the black hat brim, constitute the site of the authoritative gaze. The area they occupy in the photo is indisputably, almost excessively the primary focus of the image.

The figure of Sitting Bull is the shadow cast behind Buffalo Bill's heroic authority. Where the latter's costume rationalizes and makes viewable his form, the untailored, fringed, and elaborately decorated apparel of the Hunkpapa chief hide him away. In sharp contrast to Cody's brilliantly highlighted and directive right hand, Sitting Bull's is entirely invisible behind the fringes of his sleeve. His lower extremities are virtually lost in darkness. Most important, his face is, in comparison to Cody's, heavily obscured and seen only in three quarter view. Just one of his eyes is visible, and it is deeply shadowed. Only the high cheekbone and strong nose are highlighted, in keeping with stereotypic notions of Native American physiognomy. The conventional contrast between the "light and dark" races is deeply coded in the lighting arrangements of this photograph, and it seems to me undeniable that this visual contrast is correlated with a none too subtle message about authority and subordination.

Now it is in no way surprising that Cody, every inch a showman, should end up the hero of this advertising photograph. He was nothing if not a master of self-promotion. And it might also be said that, though placed in a subordinate position compositionally, Sitting Bull is allowed considerable dignity here, in keeping with Cody's benevolent, if by modern standards patronizing, attitude toward Indians. But it also seems to me that this photograph contains two small gestures, again one of the eye and one of the hand, that might be read as thin cracks in the conventional facade the image otherwise maintains.

For one thing, Sitting Bull's gaze has gone slightly awry. Although we cannot see very clearly exactly where he is looking, his eyeline obviously does not match Cody's gaze. While Buffalo Bill looks up and out of the plane of the photograph, suggesting a whole host of deep-seated cultural associations—aspiration to "higher" things, heroic endeavor, movement forward, Manifest Destiny—Sitting Bull appears to be looking almost along the plane of the photo and at his own eye level. In other words, he seems more firmly set within the space of the image itself, a quality reinforced by his static pose, in contrast to the relatively dynamic forward extension of Cody's arms and left leg. In short, Sitting Bull does not appear to be looking where he is supposed to look. Especially to us today, unconsciously trained by the conventions of Hollywood film, the failure of eyeline match is a particularly disconcerting "error" in the maintenance of an image's coherence. Like any violation of visual conventions, it reveals the artifice through which a text is produced. It can create a feeling of extreme discomfort, but more often it produces a vague sense that something has "gone wrong."

One of the things that has slipped a cog in this image is the smooth operation of visual authority. We might take Sitting Bull's "misdirected" glance as a small moment of resistance, or at least an indication of an alternative to Buffalo Bill's imperious gaze.[8] And, given the direction of his own self-absorbed looking, Cody cannot see this visual otherness. Although the relationships of looking are not exactly the same as in the joke I began with—Cody being not the naive easterner, but rather the knowing purveyor of the spectacle of the West *for* those easterners— still, the stagy histrionics of his pose and gesture, like the foolish misperceptions of the tenderfoot tourists, is undercut by the Indian's other "way of seeing." And, most important, these relationships are all played out in terms of a geometry of vision.

The second ambiguous gesture I would point out is the grip Sitting Bull has on the barrel of the rifle. Although shadowed and somewhat obscured, like his eye, Sitting Bull's left hand is lower and more firmly in control of the weapon than Cody's. In keeping with the ideology of reconciliation, that both men have a hand on the gun may legitimately be read as a marker of the supposed new amity between the races. But this does not necessarily disqualify a reading which recognizes at least a hint of the idea that the Indian, though visually obscured and composition-ally subordinated, really has a firmer grip on a symbolically important artifact. The rifle occupies an interesting place in the discourse of West-ern looking. It is both an optical device and a means of direct, material enactment. It is a device that implies both visual mastery and material acquisition, not to mention violent intervention that annihilates dis-tance, the latter feature linking it symbolically to those optical devices we have encountered in other texts. And of course the Winchester rifle, along with the Colt revolver, is the artifact most firmly associated with the "winning of the West." That the Indian in this image appears to have the stronger control over this important icon I choose to read as more than coincidental.

Although it is only hinted at in this publicity shot, the image of the visually obscured Indian, or the Indian as unseen seer, is a very firmly established convention in the text of the West, one with a history trace-able to James Fenimore Cooper and beyond (for an early visual repre-sentation of this motif, see Goetzmann and Goetzmann 1986:119). This shadowed, occulted Indian is often constructed as the very embodiment of optical threat, the sinister watcher with hostile intent. The connection to the previously mentioned motif of covert surveillance will, I hope, be obvious.

It is again the western film that has most firmly established this image as part of our national cultural baggage, but in Chapter 3 we shall en-counter it ethnographically in the context of living history reenactment. Also, in Chapter 2 we will see it showing up at an important moment in *The Virginian*. While I have discussed at some length the operations of optical desire as manifest in brief, mainly comic texts, the discourse of Western looking is also suffused with shadows and riddled with hid-den places. In fact, the complex interplay between apparently absolute clarity and visibility on the one hand and obscurity or ambiguity of vision on the other is at the heart of this discourse. Although they seem to be touching shoulders, that Indian may be farther away than Cody thinks.

*   *   *

To reach my next stop on this tour of minor, though emblematic sites in the discourse of Western looking, I will jump boundaries again, re-turning to the domain of folk literature, but now in a more distinctly contemporary vein than before, and with a greater emphasis on the dark undercurrents of this visual practice. Here, in something of a composite version, is a tale I have encountered regularly while teaching folklore courses at the University of Wyoming:

Up on the Alcova Reservoir, along the North Platte River, some teenagers are waterskiing one day. One of the girls is up on the skis and seems to be doing fine, when all of a sudden she falls and starts struggling in the water. The others turn the boat around and go back to pick her up, but by the time they pull her aboard she is slipping into shock. Just before she falls into a coma, she asks, "Why did you drag me through that barbed wire?" Nobody knows what she's talking about, and within a few minutes she dies.

One thing they notice is that she's got small puncture wounds all over her body. So they're trying to figure this all out, when one of them notices a log or branch floating in the water near where she fell. They go over to investigate, and as they get closer something looks strange about the thing that's floating there. It seems to be squirming. What they find out is, it's not a log at all. It's a writhing mass of live rattlesnakes! Apparently what happened was that the girl accidentally skied into them and was bitten to death. Later they hear that the water level in the reservoir had recently gone up, which probably washed a big den of rattlers out into the middle of the water.

This tale falls into the category folklorists call "urban legend" or "urban belief tale," obviously something of a misnomer here, since this story is distinctly, even actively non-urban. It does, however, share with other examples of the genre a wide distribution through the agencies of mass communication. This link between folk cultural performance and mass cultural mechanisms of transmission is in fact the most distinctive feature of the urban legend, giving it an interesting location in the general landscape of cultural production.

Although the versions I have encountered in my classes are localized to Wyoming, the story shows up outside the West and probably originated elsewhere. Apparently, the knotting behavior and the aquatic environment are alien to the natural history of the prairie rattler, the species found in this region. However, the related but non-rattling water moccasin of the southern swamplands and rivers does display something like these proclivities, and versions of the story have been collected there (Brunvand 1986:29–30).

Regardless of origins, the narrative of deadly floating rattlesnakes has definitely taken firm root in the West. As always with such stories, it exists as a rather nebulous assemblage of motifs, images, and local details, ranging from full-blown narrative accounts to vague recollections of having heard something about such an occurrence.[9] My students have associated the bizarre accident with a number of bodies of water in Wyoming besides Alcova, among them the Flaming Gorge Reservoir in the southwestern part of the state and Boysen Reservoir along the Wind River.

Based on this evidence, it is a fair assumption that something about the tale resonates with perceptions of the West held by those who reside there. I would propose that one of these resonances is with the patterns of visual practice we see operating in the other texts I have discussed. The surface elements of this story are quite different from anything we have encountered so far, and it is not so obviously *about* vision itself as the tales of magnified landscape or Cody's heroic gaze in the publicity photo. But in less direct, more symbolic ways this gruesome legend is organized around a related apparatus of visuality.

The most obvious connection lies in the motif of the unseen threat, or the misrecognition of a "reality" that in this case turns out to be a mortal danger. So far we have only encountered small hints, either disguised with humor or overlaid with explicit messages about racial harmony, that there lurks within this Western discourse of looking a position from which a hostile gaze emanates. Not just a controlling or dominating look, but the destructive exercise of visual power is an important element in this optical regime.

Some of the most familiar urban belief tales center on such motifs as the belated discovery of disgusting contaminants in fast food items, giant albino alligators lurking unseen in urban sewers, and, of course, the homicidal lunatic skulking upstairs in the dark while the oblivious baby-sitter watches television in the den. Many examples are specifically about unseen watchers or turn upon some form of visual error, and women, especially young women, are typically the victims in these tales. Perhaps it is not so surprising that a genre with such preoccupations should show up in the context of Western visuality, where complex (and conflicted) relationships of viewing are so central. In fact, we would not be completely off the mark to think of the floating snakes story as importing all the genre associations of urban legendry into this visual discourse, even if such associations might only constitute a very distant backdrop unrecognized in most enactments of the tale.

Another, and more remote set of associations floating well beneath the surface of this story are some of our shared cultural notions about rattlesnakes. These associations are themselves quite varied, with a history of their own (Wilson 1987), but the subset most relevant here is the connection made between the rattlesnake and sinister, murderous vision. Though long since abandoned by science, and no doubt only dimly recollected in the popular imagination, at one time it was a widely held belief that rattlesnakes had the power to mesmerize prey, in some accounts even humans, with their lidless, gelid stare. Even if we do not subscribe to this bit of folk zoology, it is still probably widely the case that the "rattlesnake's absence of ocular expression disturbs us and leads to inferences of malignant, cold or hot affect projected by rattlesnake staring. The whole matter of the snake's reputed ability to fascinate small creatures, or even people, comes back to its eyes more than to any other feature" (ibid.:46).

Such residual associations and remote invocations operate as deep background, but they are also real forces in the realization of discourse, lending weight and richness, though more felt than consciously articulated. In the present case, if we put together the two sets of associations I have just mentioned, the snakes might be read as the embodiment, if only through a dim symbolism, of the hidden, hostile eye. If we carry these associations forward, it does not seem outrageous to see in the puncture wounds covering the girl's body the traces not just of the snakes' fangs, but also of the penetrative gaze that is part of this whole symbolic complex. This idea that the act of looking may produce a material effect is, as we shall discover, another important element of the visuality in question.

We need not, however, go so far into the remote symbolism of this tale to find relevant discursive features. Perhaps the most obvious thing to notice, for instance, is that waterskiing has about it a self-contained structure of spectatorship and display. The skier, held at a fixed distance from a viewing position, is the focus of intense attention. Standard safety procedures dictate that the boat contain at least two people, one to drive and one to watch. For the accomplished skier, the time at the end of the tow rope is an occasion for spectacular display.

One trivially obvious feature of this arrangement strikes me as of considerable importance to the larger discursive issues. In the story at least, the tow boat is simultaneously the platform from which the spectacle of the skier is viewed and the motive force that makes that spectacle possible. In other words, the act of watching a display and the production *of* that display occupy the same space, are effectively the same thing. This notion that the act of looking actually generates its own object is crucially important to what follows. It is, for my purposes, the most relevant variation on the theme I have just mentioned, namely, that the gaze may have material efficacy.

Since I have been examining this narrative in terms of the symbolic displacements it stages, I should at least raise the possibility of a connection between the viewing position from inside the boat and the symbolic viewing position represented by the floating serpents. While overtly the act of viewing from the boat takes the form of benign, even protective spectatorship, we should keep in mind that at least in the advanced consumer social order we inhabit, all spectatorship is objectifying and appropriative. One legitimate reading of this tale is that the seemingly benign gaze from the boat has hidden and unseen within it the "hostile" intent of fixing the object of viewing as an artifact for acquisitive desire. When the occupants of the boat cannot at first understand the source of the girl's puncture wounds and when they mistake the floating rattlesnakes for a log, they are misrecognizing their own appropriative gaze.

In other words, the tale symbolically enacts not just a particular displacement, but acknowledges the very phenomenon of displacement itself, the very point of which is to avoid seeing things directly and "clearly."

And to complete this symbolic reading, I need at least to mention what will no doubt have occurred to most readers as an obvious point, namely, that the victimization of the girl has a distinctly sexual quality to it. It is almost too much a cliché to mention the phallic associations of the snakes, here almost fully literalized by the penetration of their fangs and injection of venom. Nor will it be news to those familiar with the literature on "scopophilia," the enactment of visual desire, that this story associates looking with symbolic sexual violation. I would only add the point that the complete marking of the girl's body conveys something of the special nature of optical desire. Its realization is not restricted to particular zones, but inscribes whole surfaces. In a symbolic sense, the object of desire is even more completely appropriated than in strictly sexual victimization.

What all these elements of the rattlesnake legend point us toward, it seems to me, is the modern world of commodity relationships, another issue I will expand on in subsequent chapters. It is one of the defining features of the modern commodity that it seems not to emerge from physical processes of production, but rather to materialize, magically and paradoxically, out of the very impulse of desire itself. In the terms most relevant here, to gaze at it is to make it. This consideration of the commodity form is related to one last notable aspect of the urban legend, its western setting. While it is true that in Wyoming the only bodies of water large enough to allow waterskiing are artificial, this does not prevent us from considering symbolic implications for the reservoir motif. I propose that this setting for the events connects the theme of commodification at work in the waterskiing scenario with the very landscape itself. The dammed reservoir is, after all, one of the most visible artifacts through which the arid western landscape is made productive.

Impounded both for agricultural purposes and to generate power, water is without question the defining commodity of the American West. Its control, precise measurement, and finely tuned allocation is perhaps the single most important factor in shaping the modern history of the region. That the floating rattlesnakes legend deals with a recreational use of water raises interesting questions about modes of production. This is an issue for later elaboration, but at present I will simply note that commodified leisure and spectatorship are central to the advanced capitalist mode, whereas agriculture belongs symbolically to a "prior" mode of production. The reservoir, then, is a site at which these two modes come into contact, and perhaps symbolically into conflict.

Here the motif of the barbed wire is an interesting addition. Although by no means included in most or even many versions of this narrative, that it appears at all is worth noting. Barbed wire is, of course, another icon of the American West. It, like the reservoir, is an artifact that represents the primary commodification of the landscape. It is the device through which the land could literally be divided, rationalized, and made orderly, and thereby fully "productive." That the rattlesnake victim should in her delirium mistake the reptiles, the very embodiments of nature in chaos, for this artifact most associated with the productive ordering of the western landscape is a meaningful irony that we should not overlook. Though only one evanescent motif in one version of a folk narrative, it has been my point throughout this chapter that it is in just such fugitive textual moments that a very large discursive formation may reveal something important about its inner workings. This story of floating snakes makes a connection between some of the deepest structures of optical desire and historical conflicts between modes of production, conflicts in which the "new" commodity is precisely one organized around the activities of display and spectatorship, as opposed to the older commodity form associated with primary production. And behind both these modes lies the still older presence, the dim recollection of an uncommodified landscape, nature in its primal state. In these terms, the snakes are holdovers from, and the avengers of, this prelapsarian condition, washed out of their natural habitat by the agencies of one mode of production and lying in wait to play their part in a drama that involves a new regime of commodification, one in which discourses of looking are central. That the American West, at least as a textual artifact, is one important location in the historical emergence of this regime is amply, almost obsessively demonstrated in the work of Owen Wister, an example of which we have already encountered. In our next excursion we will explore his historical moment more thoroughly.

Chapter Two
Into the West with Gun and Camera
An Excursion in Wister's Visual Moment

By 1893 Owen Wister was a fairly seasoned traveler in the American West. He began making extended summer visits in 1885, in that year to recuperate from one of those emotional collapses that eastern elites specialized in at the time, and thereafter as an avid sportsman in search of big game and trout. He made frequent pilgrimages, some for months at a time, to various parts of the West over the last fifteen years of the nineteenth century. These trips changed as time went on from manly youthful adventures to more reflective literary expeditions in search of "material," but throughout, Wyoming was Wister's favorite destination.

On July 16, 1893, two days after his thirty-third birthday and fresh from a visit to the Columbian Exposition in Chicago,[1] Wister arrived by train in the town of Rawlins, Wyoming. We find him there falling prey himself to that deception of the western landscape I have made much of in the previous chapter. He records in a journal entry this experience of the optical illusion:

John had a pleasant joke out of me. "The atmosphere is very deceitful here," said he, "how tall should you say that pile of stones is on the hill over the railroad cut?" "At least 10 or 12 feet," said I. "It's just 5, the man says." So I and my distances got laughed at. (July 16, 1893)[2]

Though far from a callow youth, Wister is still the tenderfoot from Philadelphia, object of good-natured teasing for his poorly adjusted eastern eyes, and brother to those latter-day butts of jokes we encountered in Chapter 1. By the time of this 1893 trip Wister had begun to use his western sojourns consciously as research expeditions for his nascent literary efforts. It seems reasonable to view his personal encounter with the West's "deceitful" atmosphere as one faint and early sign marking a discursive trail destined to cross and recross the textual landscape of *The Virginian* a decade later. I have already discussed that novel's episode of tall tales based on misperceptions of distance. It will be my contention here that *The Virginian*, the most classic of popular westerns, is thoroughly marked by a connecting web of optical pathways amid which the motif of visually deceptive landscape is only the most overt and epitomizing expression.

Nor do these lines of connection stop at the borders of the book. My subject in this chapter will be what I am referring to as "Wister's visual moment," implying with that term that I will view the historical experiences of the man, the social moment in which he was located, and his literary productions all as aspects of a single continuous cultural text characterized by particular ways of looking. This Wister moment offers us a fine vantage from which to view the landscape of pathways inscribing the visual regime I began to sketch out in the previous chapter. If not the absolute inauguration of this Western discourse of vision and display, the Wister moment constitutes an important early nexus of its elements. In Chapter 4 I will contrast this visual regime with some of the other visual modes that were applied to the West in the nineteenth century. These latter have come in for much commentary and seem more like broad highways of visuality than the meandering, sometimes indistinct trails I am mainly interested in following. It will be my larger historical point, though, that this "alternative," perhaps more diffuse mode of vision and display has become central in the modern text of the West, as embodied in such things as the sites we will visit in the second half of this study.

*   *   *

Perhaps the most important of all Wister's western trips was the one he took in 1891. That was the year he actively oriented his stalled literary aspirations in a new direction, looking West. He wrote his first western story, "Hank's Woman," upon his return to the East after that summer in Wyoming. In strictly literary-historical terms, Wister's resolve to become the "American Kipling" and to make the West our national landscape for epic and romance are the momentous developments precipitated by his 1891 western experience. But some other aspects of that journey are, at least for my purposes, equally noteworthy.

One of these is suggested by some entries in the seemingly exhaustive list of travel expenses Wister recorded in the front of the notebook that would serve as his journal for this trip. Among the many purchases listed are $27.00 for a pair of fieldglasses, $42.33 on guns, ammunition, and fishing tackle, and $53.25 for a "Codac." Wister went West equipped to view (and sight upon) things, and of course he loaded his optical gear into yet another device deeply invested in the activity of looking—the trans-continental railway car. The three commodity artifacts—binocu-lars, gun, camera—bespeak an array of apparatuses for looking West. Taken together they may serve as emblematic markers for large domains of social practice in which the management of vision is central, among them: military reconnaissance, recreational big game hunting, resource surveying, landscape documentation, panoramic and stereoscopic view-ing, and of course tourism. Wister did not participate directly in all these visual activities, but some of them are very much at the heart of the Wister moment.

Before we consider further the larger apparatuses of looking that enabled and conditioned this moment, another entry in Wister's 1891 journal merits notice, for it was to become the raw material out of which he fashioned the single most important passage in *The Virginian*, at least in terms of that book's visual practices. Having arrived in Casper, Wyoming, on June 11, Wister set out early the next morning toward the Powder River country along the eastern slopes of the Big Horn Mountains. He had been committed to the temporary care of a rancher named Tisdale by the friend who was hosting him on this trip and who was away at the moment on the business of roundup. At first Tisdale proved the congenial host.[3] His substantial ranch house, the volumes of Scott, Dickens, and Shakespeare on the shelves of his library, and his thousands of acres of good cattle land, much of it fenced, impressed themselves favorably on the ever class-conscious Wister. However, things soon took an ugly turn.

Having made an overnight trip to collect the mail from the town of Riverside, Wister and Tisdale set out on horseback the next day to dis-tribute it to the men working on the ranch. "We had two extra horses with us," Wister says:

I rode one, leading Syd, my horse of yesterday. Tisdale led a big sorrel, an outlaw because of his bucking habits, whom he proposes to make into a team horse. We came comfortably by the Carrs' ranch on Middle Fork, passing 3 vultures who sat on some high bluffs with wings spread out to catch the sun. A curious sight. When we passed the last gate on Carrs' ranch Tisdale roped the horses we were leading, pretty close together, & started to drive them in front of us. The sorrel got a little way ahead on the trail & decided he was not coming with us. So he ran up a steep sultry hill towing Sydney after him. (June 18, 1891)

Thus begins an account of a grueling effort by Tisdale to bring the fractious "outlaw" back under control, with Syd being pulled along as the ineffectual hostage. Wister confesses to being of little help in this business and mostly follows behind as an observer of the proceedings. As his mount begins to play out, Tisdale reveals a brutal temper. "Insane with rage," he begins to curse and kick the hapless animal, which has become too tired to move at more than a walk. When Tisdale proposes swapping for Wister's fresher horse, the easterner urges the exchange, in the hope of securing some relief for the wretched beast being brutalized by the rancher. But:

Tisdale seemed to forget about his intention of swapping. He continued to swear at his horse & kick it, and then I noticed him make several vicious grabs at its eyes. Then he got into the saddle again and the brute walked slowly forward with him some twenty yards in the direction of the vanished sorrel, leaving me dismounted & watching Tisdale's heels & fists beat the horse without pause. It stood still, too weak to move and I saw Tisdale lean forward with his arm down on its forehead. He told me that he would kill it if he had a gun but he hadn't. I watched him, dazed with disgust and horror. Suddenly the horse sank, pinning him to the ground. He could not release himself, & I ran across to him & found only his leg was caught. So I lifted the horse & he got his leg out. I asked him if he was hurt. He said no, & got up adding "I've got one eye out all right." The horse turned where he lay, and I caught a sight of his face where there was no longer any left eye, but only a sink hole of blood. (June 18, 1891)

To judge from his journal entries of the following days, Wister was profoundly repulsed by this barbarity. His thoughts were quite preoccupied by it and he agonized over his own inaction. He both grasps at self-justification, insisting on the difficult position he is in as the guest of someone doing a mutual friend a favor, and castigates himself for a "moral craven." Having maintained a stony taciturnity toward his temporary host, Wister is finally rescued from his dilemma by the arrival of Morris, the anxiously awaited friend.

Perhaps the most remarkable thing about this whole episode is that it precipitates in Wister the literary resolve that has been coalescing for some time. He turns this deepest encounter with the brutality of the American far West into a kind of literary mission. "I begin to conclude from 5 seasons of observation," he says,

that life in this negligent irresponsible wilderness tends to turn people shiftless, incompetent and cruel. I noticed in Wolcott in 1885, and I notice today a sloth in doing anything and everything that is born of the deceitful case with which make-shifts answer here. Did I believe in the efficacy of prayer I should petition to be the hand that once for all chronicled and laid bare the virtues and the vices of this extraordinary phase of American social progress. Nobody has done it. Nobody has touched anywhere near it. A few have described external sights and incidents, but the grand total thing—its rise, its hysterical unreal prosperity and its disenchanting downfall. All this & its influence on the various sorts of human character that has been subjected to it has not been hinted at by a single writer that I, at least, have heard of. The fact is, it is quite worthy of Tolstoi or George Eliot, or Dickens. Thackeray wouldn't do. (June 20, 1981)

While few today would be likely to consider Wister the West's Thackeray or even its Kipling, much less its Dickens or Tolstoy, there is no denying that his western fiction did a great deal of the original grinding that produced the modern lens through which we cannot help but view the West—the West, that is, as a grand text with national, international, indeed global currency. It seems strange, then, that so little attention has been paid to the centrality of the visual in his work. His preoccupation is not so much with the grand vistas, the big sky and sublime spectacle of the West, those visual properties that perhaps come quickest to mind, as with the gestures and problematics of looking itself. That this should be the case in so foundational a moment—this Wister moment—deserves more than passing comment.

I have suggested, on the evidence of a few journal entries, that Wister's profoundly disturbing observation of a savage horse maiming leads him to acknowledge his own desire to capture in fiction the moral order of a time and place that could produce both such brutality *and* those frontier virtues he comes to associate chauvinistically with a putatively Anglo-Saxon chivalric heritage (Wister 1987 [1895]). The particular form the maiming took, the gouging of a horse's eye, might seem merely contingent. However, in its literary reincarnation this act occupies the very center of a whole visual apparatus that defines the Wister moment, and by extension informs the modern text of the West.

The Virginian is surprisingly lacking in overtly depicted violence. Plenty of violence is implied and violent acts occur just off stage (e.g., an ambush, a lynching, a cold-blooded murder), but even the climactic moment of the pistol duel between hero and villain, archetype for countless popular westerns, comes off almost lyrically. We are only aware a gunfight is underway when "a wind seemed to blow the sleeve" of the Virginian's shirt; he replies in kind; the dastardly Trampas pitches forward into the dirt; smoke flows up from their gun barrels; and it's all over. This chartering enactment of a ritual that will be anatomized through countless replays and variations takes up no more than five lines of text.

There is, however, one crucial exception to Wister's genteel reticence toward depictions of violence. About two thirds of the way through the novel circumstances throw the hero in with a rancher named Balaam. The latter is overdue in returning two horses he has borrowed from the Virginian's employer. The cowboy and this Balaam set out on a long ride to return the animals. Already having displayed an inclination toward cruelty, the rancher decides to tether the two recalcitrant ponies together and drive them in front of him, in the interest of making better time. When one of these horses, a sorrel, takes it into his head to bolt, the grueling and futile pursuit is on. After merciless goading from his master, Pedro, the cow pony Balaam is riding, finally plays out completely. Thoroughly enraged, the rancher resorts to various forms of extreme physical abuse. Finally, he demands the use of the Virginian's horse, Monte, which the cowboy denies him in the most definite terms. To this rebuff Balaam

made no answer, but mounted Pedro; and the failing pony walked mechanically forward, while the Virginian, puzzled, stood looking after him. Balaam seemed without purpose of going anywhere, and stopped in a moment. Suddenly he was at work at something. This sight was odd and new to look at. For a few seconds it had no meaning to the Virginian as he watched. Then his mind grasped the horror, too late. Even with his cry of execration and the tiger spring that he gave to stop Balaam, the monstrosity was wrought. Pedro sank motionless, his head rolling flat on the earth. Balaam was jammed beneath him. The man had struggled to his feet before the Virginian reached the spot, and the horse then lifted his head and turned it piteously round. (240)

Wister published a short story entitled "Balaam and Pedro" in an 1893 number of *Harper's*, obviously basing it on the experience recorded in his 1891 journal. In the chronology of his writing (though not of publishing), this western "sketch" is the first place the Virginian appears—as a character ancillary to those referred to in the title. The passage just quoted comes from the reworked version, also called "Balaam and Pedro," that Wister shoehorned into the plot of the 1902 novel. Of interest here are some of the changes this episode went through as it made its way from journal to western romance. The most obvious of these is the absence from the novel of an actual description of the horse's maimed eye, an image presented quite graphically in both the earlier accounts. The well-known literary-historical explanation for this change is that Theodore Roosevelt, Wister's good friend and fellow Harvard alumnus, prevailed on him to soften the shocking scene. Wister even refers obliquely to Roosevelt's influence on the passage in dedicating the book to this illustrious friend (Roosevelt would be sworn in as president by the time *The Virginian* hit the book stalls).

In keeping with the premise that such seemingly contingent textual gestures can have a significance beyond their cause-and-effect authorial explanations, I would propose that this double loss of the horse's eye, both its literal removal and its textual absence, are important markers in the visual discourse of the Wister moment. There is a double violence here that invests this passage with particular import. The straightforward, commonsense explanations—that Wister constructs an episode around the gouging of a horse's eye because he actually saw this happen, and that he is subsequently convinced to avoid a graphic description of this act out of concern for the sensibilities of his genteel readers—such explanations are inadequate to an understanding of the larger textual processes at work.

The physical violence against an actual flesh and blood eye in this passage is the most blatant possible literalization of the disruption of vision. And it is precisely the *disruption* of looking—a disruption enacted in many forms—that underlies the whole visual mode I have taken as my subject here. Those lighthearted tall tales and practical jokes built around the theme of deceptive landscape are other outcroppings of the same underlying formation. That the episode of the unfortunate Pedro stands out so dramatically, both in its uncharacteristically overt violence and in the glaring absence installed by clumsy suppression of its key image, should lead us to recognize it as a strongly marked gesture of self-announcement—the place in Wister's novel where a discourse of the disrupted gaze declares itself most explicitly. If this passage does indeed stand at the heart of something fundamental in Wister's classic western, and if we accept that this book stands at the heart of the Wister "moment," and if we further accept that this moment is in some sense foundational to what I have been referring to as the modern text of the West, then the annunciatory act encoded in the bloody eyesocket of a brutalized horse takes on far-ranging significance. And it should come as no surprise that when we spiral out from this gruesome pivot, a whole world of disrupted looking begins to open up in *The Virginian,* and in the historical moment Wister epitomizes.

One commentator has pointed out that in revising this episode for inclusion in his novel Wister seems to compensate for the elision of the blinded eye by elaborating the overall violence of the scene (Seele 1988:444–46, n.56). I would add that the pumped up violence is pervaded by an imagery of visuality not present in the earlier versions. After Pedro is maimed, the passage continues thus:

> Then vengeance like a blast struck Balaam. The Virginian hurled him to the ground, lifted and hurled him again, lifted him and beat his face and struck his jaw. The man's strong ox-like fighting availed nothing. He fended his eyes as best he could against these sledge-hammer blows of justice. He felt blindly for his pistol. That arm was caught and wrenched backward, and crushed and doubled. He seemed to hear his own bones, and set up a hideous screaming of hate and pain. Then the pistol at last came out, and together with the hand that grasped it was instantly stamped into the dust. Once again the creature was lifted and slung so that he lay across Pedro's saddle a blurred, dingy, wet pulp. Vengeance had come and gone. The man and the horse were motionless. Around them, silence seemed to gather like a witness. (240)

Virtually the antithesis of the moral craven Wister accused himself of being in 1891, the Virginian exacts the retribution his creator failed to impose in that earlier day. The fictional western hero steps in and takes the place of the "real life" eastern tenderfoot, thereby enacting the sort of displacement that I have suggested motivates the desires of those easterners in the jokes and tall tales.

Importantly, the Virginian's violent confirmation of his own clarity of moral vision, the clarity that was lacking in the tenderfoot Wister, is itself enacted in terms of an assault on vision and a disruption of the apparatuses of looking. Balaam has to defend his eyes from the Virginian's blows, eyes already referred to as "glazed" with rage. He feels "blindly" for his pistol beneath the righteous hero's onslaught. The "sledgehammer blows of justice" exact, at least symbolically, the harsh biblical punishment of "an eye for an eye," a connection Wister may in fact have wanted us to make, given his general framing of this episode in biblical terms (see below). Nor should we miss the fact that when Balaam's pistol, along with the hand trying to aim it, gets stamped into the dust a kind of visual operation is being thwarted, since the use of a firearm involves coordinating a line of sight with the projection of matter through space.

And finally, even the description of the brutal rancher's return to consciousness treats it as the reengagement of a temporarily inoperative optical apparatus:

He [the Virginian] stood looking down at Balaam and Pedro, prone in the middle of the open tableland. Then he saw Balaam looking at him. It was the quiet stare of sight without thought or feeling, the mere visual sense alone, almost frightful in its separation from any self. But as he watched those eyes, the self came back into them. (241)

Not only has Balaam's vision been disrupted—temporarily blinded and beaten out of focus—but he becomes himself unfocused as an object for *our* looking, a "blurred, dingy, wet pulp," a "creature" whose very humanity has lost clear definition. There is at work here a subtle slippage from an imagery of disrupted optical devices, most obviously the eye itself, to disruptions of the objects of looking. Once sensitized to this shift, we can begin to see a larger pattern in which the positions from which looking proceeds and the positions toward which looking is directed circulate in a complex play of displacement and exchange.

Several types of looking are invoked in the few paragraphs of this episode. When the blows of justice have ceased to rain down, the very silence metaphorically gathers around to "witness" the punished miscreant, looking on in a quasi-legal act of visual confirmation and endorsement. The Virginian, too, stands "looking down at Balaam and Pedro, prone in the middle of the open tableland," as if contemplating a kind of static display—a pathetic tableau of physical and moral blindness. This position of detached and passive spectatorship, with nuances of both aesthetic contemplation and authoritative judgment, is one mode of looking represented in the episode.

More active forms are also evident, however. For example, after Balaam comes to, the Virginian inspects him with clinical detachment and efficiency to determine whether he is badly hurt. This "hunting for signs" on the body of a displayed subject is echoed by a hunting for signs in the landscape as the two men finally continue their pursuit of the runaway horses. They follow the animals' trail until at one point the Virginian has to dismount to inspect the ground more closely. In doing so he discovers another presence: "There's been a man camped in hyeh inside a month," he observes, "White man and two hawsses" (242).

This is, of course, an example of one of the most familiar tropes in the genre of the western, well established long before Wister's deployment of it.[4] The western hero's visual expertise as the authoritative close reader of minute signs complements his visual mastery of vast distances, that famous squint-eyed perspicacity capable of seeing through the deceptions of landscape and discerning accurately the most remote object. In a later episode of the novel, the tenderfoot narrator underscores this mastery of the distant view by confessing his own lack of it. Coming into a wide plain he sees the dark dots of far off cattle. Only when he gets much closer does he realize they are really horses. "The plainsman's eye was not yet mine," he ruefully admits. "When was I going to know, as by instinct, the different look of horses and cattle across some two or three miles of plain?" (295).

Both extremes of western visual mastery, then, the nearly microscopic and the nearly telescopic, are amply displayed by our cowboy hero. He is truly the possessor of the authoritative, knowing gaze. And though as a hired hand he is socially obligated to Balaam, the Virginian is uniformly in control of things morally, materially, and visually during the journey to the Sunk Creek Ranch. At least that is how it would seem if we allowed our deeply ingrained assumptions about the masterful frontier hero to distract us entirely from those moments at which his own visuality is disrupted. I will turn to some of these shortly.

Not only are we generally confirmed in our expectations of the Virginian's authority as a reader of macro and micro landscapes, but we are also meant to accept the moral authority of his position as definitive spectator. There are many instances in the novel where he looks on as an observer, almost always with an implicitly masterful gaze. In fact when we first see him (through the eyes of the narrator as he arrives in the West), it is as a detached observer of this sort, a spectator at the comic performance of his fellow cowboys as they try to lasso a fractious pony. "Then for the first time," says this narrator, "I noticed a man who sat on the high gate of the corral, looking on" (2). The Virginian, as yet unnamed, immediately demonstrates his mastery of the situation by casually accomplishing the task his companions could not.

I will return to this opening scene of the novel, since it displays other aspects of the visuality I am concerned with. It is sufficient here, though, to see how the role of master observer, combined with that of the expert reader of signs and landscapes, constitutes the locus of authoritative looking, this position being the primary object of desire in the novel—and I would argue in the Wister moment generally. Since the Virginian is the primary occupier of this position, the points where his visual authority slips, where he is even slightly destabilized in this role, call out for notice. Fleeting perhaps, but still revealing, is that critical moment of the hero's visual confusion when Pedro is being blinded: "Suddenly he [Balaam] was at work at something. This sight was odd and new to look at." Of course the intention here is to enhance the Virginian's moral authority as someone for whom such cruelty is so alien that he cannot at first even comprehend what he is seeing. However, we should not miss the hint of a spectacular unveiling in this moment of suddenly recognized brutality. The display of Balaam's perfidy, this something "odd and new to look at," has about it the quality of an unappropriated, not yet mastered spectacle. As such, it is an object of looking that evokes at least a small charge of desire.

In terms of the visual symbology, the Virginian's belated "tiger spring" to forestall Balaam's crime is prompted not only by revulsion but also by attraction. It is the enactment of his desire to acquire and control this not yet mastered object of looking which titillates the eye with its novelty. At this point in *The Virginian*, then, a point which I have proposed is quite central to a much larger discourse, the iconic embodiment of authoritative western looking has more than a bit of the naive spectator about him. A glimpse of those deluded eastern tourists and tenderfeet, at least in terms of their position in the visual economy, peeps through the seemingly placid facade of the Virginian's knowing gaze.

The temporary inability of the hero clearly to "see" (read: control or possess) an act that itself quite literally mars vision is a kind of condensed inscription of a mode of spectatorship endemic to the nascent modernity of Wister's moment. Much has been made, of course, of Wister's deep nostalgia for a fast departing "old West," a heroic age he felt he had just glimpsed as its curtain was being rung down. For all this romantic looking backward, however, his work (and his moment more generally) is saturated with emergent structures that are to become more and more insistent as the new century progresses, so that by our own day they are virtually diagnostic of our cultural life. And, as I have been proposing here, a dispersed imagery of disrupted visuality is one of the most important discourses in this new order. The passage in Wister's novel where an act that physically disrupts vision is itself depicted as a visually mystifying spectacle takes on, then, particular symbolic force. Like the joke with which I began, it, too, epitomizes the layering of visual acts and displays and reflects the ceaseless circulation among positions in the visual economy, from spectator to spectacle and back again.

The overall trajectory of the horse maiming scene could be understood as a kind of eruption of one mode of spectatorship—unstable, desiring, motivated—followed by its containing displacement into another —static, cool, masterful. The Virginian starts as the victim of a visual shock, briefly paralyzed and then jolted into motion by the brutal novelty of this strange new thing to look at. The scene more or less concludes with him reinstalled in his wonted position as the knowing observer, looking down with aesthetic/judicial detachment at a static display. In between these two spectatorial positions, the overtly violent exchange of reciprocal blindings symbolically registers the more subtle violence of the discursive upheaval. The hero's relentless assault on Balaam is retribution both for the overt crime against an actual eye and for the deeper crime against the stability of the spectatorial position the Virginian represents. Blindness, literal or figurative, circulates from Balaam's assault on Pedro, to the mystified Virginian, and then back to Balaam. Again, it is precisely such circulation and instability, spectator slipping into spectacle, acts of looking or the disruption of looking themselves positioned as displays to be looked at, visual plenitude discomfited by the optics of desire, that defines the discourse of Western looking.

The episode of Pedro's blinding, for all its prominence as a rather shocking outburst of graphic violence, might seem too transitory to carry the burden of analysis I have imposed on it, were its elements and implications not echoed, elaborated, and in various ways played out at many other points in the novel, and, as we shall see, in other of Wister's fiction, not to mention in his social moment more generally. Perhaps the most obvious of these extrapolations is to be seen in the conclusion of the "Balaam and Pedro" chapter itself. In considering how this is so, we might begin with the rather ham-handed biblical allusion Wister imposes on his material. How deeply he might have expected his audience to trace the reference to the Old Testament Balaam and the story about his unjust mistreatment of his donkey (Numbers 22:2–24:25) is less to the point here than that the biblical narrative is thoroughly suffused with "raw material" resonant with the larger discursive project of Wister's novel.

The gist of the story is that Balaam, a well-known seer with reliable abilities in issuing both curses and blessings, is hired by the king of Moab to come and curse the Israelites, who have arrived in large numbers at the border of his kingdom and threaten to invade. The catch is that Balaam's efficacy comes directly from the word of God, he being merely the conduit for the divine Will. He can only curse or bless as God decrees. By naming his rancher Balaam, the overt connection Wister makes is to the first episode of the biblical story, in which the seer beats the ass he is riding because the animal balks. This occurs three times, the donkey becoming more difficult in each case. What Balaam does not realize, what he is literally unable to see, is that the Angel of the Lord, brandishing a sword, has come down to block the road. At the third repetition God grants the ass the ability to speak, which he uses to complain of the harsh treatment. At that moment "the Lord opened Balaam's eyes" (22:31) and he finally sees the Angel, who tells him that if the donkey had not shied off the road, he would have struck Balaam down.

In a brief but telling commentary on this biblical narrative, Robert Alter points out that the first word in the Hebrew text is "to see," which serves, through numerous variations, as the *Leitwort*, that is, the unifying element, of the whole tale (Alter 1981:104–7). Seeing of many sorts, from simple looking to preternatural vision, is what the story is "about." In this regard, his invocation of the biblical narrative is perhaps more relevant than Wister was himself fully aware. In keeping with my premises about the operations of discourse, we could say that the larger textuality of which Wister was as much a creature as a creator is "responsible" for the deeper implications of the allusion.

Most to the point, however, is that Pedro, even though bereft of one eye, is like the biblical ass in having a higher ability to see. Continuing on their way in pursuit of the outlaw horses, the Virginian and Balaam come to a point on the trail where the woods reach all the way down to the edges of the watercourse they are following. The hero, once again seemingly in full command of the situation, instructs Balaam to make camp in a meadow bordering the woods while he rides up into the trees to make sure the renegade animals keep to the path that will eventually open onto their home territory, at which point they can be counted on to make their own way to the Judge's ranch.

Left with Balaam, Pedro suddenly starts to behave oddly. Inexplicably he shies "where there was not even a stone in the trail" (245). And then, seeming to lose control, he rushes out to stand in the middle of the stream, perhaps, Balaam surmises, with the intention of making his own escape and compounding their difficulties. To forestall this, Balaam attempts to fire his pistol in front of Pedro to turn him back. Unfortunately for the pathetic animal, Balaam misses his aim and shatters the horse's foreleg. But precisely at this moment of displaying yet again his faulty vision, Balaam's eyes are suddenly opened. For in this split second he divines what Pedro has "seen" — "the Indians; but too late" (246).

As the two men have proceeded on their journey a series of events have come together to create a sense of foreboding that they both feel but neither expresses. The Virginian's discovery of the signs (including a piece of red flannel) that a "white man" had been on this trail recalls reports of a lone trapper who had recently entered these mountains but never come out. A buzzard rises from a marsh and stays circling above, in one of its passes dropping another rag of red cloth. Most ominously of all, for an hour before coming to their camping spot the two travelers hear the unseasonable calls of a pair of owls that seem to be paralleling their journey from the bordering woods. In the flash of insight that accompanies the shot with which he seals Pedro's fate, Balaam connects these things with the rumors that some supposedly pacified Indians have not returned to the reservation after their hunting season in the Bow Leg Mountains. Like the biblical ass, Pedro has saved Balaam's life with his higher ability to see, for had the rancher entered the woods he would have been ambushed, the presumed fate of the lone prospector. The relevant point here, of course, is that both Balaam and the Virginian have become the unwitting objects of a hostile, hidden gaze.

In the magazine sketch version of this episode, the last we see of the Virginian is his departure into the trees in pursuit of the horses. Not yet established as the iconic hero he was to become, Wister leaves the cowboy to a presumably dire fate. In the novel however, through perhaps the clumsiest plot turn in a frequently ragged narrative, we next come upon the Virginian as he lies critically wounded near a spring, the very one he has frequented in his rides with the schoolmarm Molly Wood. In an outrageous coincidence reminiscent of *The Virginian*'s dime library precursors, an emotionally agitated Miss Wood rides out to this same spring just as the hero is languishing there on the verge of bleeding to death. She has recently decided to flee back to Vermont to escape his courtship, denying her true feelings in order to perpetuate the false codes of social decorum characteristic of the morally enervated East. Instead, of course, she rescues her fallen champion and nurses him back to health, setting in motion the events that lead finally to the happy resolution of their romance.

We might choose to see this rather disconcerting juxtaposition of the novel's most graphically violent episode with perhaps its most sentimental as the place where the two modes of Wister's writing grind together with especially noticeable strain. His early inclination toward a realist sensibility comes up hard against the romantic impulse, a combination that characterizes much of the popular tradition of the twentieth-century western. In keeping with the approach I have been taking here, however, it is legitimate to view the implicit fate of the Virginian in the magazine story as still an active, if ghostly presence hovering in the background of the novel, just as the over-timid tenderfoot of Wister's journal lurks behind the compensatory figure of the avenging cowboy hero onto whom he projects the moral decisiveness he could not himself muster. In other words, the larger textuality I have been referring to as the Wister moment has all these elements equally and simultaneously in play, requiring us to read them together.

In taking this approach, then, it makes sense to say that the Virginian does indeed meet his end in those ominous woods of the Bow Leg Mountains, and it is a death consistent with the protocols of visuality I have been at pains to unpack. The hero's "demise," hidden off stage under the obscuring cover of trees, brings to a kind of conclusion the spectatorial drama begun with Pedro's blinding, which as we have seen is itself "hidden" from the reader's view.

I have already pointed to ways the visual mastery that is a presumed hallmark of the western hero suffers moments of slippage, most notably when the Virginian briefly occupies the unsteady position of the mystified spectator in the presence of a novel object of looking. The conclusion of this episode calls into question his mastery much more definitively. One rather subtle anticipation of this outcome is the hint of an alignment between hero and villain, previously constructed as absolute opposites in the moral economy of the narrative. Although Balaam has been the very embodiment of blindness, both literal and figurative, and the Virginian the paragon of the knowing gaze, they come to share a position as victims of another's look, specifically, objects of covert surveillance. As their sense of an unseen threat grows, they actually become glad for one another's company. And, whether fully intended or not, Wister sets up a small echo between them in expressly visual terms. When the Virginian's spectatorial gaze suddenly "comes into focus" on Balaam's brutal display, it is "too late" to forestall the crime against vision. Likewise, when the scales finally fall from Balaam's eyes and he suddenly recognizes Pedro's odd behavior for the warning it is, this also comes "too late," either to avoid ruining the ill-fated pony or to save the Virginian.

The small associations between the hero and villain are additional slight tremors in the stability of visual mastery. Absolute mastery means, among other things, that the visual field is fully "within view" of the mastering gaze. But this knowing eye also presumes itself to be unchallenged by a gaze from another source, another way of looking. When such a presence makes itself felt as an independent visual locus, the field of looking becomes contaminated and destabilized. It is forced to acknowledge its own incompleteness, its lack of that plenitude which means the end of desire. Covert surveillance is perhaps the clearest instance of such disruption, and when he becomes the object of surveillance the Virginian's visual plenitude, his mastery, is thoroughly undermined. His symbolic, unseen "death" at the hands of those who have been watching him from ambush completes the pattern in which acts of direct physical violence serve as correlatives for assaults on the stabilities of discourse. When the Virginian is "resurrected" at the spring it is also a revival of that mode of visuality we have encountered in the opening Medicine Bow episode (see Chapter 1), one in which the genteel exchange of glances, the blushing avoidance of eye contact, and other such visual gestures enact the social codes of sentimental romance. The whole novel, in fact, alternates between these two optical regimes, one of them with a long-established literary tradition, the other an emerging twentieth-century synthesis that combines pre-existing visual tropes with entirely new modes of visual experience.[5]

One of the familiar motifs of this latter discourse we have already encountered in the paradigmatic joke with which I began this study. We will come upon it again as a key structuring element in the Fort Laramie living history exercise that will be the subject of the next chapter. I am referring to the association of Indians with the dominant, and implicitly hostile, viewing position of surveillance. The Sitting Bull/Buffalo Bill promotional photo is, in my reading of it, an interesting representation of essentially the same optical relationships. This positioning of the iconic Indian as an unseen surveillant presence is of course an established literary motif well before Wister, the Leatherstocking saga being perhaps its locus classicus in American letters. But there is a sense in which this Indian-as-icon becomes a "new" location when drawn into the orbit of the larger discursive field that is coalescing around the turn of the century and registering quite insistently in the Wister moment.

Emergent discourses are not necessarily unprecedented in all their textual elements and concrete manifestations, that is, they are not necessarily absolute departures from previous procedures. Novelty may reside, at least in part, in new arrangements, new structurings of established elements, and new relationships to social/historical context. The unseen, surveillant Indian needs to be "read" in relation to those other features of visual positioning—the circulations of spectatorship and display, the destabilizing of authoritative looking through agencies of desire—that I have been attempting to isolate as distinctive of a particular mode of modern visuality. The introduction of the Indian ambush in Wister's novel must be viewed in the context of the whole episode it culminates, an episode that is organized precisely around complex disruptions and destabilizations of looking. In fact, it must be viewed in the whole context of Wister's literary production. As we will see, in a late piece of short fiction he repositions the Indian in yet another permutation of the elements that constitute the visual discourse we have been trailing. Before looking beyond *The Virginian*, however, I want to look backward briefly, to the very first of Wister's published stories. It will point us outside his literary texts to an aspect of social experience that stands, it seems to me, at the heart of Wister's moment.

*   *   *

"Hank's Woman" is Wister's first western story, its original draft almost completed at one sitting shortly after he returned from the 1891 Wyoming trip. A rather bleak tale of abandonment and moral decay, it is very much in the realist mode. Although the as yet uncreated Virginian did not figure in the first version, in revising it for a later collection of his short fiction Wister refashioned the tale to bring in the Virginian as a central player. The events of the story ostensibly occur while the hero is on hiatus from his job at Judge Henry's ranch, a circumstance alluded to in the novel. While on this self-imposed furlough he has invited the eastern tenderfoot to come back West for a hunting trip. The dramatic center of gravity falls in the second half of "Hank's Woman," where the tenderfoot observes directly how a pious, working class immigrant is brought down by the degeneracy of the man she has imprudently married in a moment of dire need. However, it is a seemingly marginal, comic passage in the first part of the tale that is most relevant here. Having stopped to do some fishing on their way to hunt elk and mountain sheep, the companions fall into conversation about various matters. The Virginian recounts a recent experience he has had visiting that most remarkable of American places, Yellowstone National Park, which on the fictive timeline of this story is little more than a decade old:

I had been seein' this hyeh Yellowstone Park, takin' in its geysers, and this and that, for my enjoyment; and when I found out what they claimed about its strange sights to be pretty near so, I landed up at Galena Creek to watch the boys prospectin'. (Wister 1988 [1894]:400)

Enjoying his weeks of leisure, the Virginian tells how he lounged around Mammoth Hot Springs, at the northern edge of the Park. "And," he says, "I got plumb interested in the tourists. For I had partly forgot about Eastern people. And hyeh they came fresh every day to remind a man of the great size of his country" (400). Most revealing is what he has to say about the operations at the big tourist hotel that has opened to accommodate the influx of eastern visitors:

And one noon I was on the front poach of the big hotel they have opened at the Mammoth Springs for tourists, and the hotel kid, bein' on the watchout, he sees the dust comin' up the hill, and he yells out, "Stage!"

Yu've not saw that hotel yet, seh? Well, when the kid says "Stage," the conse-
quences is most sudden. About as con-spicuous, yu' may say, as when Old Faithful Geyser lets loose. Yu' see, one batch o' tourists pulls out right after breakfast
for Norris Basin, leavin' things empty and yawnin'. By noon the whole hotel outfit has been slumberin' in its chairs steady for three hours. Maybe yu' might hear
a fly buzz, but maybe not. Everything's liable to be restin', barrin' the kid. He's
a-watchin out. Then he sees the dust, and he says, "Stage!" and it touches the
folks off like a hot pokeh. The Syndicate manager he lopes to a lookin'-glass,
and then organizes himself behind the book; and the young photograph chap
bounces out o' his private door like one o' them cuckoo-clocks; and the fos-
sil man claws his specimens and curiosities into shape, and the porters line up
same as a parade, and away goes the piano and fiddles upstairs. It is mighty con-
spicuous. (400–401)

I quote this passage at length to make the point that the very first of
Wister's western stories begins in the context of an emerging modern
tourism, specifically, mass commercial tourism of the American West.
Although "Hank's Woman" is most centrally a morality tale about the
decline of this region as it passes out of its heroic age, it also provides
a glimpse of emergent social and economic relations, however marginal
their depiction is to the main plot. Examining it a little more closely,
one discovers that the story actually captures some of the complexity of
the emerging relations of tourist production, at the core of which is a
complex geometry of visual relationships.

The story registers an important transition, or an overlapping of
phases in the development of western tourism, and thereby registers as
well a shift in the visual economy of looking West. It should not surprise
us that in its inaugural moment Wister's fiction reflects these conditions
of cultural production, for he was himself very much a participant in
the transformation of modes of looking epitomized by the emergence
of the modern "tourist gaze" (Urry 1990). I hasten to add, though, that
I view the reorientation of tourist optics reflected in Wister's work as a
social, institutional, and economic concomitant to a pervasive shift in
the visual order generally, rather than as a primary cause of that shift,
having already rejected unilinear historical explanations as inappropriate to the analysis of large-scale discourses. Rather than seeing certain
patterns of looking as mere symptoms of modern tourism, I will treat
particular structures of tourism as part of the enabling apparatus for the
distinct, complex visual discourse that underlies the Wister moment.

Although one cannot determine absolute categories, it could be said
that Wister's experience in the West drew upon at least three modes
of tourist looking. Two of these were well entrenched cultural systems
prior to Wister's participation in them; the third was emerging roughly
at the same time he was formulating his fictional West. Most importantly, his moment is characterized by the overlapping of and conten-

tion among these modes. Of the three, the most residual by the time he started publishing his short fiction is reflected in a letter he wrote to his mother while on his pivotal 1891 excursion. He has himself made his way to Yellowstone Park and is here describing the Grand Canyon of the Yellowstone River:

The place is at once romantic, exquisite, and wholly sublime. The South is not in it, nor anything of Homer, but you can easily believe Monsarrat is round the next corner or expect to see the Gods stretch a rainbow somewhere and march across to Walhalla. I am reminded of certain of the most beautiful passages in Wagner's trilogy. (Wister 1958:127–28)

Here are the conventional associations characteristic of the luxury railroad excursions to the far West undertaken by an eastern elite whose idea of leisure travel was thoroughly conditioned by the European grand tour model and who were not daunted by the considerable travel expenses. With the post-bellum development of the trans-Mississippi rail system, an impressive infrastructure of deluxe amenities grew up quickly —opulent palace cars, grand resort hotels designed for maximum visual effect, gourmet dining, carriage excursions, spa facilities, elite entertainments, and so on. This mode of tourist experience was highly literary in its inspiration and, as reflected in the passage from Wister's journal, relied on the touchstones of European high culture for creation of its visual coherence. It privileged above all the aesthetic categories of the sublime and the picturesque.

I will have more to say about this mode of looking in Chapter 4, but for immediate purposes it is sufficient to observe that this touristic tradition depended on a radical restriction of view. The desired emotional effects of sublimity and picturesqueness presupposed artistic framing and a stable vantage point. Although the goal of visual experience in this mode is some sort of emotional transport, whether ecstasy in the case of the sublime or the more modest delectation appropriate to picturesque views, a high degree of management is involved. The elite tourist apparatus that thrived in the three decades following the Civil War was devoted to providing relatively effortless access to these sorts of experiences, which in fact depended on maintaining considerable distance from the material realities of the West. As Earl Pomeroy describes it, a typical "activity" of this brand of tourism would be to sit and view snow-capped peaks through the glazed porch windows of a massive resort hotel, presumably while awaiting notice that the next gourmet meal was available for service (Pomeroy 1957:19–24).

It is perhaps indicative of Wister's position along a fault line in the unstable cultural landscape of late nineteenth and early twentieth-century America that he participates in this white glove tourism, at least through some of the language he uses in his journals and letters, while also disdaining it. The central drama of "Hank's Woman," for example, begins when a wealthy eastern matron, having arrived in Yellowstone on her husband's private railroad car, callously and unjustly dismisses her lady's maid, leaving this Austrian immigrant to her own pitiful devices, "out of a job and afoot a long, long ways from her own range" (402). In Wister's cosmos, this particular brand of elite western tourism is an extension of an effete, feminized eastern culture. Though not emphasized in his fiction, the emblematic optical device here is the Pullman car window, the framing apparatus through which the encapsulated observer surveys from a distance the panorama of a sublime and picturesque West. This "Pullman tourist . . . had his heyday in the eighties, when the West seemed almost his exclusive province. Then a larger tourist public began to move in" (Pomeroy 1957:29–30).

Hardly less elite, but predating the arrival of railroads, thoroughly male, and more actively engaged with the material substance of the West is the longstanding tradition of sportsman tourism, with its central activities of hunting and fishing. Unlike its genteel, resort-based counterpart, this brand of elite tourism had among its goals the pursuit of adventure and manly vigor through arduous travel and the life of the camp. Although hardly acknowledged in the popular imagination, this hunter-tourist was a regular and common feature of the nineteenth-century American West. He played a part, if an ancillary one, in most of the enterprises around which our collective epic reconstructions are built:

He is almost a regular fixture of the Western Army post, where the officers and their wives are glad for a change of society; occasionally by special permission he follows a military expedition in the field. He likewise follows the fur traders and railroad surveyors and builders, and when the railroad is built he shortly rides it with his trophies. He is guest at farmhouse and cattle ranch; often he becomes a rancher and is host to his friends. (Pomeroy 1957:74)

Along with his quasi-military aspect, this type of sportsman also has much in common with the entrepreneurial, appropriating endeavors of the developer, land speculator, and scientific resource surveyor. It is no accident that more than a few of these elite hunter-tourists invested, and in some cases took up residence, in the West, buying large ranches and participating in the cattle boom that was completing its moment of crisis just at the time Wister was making his earliest visits.

Especially on his early trips, Wister operated primarily in this mode of sporting tourism. Not surprisingly, it is the mode he presents most often in his fiction. In fact his signature narrator, the eastern tenderfoot, is in most respects an incarnation of this hunter-tourist. He is witness to the events of "Hank's Woman" while being guided on a hunting trip;

he blunders into one of the more important episodes of *The Virginian,* where a pair of cattle rustlers are about to be lynched, while on his way to join the cowboy hero for some hunting; and as we will see, Wister's late story "Bad Medicine" involves another fateful hunting expedition into the Yellowstone country.

Of the optical devices Wister purchased in anticipation of his 1891 trip, the field glasses and, of course, the guns are the emblems of this second type of elite tourism, and they reflect the military antecedents on which it is based. Though at bottom martial in its style and procedures, it should not be assumed that this mode of early western tourism is simply the "savage" antithesis of the genteel palace car and resort system of recreational travel. In fact, they overlap in many respects. By Wister's own day, for example, both modes depended on elite rail transportation. Nor are they absolutely contrastive in their visual procedures. In his journal accounts of actual hunting forays, Wister mixes ecstatic descriptions of sky and mountain views, drawing on the conventions of the sublime and picturesque, with detailed reports on the hunting procedures he followed (e.g., Wister 1958:48–60).

What distinguishes sporting tourism as a visual mode, however, is its concrete materialization of the act of seeing. Through the visual processes of sighting, stalking, and bagging one's quarry, the hunter-tourist accomplishes an intervention in the material world that has as its intended outcome the production of a display. The elite tourism of the palace cars, grand hotels, and excursions to scenic overlooks had the effect of reproducing eastern drawing rooms, picture windows, and artwork frames in the midst of the western landscape, which could thereby be viewed in luxurious comfort (both physical and discursive). The hunter-tourist accumulated, through arduous and even heroic effort, artifacts belonging to and symbolic of this landscape, transporting them back to the private clubs, dens, and smoking rooms of the East, where they were arranged in emblematic, artful, museum-like displays expressive of the West.

Wister's journal accounts of hunting are interesting compendiums of the visual procedures through which transportable pieces of the West are appropriated. In his detailed chronicle of hunting mountain sheep in the Teton Mountains in 1888, on his third trip to Wyoming, he records a complex apparatus of visual operations: using field glasses to locate the distant quarry and distinguish it from the background landscape, the cat-and-mouse process of stalking in which seeing while remaining unseen is the main task, and, finally, fixing the prey in the sights of his rifle so that it can be materially transformed from quarry into trophy, an item for symbolic display elsewhere (Wister 1958: 75–85). It is this play of visual codes, procedures and technologies to accomplish the material production of a display that distinguishes sporting tourism as a visual practice. The materialization of the visual through the deployment of a firearm is its definitive gesture, setting it somewhat apart from both the detached visuality of resort tourism, but also from the dematerialized visual production of a third form, the one which is emergent in Wister's own moment and which he both resists and heralds in his personal experience of the West and in his fiction.

But before turning to this third mode, I want to mention one final common feature, an abstract, structural element, of the two forms of tourism I have been talking about to this point. It is simply that as discursive practices these modes of tourism can be characterized as "monocular." Though both are dependent on complex institutions, economic infrastructures, and a whole array of preexisiting verbal and visual tropes and conventions, at their core they deploy a simple arrangement of the gaze: a single viewing subject focused intensely on an isolated object of looking, the sublime or picturesque view in one case, the quarry or potential trophy in the other.

Of course they differ in that the latter entails a more dynamic, materially acquisitive relationship between the subject and the object of looking, but neither is significantly troubled by any invasion of the visual field by contaminating elements—oblique gazes from other locations. In the case of hunting, the quarry may see and return the gaze of the stalker, but it is still a closed dyadic relationship of looking. And it is perhaps not irrelevant to mention that when the Indian appears in Wister's journal accounts of his early hunting trips to Wyoming, it is as the guide who serves only as a kind of enhancement of the hunter's own vision, a kind of magnifying device like the field glasses, improving the hunter's ability to track and spot game. In the journals, this figure is never presented as in any way disruptive of "normal" visual procedures. He is, one might say, the Sitting Bull of the promotional photo discussed in Chapter 1, minus the hints of an alternative gaze that are encoded in that figure.

It is to a third mode of touristic experience that we must look to find the complications of visuality evident in the array of texts I have examined to this point. If his 1891 tour of Wyoming was the watershed year of Wister's literary career, it was also the year in which we begin to see a shift in his tourist's gaze. He continues in his role as elite hunter-tourist, but it is precisely in this role that he is able to observe another, newer mode.

After his disturbing encounter with Tisdale in eastern Wyoming in June, Wister makes his way in early July to Fort Washakie, on the Wind River Indian Reservation. There a hunting party is assembled, with guides and the necessary camping equipment. The next month is devoted to hunting through the Wind River country, following a route that eventually leads them into the back regions of Yellowstone Park. The journal entries from these weeks, and his frequent letters to his mother, are a telling mix of romantic nature descriptions, self-conscious "literary impressions," hunting anecdotes, and, most important here, commentaries on the middle class tourists who are turning up in ever greater numbers in Yellowstone (Wister 1958:119–30). On September 1, while stopping at the tourist hotel in the Upper Geyser Basin, Wister records essentially the scene that he has the Virginian describe in the opening episode of "Hank's Woman." Because he has come in from the back country and is operating on his own rather casual timetable, Wister as elite hunter-tourist is in a position to observe the sudden animation of the commercial apparatus at the hotel as it makes itself ready for the arrival of the stage bringing a load of bourgeois tourists from the train. As his fictional counterpart, the Virginian in "Hank's Woman" is quite explicit about the fact that, after seeing the Park sights himself, he hangs around to observe the tourists.

To characterize the situation here abstractly, it entails one mode of tourism (increasingly residual) serving as the vantage point from which another (emergent) touristic mode may be observed. Furthermore, this latter form of touristic looking is itself directed toward a display that exists precisely to be received as the object of spectatorship. One might even say there is a sense in which the very act of looking in this new tourist mode *produces* the object of its own attention. Wister's (and the Virginian's) account of the almost magically vivified hotel, which one easily imagines going through its routine on a regular schedule, is a rather direct expression of a very general principle at the heart of modern tourism: its inextricable linkage of the subject and object of looking, wherein the production of the spectacle and its consumption, the making of the display and seeing the display, are hardly distinguishable.

As a kind of "meta-spectator" to this very modern arrangement of spectatorial visuality, Wister is by turns patronizingly tolerant and scathingly derisive. As he is coming into to the Park he observes:

Lots of outfits & people passing on the road & children screaming. This park is an immense thing for the American bourgeoisie. Popper takes Mommer & the children in a big wagon with two mules & their kitchen & beds & forth they trundle hundreds of miles and summer in the Park. Nothing like this ever existed before, I think. (August 11, 1891)

But while this democratic generosity applies in the abstract, the bourgeois tourist does not fare so well in the particular encounter:

Then a woman at the Golden Gate (where the view is fine) asked what the stage was stopping for & was told it was for the view—"That's enough," I heard her say instantly. "Drive on. We ain't [got] time." Also a young girl at the Hot Springs swinging her very nice feet as she tipped her chair back & asked the porter about the sights at the Springs—She broke off suddenly—"Well, *say,* ken ya' buy silk caps anywhere round here?" (September 1, 1891)

In this seeming ambivalence about the "new" Yellowstone tourist we might recognize a displacement of Wister's own rather unstable and multivalent position. In observing one touristic mode from the location of another, he is enacting a layering of visual procedures, looking at other acts of looking, that is structurally similar to some of the complex visual arrangements staged in his classic novel. My point is not that this aspect of Wister's own social experience "explains" or is allegorized in his fiction, but rather that they constitute redundant enactments of the larger historical practice in which they both arise.

And it is not the end of my account of visual complexities in Wister's historical moment to recognize that he occupies a position in one form of tourism from which he is able to observe another. I have already suggested that at least in some contexts (especially his letters to his mother) he deploys the conventions of genteel, "grand tour" tourism, conventions reinforced no doubt by his own European travel. Even more so is he a participant in, and not just an observer of, the bourgeois tourism that he patronizes and pillories in his journals and fiction.[6] Or to put it another way, Wister's social location is ambiguous and mystified as a result of his straddling several cultural fault lines. Though his identity as hunter-tourist might seem a stable and from his point of view a superior position in the cultural economy of turn-of-the-century tourism, Wister in fact "circulates" among a number of discursive locales.

On his way from the Wind River Reservation to Yellowstone, a month to the day after the harrowing drama of the horse blinding, Wister reports in his journal a side trip he took to Warm Springs Canyon, near the town of Dubois, Wyoming. He is thoroughly enchanted by this remarkable site, a deep gorge in which are to be seen two natural rock bridges. "It is impossible to get down to the water there," he tells us, "but we shall try tomorrow, *for I greatly desire a photograph of this place*" (emphasis added). Later he makes it down, with much difficulty, and is not disappointed by the experience. And at this point he expresses the kind of sentiment that reflects a very modern way of looking:

. . . thank the Lord, it is nameless and unknown save to Indians, cowboys, and horse thieves. . . . Some day, no doubt when civilization crawls here, this poor creek with its cañon and natural bridges will echo with the howling of the summer mob, who will have easy paths made for them, and staircases, and elevators perhaps too. There will be signposts directing you to Minerva Terrace, Calypso Garden, Siren Grotto, for every unfortunate ledge and point will be saddled with a baleful name rotten with inappropriateness. I hope at least some of the photographs I took will succeed. (July 18, 1891)

The unintentional irony is perhaps obvious. Wister here enacts in a couple of sentences the structure of visuality I have been proposing. He relates to this site in what will fast become a conventionally touristic fashion. He finds his way, after difficult travel, to a viewing position from which he can mark the site with the tourist snapshot. But virtually at the same time he adopts in imagination a viewing position outside his own act and from which he "sees" the anticipated tourist hordes that will come to view the site once it has been packaged more conveniently. What we encounter here is the dissociation of the gaze, its splitting so to speak, into a look that directly confronts and records the site, and a look that gazes down from a superior position at this first sort of looking. Although he misrecognizes himself as belonging to the "authentic" western company of Indians, cowboys, and horsethieves (and we might add hunter-tourists) who know of this place, his Kodak is in fact the badge of his membership in that large company yet to come. This camera is the third optical device Wister records at the beginning of his 1891 journal, and it belongs to the set of artifacts—the stairs, the elevator, the pre-packaged and named views and natural features—that accommodate the "summer mob."

The device Wister refers to is a roll-film box camera. First introduced to the general market by Kodak only a few years earlier (1888), the model Wister apparently bought could capture up to one hundred shots and required none of the technical knowledge of wet-plate photography that had dominated before Eastman's innovations of the 1880s (Gardner 1985:14–15). When the roll was filled with exposures, the whole camera would be sent to the processing facility in Rochester, New York. The film would be removed and developed and a new roll inserted. If in his early trips to Wyoming Wister participated in the late stages of elite sporting tourism, starting in 1891 he belongs as well to the first generation of so-called *Kodakers*, the avant garde of what would become mass, truly touristic, snapshot photographers. Whereas in some of his early journal entries we find Wister regretting his lack of the painterly skills that would allow him to capture visually a landscape which defied verbal description, after 1891 he can be heard to express what has become a universal tourist lament: "I wish I'd had my camera with me."

It is perhaps worth noting that the camera is a fundamentally different sort of optical device from the others on Wister's equipment list. Whereas the fieldglasses and rifle perform the enhancing functions of isolation, alignment, magnification, and clarification, the camera frames and inscribes. The first two operate as extensions of an actual eye, while the latter substitutes for the operations of vision itself. To characterize the distinction in another way, guns and binoculars are visual tools, while the camera is a visual apparatus, a distinction that implies a fundamental difference in the relationship between the artifact and the human agency that deploys it. Tools amplify human actions and are under the control of the user. Apparatuses locate the human agent in a larger network of social and material relations which she or he does not, in fact, control, even though this may not be immediately apparent (Crary [paraphrasing Marx] 1993:129–31). The Kodak box camera that Wister used was not fully under his control in at least two obvious ways. It was, both literally and metaphorically, a black box technology, as are cameras for most of their users today. That is, the actual mechanisms and processes of production are unobservable, largely obscure to the users, and need not be understood to produce the desired result. In fact, the easy-to-use snapshot camera Kodak made available to middle class consumers at the end of the nineteenth century, and which Wister wasted no time in obtaining, may be one of the first such black box devices to come into common use by the general public.

And the functioning of this apparatus was also outside the user's control in that the actual processing of the images occurred at a location and through industrial mechanisms remote from the primary act of taking the picture. This is still true in many respects today, though it was especially obvious in the first phase of mass snapshot photography. One pointed the black box, pushed a button, and turned an exterior crank. After one had done so a specified number of times, the box left one's possession, only to return ready for further use and accompanied by a set of inscribed images, all as if by magic and with only a preset fee to indicate the photographer's participation in a process where the line between production and consumption is devilishly difficult to locate.

There is one final aspect of this black box that should not escape our notice, namely, its inherently covert nature. Although the field glasses and rifle might be used covertly and in contexts of surveillance, the camera has a fundamental covertness built into its material substance. Its inscription process goes on of necessity in a dark, unseen place. And this inherent covertness of the device in its basic material operations was very quickly reproduced in its social use. It wasn't long before the idea of the "detective" or button-hole camera was developed, a black box designed to be used covertly for purposes of surveillance, or in a more benign characterization, to take candid shots.

Wister's Kodak, then, is the emblematic artifact of the new arrangements of seeing that I have proposed are emerging in his historical moment. And the little episode at Warm Springs Canyon is a rather direct expression of the complexities in this new visual discourse. In imagining the future of this site, Wister "produces" an image of modern mass tourism as itself a kind of spectacle, of which he is the outside observer. In doing so he anticipates the scene of sudden animation at the Yellowstone hotel that he will observe just a few days later and subsequently reproduce in his fiction, placing the Virginian in the role of meta-spectator (surveillor?) at a scene of touristic spectatorship/display. What Wister does not recognize, of course, is that his desire to get his snapshot of Warm Springs Canyon is the quintessential gesture of precisely that modern mass tourism he anticipates so pessimistically. He is already part of the spectacle that he imagines as yet to come. One might say he is both the observer of its emergence and simultaneously one of its harbingers. Eventually, through his fiction, he also becomes one of its most effective, if unintentional purveyors.

* * *

I hope it will be apparent by this point that there is a deeply rooted connection between Owen Wister's fiction, especially his classic novel, and his own enactment of the complex social formations emerging in his day and registering particularly in the overlap of the various tourist modes. The connection goes far beyond the fact that he traveled in the West and based his fiction on direct observation. Nor is it adequate to think of the connection merely in cause and effect terms: the emergent social relations informing the literature and becoming manifest in indirect and symbolic ways. I am proposing that it is more productive to think of the whole Wister moment as suffused with a common discourse, one that is emerging *in* his cultural moment (though hardly unique to him) and is manifest especially as a complex arrangement of visual practices and structures. All the elements we have encountered— the recurring situation of one gaze being directed toward other acts of looking, the frequent confusion of or slippage between subject and object of looking, the recurring motif of disrupted or distorted or hostile vision, the layering of spectatorship and surveillance, the seeming magic of a gaze that produces the very spectacle it sees—such are the elements of an extensive discursive field that pervades Wister's moment and continues to inform the comprehensive text of the West as we encounter it today.

To conclude my consideration of Wister and his cultural moment, I want to move back one last time to his fiction, and especially to a late story that seems to me a remarkably overt representation of the discursive elements I have been talking about here, especially in its explicit thematization of the camera and photography in a touristic context. As a preliminary, we might take note that photography and quasi-photographic arrangements crop up here and there in *The Virginian*, though they could hardly be said to constitute a coherent theme. I have already referred to the first glimpse we get of the Virginian, through the eyes of the tenderfoot narrator as he arrives by train at Medicine Bow. The first line of the book refers to a tourist photo opportunity: "Some notable sight was drawing the passengers, both men and women, to the window; and therefore I rose and crossed the car to see what it was." This is a Kodak moment awaiting, in terms of the novel's time frame, the arrival of the not-yet-available recording apparatus, though of course Wister had been taking snapshots of the West for a decade by the time he published *The Virginian*. And more than a few of his images capture the sort of activity the tenderfoot witnesses from the train, for what he sees is the cowboy hero displaying his work skills. The train window provides a quasi-photographic frame for this premier icon of the West.

At his first close-up view of his future friend, who is now standing at ease on the station platform, the narrator's impression is of "a slim young giant, more beautiful than pictures" (3). Not surprisingly, the Virginian is repeatedly positioned as if he were a photographic subject, both by implications of pose, framing, and context, and in one case quite literally. As the romance between schoolmarm Molly Wood and her ardent suitor progresses, there comes a moment when she feels the need to return for a fortifying visit with her family in the East. While she is there, her elderly aunt, one of the few sympathetic members of Molly's eastern kin, divines that her niece has "met someone" out in Wyoming. With characteristic directness she says, "let me see his picture" (201). We learn that in fact Molly has brought with her a number of "Western views" to show the home folks. With one exception, "They were views of scenery and of cattle round-ups, and other scenes characteristic of ranch life" (202). In this they corresponded to many of the photographs Wister himself took on his western tours. One, however, was a portrait, and this she had kept back from the members of her family. It was, of course, an image of the Virginian. "It was full length, displaying him in all his cow-boy trappings,—leathern chaps, the belt and pistol, and in his hand a coil of rope" (202).

The source of these photos is not made clear. Are we to assume that Wister has anachronistically provided Miss Wood with the sort of snapshot camera he himself used extensively to record "Western views"? There is in any case a hint of the tourist's gaze in her photographic collection. And although the hero's photo is certainly a marker of her personal feelings about the actual human being who is its subject, it also has the qualities of a typifying souvenir postcard—the perfect image of the "Cowboy in His Regalia." And this is how the aunt first reacts to the photo, accusing her niece of having fallen in love with the clothes.

Perhaps the most telling example of how the cowboy hero is constructed as a touristic spectacle occurs in another situation associated with the railroad, one which has distinctly touristic "photo-op" qualities to it, though in this case no actual camera is in evidence. Over the course of several chapters Wister develops an episode in which he reveals the Virginian's superior abilities as a leader of men. Having been put in charge of a herd of cattle to be sold on the Chicago market, the hero is returning to the Judge's ranch with his cowhands when a crisis arises. Their train is approaching Montana goldfields where there have been recent reports of rich strikes. This news has put the easily influenced crew in mind of abandoning the cattle ranges and seeking their fortunes as miners. The always treacherous Trampas has been fomenting mutiny, with the intention of discrediting the Virginian, or perhaps worse.

Though the possibility of physical violence is in the air, the conflict ends up taking the form of a test of wits in which the two antagonists compete over who can tell the most outrageous lie and get his opponent to swallow it. The tide has turned in Trampas's favor after he takes the Virginian in with a tall tale about the speed of trains. The climax of this episode occurs when their own train is temporarily halted by a washed out bridge. Several other trains are also there awaiting the repairs. It is at this point that the Virginian displays his superior verbal and mental abilities by fooling Trampas and the whole outfit with his masterfully deadpanned story about boom and bust in the frog leg market and frog ranching in Tulare, California.

The relevant issue here is not the story itself, but the situation in which the Virginian conducts his performance. With the delay of several trains, food has become scarce both in the dining cars and in the small settlement near which they are stalled. The Virginian gathers up gunnysacks of frogs from the sloughs along the right of way and sets up an operation to sell fried frogs' legs to the hungry passengers. All the while he slowly builds his epic lie about the rise and fall of a frog raising industry, a kind of absurdist parody of cattle ranching. His own companions, including Trampas, are completely hoodwinked by his tale, but they themselves become the object of a secondary audience—the eastern tourists who have stepped down from their Pullman cars to witness this performance of western local color. The situation actually reverses the normal audience arrangement of the western tall tale, in which the local performer tells his "windy" to one or more gullible outsiders (classically, easterners), while a secondary audience made up of locals observes the proceedings, maintaining poker faces as long as possible. The eventual discomfiture of Trampas and the crew is especially acute precisely because their gullibility has been put on display for eastern tourists.

The whole scene is viewed by these easterners as a picturesque example, as if it were a staged display, of "authentic" western verbal art, manners, and character types. "All eyes watched the Virginian and gave him their entire sympathy" (152). "Oh, I must call my wife!" exclaims one of the eastern onlookers. "This is what I came West for" (151). When one of the genteel travelers is scandalized by the proceedings, her husband advises her to stay and "see it out. This beats the geysers or anything we're likely to find in the Yellowstone" (152).

In this last remark the Virginian's performance is compared directly—and favorably—to the premier tourist destination in the West, and implicitly at least the iconic cowboy's worthiness for photographic capture is comparable to the geysers. Here, then, the Virginian is constructed expressly as a spectacle for the tourist gaze, a reversal of his role as an observer of Yellowstone tourists that we saw in "Hank's Woman." His triumph as "king" of the cowboy verbal art of lying occurs precisely at the moment he himself becomes a western tourist attraction, and in fact depends upon that circumstance. If the fictionalized Pullman car travelers belong historically to the phase of genteel, upper class leisure, Wister's construction, both implicit and explicit, of the Virginian as eminently photogenic edges him at least slightly into the context of the emergent mass tourism that we have seen Wister himself deeply engaged with. The complicated discourse of layered and disrupted vision that I have argued is pervasive in the novel is accompanied by at least a marginal acknowledgment of a concrete social and economic formation, modern tourism, that is one of its clearest institutional sites of enactment.

There is at least one place in Wister's oeuvre where he makes quite explicit the sort of discursive connections that have to be coaxed out of their rather indirect embodiments in *The Virginian*. The late story "Bad Medicine" (Wister 1928:1–48),[7] published in his last collection of short fiction, follows yet again the eastern hunter-tourist as he travels from Fort Washakie into Yellowstone, as Wister had done on his 1891 trip. And like Wister in that watershed year, this story's narrator carries with him a Kodak. But now it has become laden with a symbolic significance we have not encountered before. In fact, issues of mass tourism, visuality, and photographic inscription are central to the tale. And as the title suggests, the figure of the Indian reappears, but now as more than a clumsy plot device and an abstract embodiment of covert surveillance.

The story begins with an attempt at photographic ambush. The hunter-tourist narrator is just arriving at Fort Washakie, on the Wind River Indian Reservation, where he has sent word ahead that he is in search of a hunting guide. As his stage arrives, he is enchanted by the sight of a regal Indian sitting in full ceremonial dress and playing traditional melodies on a wooden flute. A young boy, his son as it turns out, sits beside the man. Both seem completely lost in the music. The narrator's response is the definitive gesture of modern mass tourism:

I seized my kodak, stood forward by the horses, aimed it at the group, the boy saw me, came to life with a jerk, the chief's arm flung itself over his face, and both had vanished noiselessly in their moccasins among the trees. (3)

The stage driver's comment on this scene makes explicit the inherent covertness of the tourist's candid snapshot: "You'd have ought t've hid behind the stage." This late story of Wister's is expressly about the effects of the arrival of "civilization" in the West, which in his fictional universe are uniformly negative. Particularly unusual in this case, though, is his rather explicit acknowledgment that a certain structure of visuality—the surface manifestation of which is modern, fully commmodified tourism—is itself a force of fundamental transformation, and not just a nuisance destined to clutter a pristine landscape. The emblematic embodiment of this force is the tourist's Kodak, characterized as "the eye of civilization." Although he is the one who introduces this tainted artifact into the western scene, the eastern tenderfoot narrator continues to be presented sympathetically as the locus of wider understanding, which might lead us to question whether Wister fully recognized the importance of his own participation in the modern discourse of looking West that his story criticizes.

We have seen that the Indian serves widely as the embodiment of the external, covert, and usually hostile gaze that is integral to the regime of visuality informing Wister's moment. In keeping with this regime's general principle of reversal, displacement, or circulation of viewing positions and sites of display, in "Bad Medicine" it is the iconic Indian that becomes the object of looking, and the dramatic development of the narrative centers on the deleterious effects on this figure caused by "the baleful eye of the machine." The theme of noble savage ruined by the forces of civilization is of course very old indeed. But, its clichéd theme notwithstanding, what makes Wister's story interesting in the present context is that relations of looking constitute the stage on which the drama plays out.

In rough outline, the tale is about Sun Road, a magnificent Shoshone "prince" who at first flees the camera as "bad medicine" but slowly comes to accept and then actively to court its attention. Respectful of the Indian's wishes, at least in part out of a desire to secure his services as a hunting guide, the narrator does not again attempt to photograph him or his son, Little Chief Hare. However, the Kodak is a constant presence on the hunting trip, and as the hunting party comes closer to the tourist centers of Yellowstone, avid Kodakers abound.[8] Eventually, Sun Road comes to relish the visual attention he is constantly being afforded and his initial reticence to be photographed transforms into a rather shameless, from the narrator's point of view, solicitation of the camera. He has also slowly overcome his "superstitious" fears about the supernatural dangers of Yellowstone itself, accounts of which have supposedly come down through traditional legend. The ironic, if also excessively melodramatic conclusion of these developments is that Sun Road meets his death just at the moment an "official photographer" at Old Faithful is taking his picture for reproduction and sale. Having been posed in front of the single most famous sight in Yellowstone, Sun Road is surprised by the simultaneous ignition of the photographer's flash powder in front of him and the eruption of Old Faithful at his back. In his dismay he ventures out onto the thin crust of the geyser basin and disappears into the steaming cavity of the geyser. The narrator makes the point explicit for us that Sun Road has indeed lost something of his spiritual substance, but it is as a result of the "malevolent" influence of the Kodaks, which have "drained out of him a portion of himself," an effect the narrator likens, tellingly, to a loss of "spiritual virginity" (40–41).

With this as its general narrative shape, certain details of this odd story express very succinctly some aspects of the visual discourse upon which I have been focusing. I have already mentioned the reversal in the positioning of the Indian, from the lurking surveillant presence with hostile intent we encountered in *The Virginian* to the victim of a visual apparatus that has a fundamental covertness built into it. It would be a mistake, I think, to give conceptual priority to one or the other of these positions. Rather, in terms of discursive operations, they should be read as simultaneous, mutually determining, and in a state of constant alternation or displacement. The gun and the camera, the respective visual artifacts emblematic of these two positions, are not substitutes for one another, nor are they merely equatable symbols. As gestures in an ongoing discourse, they circulate meaning between them in their relationship of similarity and difference, creating ever widening circles of association: the visual tool that aligns the eye displaces/is displaced by the visual apparatus that imitates the eye; direct material intervention in the world (violent ambush or bagging a trophy) displaces/is displaced by the inscription of views of the world; the locus of the covert gaze is in one case a position in the "natural" landscape (out of sight in the woods or behind a ridge) and in the other a function of a commodified black box device. It is precisely a characterizing feature of the visual discourse under consideration here that it depends on such circulation and instability of positioning, rather than on maintaining seemingly fixed arrangements of the gaze, as do some other scopic regimes (see Chapter 4).

Consistent with this quality of circulation and displacement, the operation of visual desire is especially evident in this discourse of looking, an issue already raised by a number of the individual texts we have encountered. "Bad Medicine" depicts this visual desire in a particularly interesting way, mapping it onto an erotics of interracial attraction. Although increasingly drawn to the gaze of the camera as it creates a position for him as a tourist spectacle (cf. the tourist gaze as producer of the "viewability" of the Yellowstone hotel in "Hank's Woman"), Sun Road only finally agrees to be photographed when a woman fixes him in her desiring gaze.

And it is not just any woman. "At the canyon, out on Inspiration Point," the narrator informs us, "I noticed a young lady watching Sun Road more than she watched the view. She was lovely. Her looks and her dress suggested a type much superior to the common, loud-voiced tourist" (34–35). Here once again the genteel, upper-class traveler makes her appearance, though in this case as a young and lovely woman whose refinements are to her credit and whose superior sensitivities prevent her, unlike the tourist rabble, from intruding on Sun Road's privacy.

She spoke low, with the voice of gentlefolk: "How handsome, how superb! He is a part of all this. How I should like to see him in Indian dress! I shouldn't think of taking his picture without his permission, and I would never find the courage to ask him." (35)

The "all this" Sun Road is part of, of course, is the sublime view that was the specialty of the tourist mode this young woman represents. That she too, like the hunter-tourist narrator and the loud-voiced mob, carries the emblem of the new visual order is a good indicator of how far this regime has penetrated Wister's fictional universe. And Sun Road's assimilation to the scenic, photogenic landscape is another indicator of the shift in tourist looking.

After this encounter, the hunting party turned tour group makes its way to the Mammoth Hot Springs, where they find tourists once again in abundance. Sun Road, now fully aware of the figure he is cutting in this environment, makes his appearance in buckskin dress. The ironies begin to stack up as he enters the lobby of the hotel and goes to the souvenir counter, where "odds and ends of the West" were sold. He buys some of these, carved figures "of soldiers and cowboys and ponies," as a present for Little Chief Hare. And who should be standing there as well but the young woman from the Canyon of the Yellowstone. She is in the process of purchasing some of the mass produced photos of Indians they have for sale and is disappointed to find out that Sun Road is not represented. Our narrator, observing from a distance, remarks that Sun Road looks at her "as any man looks at a beautiful woman."

A short while later their paths cross again, and this time the crucial deal is struck. On finding out that Sun Road knows some of the people represented in the photos she has purchased, including his own grandfather, Chief Washakie, she inquires, "Has no one wished for a likeness of you?" "Do you wish it?" is his reply. When he learns of her desire in this regard, he says simply, "I like you to do what you wish." "It—it will only be very small. Not like these you buy," she assures him (37–38).

This whole episode of tourist encounter conflates an implied sexual attraction across racial, class, and regional lines with the geometry of visual desire and appropriation we have already noticed in a variety of other western texts. Although not strictly speaking an economic transaction, the shadow of image commodification hovers over the scene, and indeed over the whole story. I would invoke here the text with which I began this study, the joke about the "distant" Indian in which the hidden desire of the eastern tourist is to occupy the position of visual authority and completion. The touristic desire in Wister's story is for the flattened, commodified image of this presumed locus of the "knowing gaze." Or perhaps more accurately, the Indian of "Bad Medicine" becomes not just a commodified "view" but the very embodiment of commodified looking in general, wherein the constant movement of subjects and objects of looking, their ceaseless displacements of one another, constitute the very soul of the commodity form.

There is a telling moment in this regard near the beginning of the story, before the hunting party leaves Fort Washakie. Just after his Kodak has frightened Sun Road off, the narrator goes into the post trader's store. There he discusses with the proprietor his confusion over the fact that while this Indian has fled the camera, others obviously have not, since right there in the store he has "some photographs exposed conspicuously for sale," some of the same ones, the reader discovers later, displayed at the souvenir counter in the Mammoth hotel. The post trader allows as how one never can tell. Some cling to the old superstitions, while others have gotten used to the new device, and in some cases "a dollar will persuade them." The narrator says, "I'll give five to get that picture" (4). And it is finally at this point of economic calculation of his image that we are made aware of Sun Road's identity. Here is another case, I think, in which an object of looking is called into being precisely through the agency of the touristic (commodified) gaze.

The twists and turns of this already complex discourse of commodified visuality become even more tortuous a few pages later. His concerns about the camera having been allayed, Sun Road agrees to serve as hunting guide, only to discover that the trip will end in Yellowstone, a place of very bad medicine. Thus both the premier tourist attraction of the American West and the device most associated with tourist inscription are connected to destructive forces in an imagined Native American belief system. As Sun Road is weaned from his faith in the efficacy of these invisible supernatural forces, he becomes the victim of another "invisible" force, that is, the mystified agencies of capital that underlie the commodity form. The colonizing power of capital is displayed most explicitly, perhaps, when the frustrated narrator seeks to overcome Sun Road's traditional beliefs about Yellowstone by offering him twice the normal fee for his services as guide.

As Sun Road hesitates to commit himself to a trip into spiritually dangerous territory, the parties to this business transaction stand in uncomfortable silence in the post trader's store. In this moment we are offered a brief inventory of the available trade goods: "coats, shirts, dark overalls, bright scarfs, the rough-dried pelts of bears, foxes, and coyotes, and hides soft tanned, hung from the hooks in the dimness"; and then most significantly, "near by, the photographed faces of Washakie and Sharp Nose stared at us with haughty aloofness" (13).

Here is another of those diagnostic moments, like the opening joke or the horse blinding episode in *The Virginian*, where large domains of a discourse/practice seem to concentrate in a small space, collapsing together elements that elsewhere are scattered more thinly and expressed with more distinct separation. The "haughty aloofness" of the Indian observer invokes the association of a superior, knowing gaze, but here its ironic expression is in the form of a commodified tourist image meant to be purchased and *looked at* and displayed. What these ironic Indian "watchers" observe is a social and economic negotiation over Sun Road's positioning in the tourist service industry, which will eventually transform him into a photogenic display himself. The colonizing capitalist underpinnings of this process are not far beneath the surface of this passage, expressed, for example, in the juxtaposition of the imported, mass produced apparel with the pelts and hides of indigenous manufacture, all equally available for economic exchange.

And if this scene condenses the key elements of display, visuality, exchange, and circulation of the gaze, such is even more true of the climactic moment of Sun Road's death. By falling into the well of Old Faithful geyser, he quite literally merges with an apparatus that embodies the whole discourse of looking West. If Yellowstone is the premier tourist destination of the American West, then Old Faithful is its regularly beating heart. This geyser is of course impressive as a spectacular display, building audibly to its sudden climax of revealed power. It is a sight especially "odd and new to look at" for the novice tourist. But beyond this, it has the feature of remarkable regularity that allows for its powerful natural forces to be integrated with the regular scheduling of tourist circulation. This uncannily machine-like quality makes

Old Faithful quite literally a component in the visual apparatus of the tourist gaze. The gesture of making the "official," which is to say the fully commodified image of Sun Road in front of the quintessential tourist spectacle is about as complete an embodiment of the visual regime in question as one could devise.

As ludicrously melodramatic as it might seem in purely narrative terms, that Sun Road should fall into the geyser has a conceptual aptness to it. He quite literally disappears into the apparatus at the very instant of his visual inscription. If he comes into being as a "real" person out of the hunter-tourist's desire to appropriate his image, there is a basic fitness to his disappearance at the moment that image is officially secured. The final irony is that the only traces of him left behind (except for photographic images) are his red scarf, emblem of his status as spectacular display, and the tourist souvenirs he has purchased for his son. These the narrator sees floating down in the heaving water of the geyser's well.

It is worth noting, perhaps, that these artifacts are carved wooden figures of soldiers, cowboys, and ponies. Is it too much to suggest that in this small collection of children's toys we have expressed the loss of a way of life under the effects of colonization? Soldiers and cowboys are, after all, the colonial agents par excellence, at least in the popular imagination that Wister was himself so involved in creating. That these figures should show up in the form of tourist souvenirs, and this in the very context of the Indian being reduced to a commodified image, suggests that in the Wister moment we find ourselves in a new (postcolonial?) stage of domination in which a new order of visuality obtains.

Chapter Three
"That's What Worries Me, It's Too Quiet"
An Ethnographic Excursion

Son, I can tell you what an Indian will do to you, but with a woman you can never tell.

Gary Cooper as Wild Bill Hickok
in Cecil B. DeMille's *The Plainsman,* 1936

I had occasion some years ago to decapitate four live chickens. The assigned method was not the hatchet and chopping block, nor the deft flick of the wrist to snap the spinal cord. Instead, I was instructed to hold each bird's body to the ground, place a foot on its neck, and with one firm tug detach the head. Gruesome as it sounds, this approach is quite efficient. Hardly less humane than the other methods, it avoids the unseemly spectacle of headless poultry flapping about until involuntary nervous responses subside. One visceral tremor, only detectable if you are holding the hen, and it's all over. In fact, this method was chosen because the use of a hatchet in a previous performance of this task resulted in a display unsettling to some of its observers.

As I and a couple of fellow executioners performed these duties under a blazing sun, we wore the woolen uniforms of privates in the frontier army, circa May 1876. Our detail was watched from the top of a low hill by a small group of women dressed in approximations of the late nineteenth-century frontier apparel working class women would have worn. We were all participants in a living history exercise conducted over a period of five days in May 1985, at Fort Laramie, a National Historic Site located near the eastern border of Wyoming, at the confluence of the Laramie and North Platte Rivers.

Although a bit off main pathways, Fort Laramie is a popular secondary destination in the national tourist network and a primary site for many regional vacationers. It certainly has claim to considerable historical significance. Euro-American occupation dates back to the fur trading period, but it is as a military outpost that the site is mainly preserved and interpreted. Fort Laramie occupied a strategically important position on the Oregon Trail, its main function being to provide supplies and protection for the overland emigrant looking West to a new life. The Fort was also the site of the 1868 treaty that established the original Sioux reservation, a parcel stretching from the Missouri River to the western border of Dakota Territory. This agreement also reserved the whole Powder River Basin, from the summit of the Big Horn Mountains eastward to the Black Hills, for exclusive use of those Indians wishing to continue the traditional way of life sustained by the buffalo hunt.

Like so many before it, this treaty was breached in short order, a process accelerated by the 1874 military expedition that confirmed rumors of Black Hills gold. It was out of conflicts subsequent to the Fort Laramie Treaty that the events of the so-called Sioux War (1876–81) grew. George Armstrong Custer commanded the Black Hills expedition; his defeat at the Little Big Horn River in late June of 1876 is easily the most emblematic event of the period. The living history exercise at Fort Laramie was set in May of that year, by which time the major campaign against the Sioux was well underway. Fort Laramie was a link in the supply chain for this operation, and in late May General George Crook marched all but twenty-nine of the Fort's soldiers northward to form one of three prongs in the strategy that was supposed to encircle and crush the unpacified Sioux and Cheyenne. After an inconclusive battle on June 17 along Rosebud Creek, Crook's column fell back and played no further role, except by its absence, in the actions leading to Custer's defeat.

But these momentous events of national cultural significance (Slotkin 1985:435–532) constitute only the dim background of the living history exercise I will give an account of here. Its focus was daily life on the frontier military outpost as lived by those on the lowest rungs of the military ladder—the infantry private and the resident civilian laundress, the latter being the only female role with official status in the frontier military. Even officers' wives and children were marginal appendages with no real standing. The laundresses constituted a contract labor force paid from the salaries of the individual soldiers for whom they did washing.

Most of the participants in the exercise, then, occupied the role of either infantry private or military laundress, with strict gender division maintained.[1] Participation carried with it three hours of academic credit from the Department of Geography and Recreation at the University of Wyoming. The exercise was also accredited by the National Park Service as legitimate living history training for its personnel. The regular interpretive program at Fort Laramie makes extensive use of living history methods. The instructors for the course portrayed the roles of non-commissioned officers, the primary instructor adopting the persona of a first sergeant. Only one commissioned officer was portrayed, and in keeping with the historical record he stayed aloof from the regular activities of the common soldier.

The five days of the exercise were preceded by classroom work that addressed the methods of living history reenactment and provided background readings on life in the frontier military. The main task of participants was to develop a credible "first person" historical persona and to "inhabit" this character as fully as possible during the activities at Fort Laramie. The living history philosophy guiding the course maintains that this sort of experience provides deeper insights into the material substance, and by extension into the mindset of a past period, than is possible using written texts alone. The smells, tastes, and textures become directly accessible. It was in the episode with the chickens that I personally came closest to this ideal, feeling their death throes and trying to choke down the stew in which they were featured that evening for dinner. All the banal otherness of the past lived for me most vividly in these mundane moments. But this episode in the exercise also comes back to me as the point at which I felt the apparatus of display and spectacle most strongly. Being personally on show in an uncomfortable moment of exposure while performing an unsavory act brought home to me my own implication in an already established structure of looking.

*   *   *

It is mid-day on Monday, just before the actual opening of the exercise, which is referred to officially as the "Camp of Instruction," the nineteenth-century name for the equivalent of modern boot camp. The participants, some thirty-five in all, with a few more men than women and ranging in age from early twenties to early sixties, are gathered behind the restored cavalry barracks, where the males will be quartered. We have completed a morning orientation tour and are having a last modern meal (hot dogs) before putting on the first persons we are supposed to inhabit for the next five days.

I am sitting with two participants who have gone through the exercise previously. One of them has also worked as a living history interpreter at the Fort. Without preamble, the other of the two says, "I've got a joke you'll like." He proceeds to offer a risqué variation on an old chestnut involving the Lone Ranger and Tonto. Here it is in recollected paraphrase:

The Lone Ranger and Tonto are surrounded by Indians. No matter what they do, they are losing the fight and it looks bad for them. There doesn't seem to be any hope, but the Lone Ranger goes over to his horse Silver and whispers some-thing in his ear. Silver takes off at a gallop and succeeds in getting away through the Indian lines. So the two of them keep fighting, and just as they are about at the end of their rope, here comes the horse galloping back. And there's a beau-tiful blond riding him! When he arrives, the Lone Ranger looks over and shakes his head: "Stupid horse!! I said 'posse,' 'POSSE'!!"

This elicits some polite if not very enthusiastic laughter, and the other of my two companions says this reminds him of another one. He pro-ceeds to tell the classic Lone Ranger and Tonto joke. Same setup as be-fore, but in this case, when their cause looks lost, the Lone Ranger turns to Tonto and says, "Well, old friend, what do we do now?" Tonto replies, "What do you mean 'WE', whiteman?" About the time this exchange of jokes is going on, I am noticing that the male and female participants are completely segregated in their seating, the men clustering in small groups of from two to four, the women all gathered separately in one large circle.[2]

I have already confessed my faith in the idea that the most evanes-cent, seemingly trivial gestures, for example, a brief exchange of jokes or the ad hoc seating arrangements at a hot-dog lunch, may have com-pressed within them a great deal of discursive significance. In retrospect, the little scene I have just described seems to me to bear an interest-ing anticipatory relationship to the living history exercise that followed it. Most obviously, issues of racial and gender relationships are at play in the jokes, and as we will see, they operate as important structuring elements in the exercise. These are not conscious historical themes the instructors set out to examine (though the history of gender relations does figure explicitly in the instruction). Rather, they move in a track alongside the living history reenactment per se, and in large measure outside its awareness. One might say that this thread of discourse uses the imagery, the scenarios, the settings, and the language of the frontier military reenactment to realize its own ends. And these ends are rooted in an advanced consumer culture, not in the marginal existence of the military underclass in the Indian Wars period.

Most important here, the themes and scenarios of the Fort Laramie exercise were played out in terms of visual experience. As an academic course and a mechanism for teaching living history interpretation, the exercise constantly called on participants to occupy varying positions of spectatorship and display. And these positions were organized, as we shall see, in terms of gender and race. The paradox, of course, is that these pervasive enactments of spectacle, heavily influenced by such things as film westerns and other mass cultural sources, are both the main reason for the exercise in the first place and in most cases the elements least "authentic" to the historical period being interpreted. To have everything organized as some sort of picturesque display for this or that audience, virtually the raison d'être of public living history interpretation, is the aspect of the exercise least consistent with all that the participants learn about the drudgery and banality of frontier military life. In other words, the explicit goals of the exercise—to counteract misperceptions about a past way of life and to present a fuller picture— are in some measure contradicted by the very procedures inherent in living history practice.

Of course this is not a circumstance unique to the Fort Laramie exercise. It is itself a historical condition built into the modern institutional context of living history. And to make this basic point is not to deny that living history can be a compelling mode of historical expression. The Fort Laramie exercise in fact did a good job of providing the conditions for imaginative encounters with the textures of the past. To experience the dry chill and utter darkness inside a nineteenth-century army barracks on the high plains of Wyoming in May is certainly to know something about an historical moment. But my interest here is how the production of these conditions is organized around a very modern discourse of looking. And that brings me back to the joke exchange.

The first Lone Ranger and Tonto joke employs an image—the beautiful woman borne on the pure white stallion—that is about as complete an adolescent male fantasy as one could imagine.[3] Though explicitly described as blond in this telling, that the woman is white could literally go without saying, since cultural convention leads us to take it for granted—just as "beautiful blond" automatically indicates female gender. At the core of the joke, then, is the pervasively familiar icon of the woman on display for and under the control of white male potency, symbolized to the point of parody by the Lone Ranger's white stallion.

And as if this image alone were not enough, Silver bears this silent, presumably assenting object of male desire through the hostile forces of a dark race to present her triumphantly to his white master. The whole setup seems to invoke, and carry to ludicrous extreme, all the conventions of white male authority that inform so much of our mass cultural discourse, pulp and B film westerns being perhaps the most apposite examples here. I hardly need add that the conventional arrangements of modern visuality, with the object of visual desire observed from a viewing position coded as male (Mulvey 1989:14–38), are fully, even excessively in force. The affinity of this scene with the water-skiing legend should not go unremarked.

But to stop there in a reading of this joke is to miss its point. This comically exaggerated scene of the triumphant display and delivery of the female trophy to the white male hero through the symbolic extension of his own potency and in the face of the surrounding threat of hostile "others" is constructed precisely to be deflated. The joke sets up, again with the elegant compression characteristic of folk expression, virtually a paradigmatic icon of male authority and control, and then thumbs its nose at it.

And furthermore, if we accept even the most basic of deconstructive principles, the joke's punchline may be taken as a remarkably concise folk expression of the idea that authoritative control over meaning is never complete, since meaning is always in the process of sliding to some other place. As the symbolic embodiment of virile mastery and power, the white stallion is a dream come true—the phallus that understands language, responds to commands, and goes off on dangerous missions. The joke's humor derives from the fact that Silver almost gets it right, but not quite. The slippage of one phoneme transforms the hero's male rescuers into female sexuality, presumably with disastrous results. The real disaster, of course, is that the absolute authority of white male potency, which is equated with control over linguistic meaning, is thoroughly undermined. All it takes is the smallest chink to bring the whole edifice down. And once this breach is established through the introduction of female sexuality, it is only a matter of time before the hostile alien force, represented by the besieging Indians, will come sweeping in.

While I certainly do not deny that this joke is patently demeaning in its synecdochic dismemberment and reduction of women to their sexuality, I am proposing that at its core it is an acknowledgment of the instability of white male dominance. A certain anxiety, even paranoia lies behind the open parody in which perhaps the "whitest" of all pop culture western heroes, especially if we take his pure white stallion as his extension, becomes the goat. Such a reading extends to and is supported by the second Lone Ranger and Tonto joke performed in this brief exchange. In fact, the second joke, which I take to be the "original" one of this cycle, seems like a completion of the symbolic scenario established in the first. Where Tonto is a silent cipher in the "posse" joke, here he dominates. The hero's complacent assumptions about his faithful, subaltern companion are shown up as fatally flawed when Tonto asserts his racial identity, allying himself with the threat from outside, the threat of difference. In claiming his racial allegiance, Tonto reduces the Lone Ranger from the individualized hero, "kimosabe," to the generic "whiteman," a drastic reduction of his meaning, and hence of his power. Once again, the quintessential Anglo male hero becomes the butt of the humor, puncturing the facade of his authority.

Between them these two jokes enact a geometry of gender and racial difference. Except for the icon-like display of the female object of desire in the first joke, explicitly visual discourse is not a strong element in these narrative performances. However, the reenactment exercise that followed them shifts their gender/racial geometry into the context of looking and display endemic to living history. To put it in simplest terms, in the Fort Laramie exercise the figure of the Anglo male is consistently displaced from its culturally assumed position as authoritative viewer to a position as the object of another's gaze. This other viewer is sometimes marked as female, sometimes as Indian. The important point is that the figure of the (potentially heroic) white man is subject to the evaluative and, at a climactic moment, actively hostile gaze of these others. As in the jokes, his is not the uniformly controlling position of the "look that knows." Rather, he frequently becomes the victim of such a look. It is this aspect of the Fort Laramie living history exercise that connects it to the larger Western discourse of looking I have attempted to tease out of the verbal texts in previous chapters.

The nonce seating arrangements at the hot-dog lunch might be read as a subtle anticipation of these symbolic relations. As we will see, it was a recurring practice throughout the exercise to locate the whole group of laundresses as spectators for male displays of various sorts. Not only did the spontaneous seating reflect the strict gender separation operative throughout, but by sitting in a single circle while the men distributed themselves in small groups the women perhaps "predicted" the fact that their participation in the exercise entailed serving as a collective in-house audience for the more diverse and individualized male activities. Frequently, the laundresses did things as a single group. The men, on the other hand, were often divided into smaller units to reenact such activities as fatigue details and guard duty. It was common for them to be scattered around the whole site, while the women tended to stay within "washtub row," the laundress compound, when they were not being deployed as an audience for some sort of male display.

Highlighted against this background of gender coded display and spectatorship, a subject to which I will return, the climax of the whole event was an overnight bivouac in which only the men participated. It was itself climaxed by an attack from an unseen party of "hostiles." The implications of all these elements for the discourse of Western looking need further discussion, but first a bit more ethnographic detail on the sequence of events will be helpful.

*   *   *

Beginning at about mid-day on Monday and ending roughly the same time the next Saturday, the Fort Laramie Camp of Instruction exercise was organized according to a loose script of activities intended to give some sense of the range of experiences one might have had as an infantry private or a military laundress at this western outpost. This means, of course, that what were apparently the two main qualities of this life, monotonous drudgery and boredom, could not be recovered. This, too, is a feature endemic to public living history, since even the most mundane of activities needs to be made "viewable" in some way. Whole spheres of life are simply unavailable in any direct way in living history reenactment. This is especially true of the most intimate and personal aspects of life: sexuality, waste elimination, illness, death, to mention a few. Aspects of these domains may be hinted at and ceremonial accompaniments to them may be reenacted (e.g., funerals and weddings), but the central activities themselves remain outside of view.

Along with these "unavailable" subjects, "real time" durations can only be conveyed in a very limited range of activities. While a whole crop may be grown and harvested at a living history agricultural site, as a performance for the public only small segments of this activity can be observed by any one spectator. The visitor stitches these pieces together with the other fragments of recreated life to form an inherently "fictive" text, fictive in the sense that the "real" life of the past is selected according to certain themes, organized into scenes and narrative sequences, and condensed or, less typically, expanded in time and space to make it "watchable" in a way that real life rarely is.

The Fort Laramie exercise was organized around a number of pre-planned "scenarios," very loosely scripted narrative sequences of activities intended to illustrate significant aspects of camp life. The enrolled participants were, for the most part, not informed in advance about these set pieces. Participants were expected to go along as guided by the instructors, all maintaining their first person identities. One of the parameters was that these fictive personas should be manufactured from scratch, based on general historical knowledge rather than on actual historical personages who may have left a mark in the historical record (e.g., in diaries). We were taught that the best approach would be to base one's historical identity on aspects of one's own life, but reframed to fit a late nineteenth-century context. The idea was to develop a fully rounded character, but not one so alien as to be difficult to maintain in concrete interactions. The more knowledgeable one became about the period and the more adept at reenactment, the more successful one would be at sustaining a remote persona. One of the instructors, for example, a very experienced reenactor of frontier military life, portrayed an Irish immigrant and seasoned veteran of previous western campaigns. He included a credible Irish accent and a repertoire of obscene military folklore among his reenactment gear. While it was frequently emphasized in the classroom instruction that living history reenactment is not theater, since one is supposed to go beyond mere play acting, still, this sort of living history resembles in many respects a kind of improvisational drama, where loose situations are established and one is expected to respond to them in keeping with the character one has adopted.

As a technical living history term, "scenario" seems particularly appropriate. It combines notions of narrative arrangement with physically enacted, visually accessible expression. Here is a partial list of the scenarios included in the Fort Laramie exercise:

- an evening of dancing in the barracks
- payday
- a military funeral
- a visit to the laundress area for "tea" (pie and lemonade)
- barracks inspection (marked by the pre-planned tirade of a sergeant who discovers "contraband")
- an evening of guard duty (highlighted by a fire alarm)
- an evening at the enlisted men's bar (including amateur melodrama)
- overnight bivouac (including several sub-scenarios, all climaxed by an "Indian attack")
- weekly bath
- practice firing of an artillery piece (demonstration by NPS personnel)
- formal retreat parade (the high ceremonial moment)

Along with these narratively shaped events, the soldiers regularly performed fatigue duties, that is, work details of various sorts. These were carried out in small groups and included such things as cleaning the corral, sweeping the barracks, firewood detail, and breadmaking (the primary staple of the enlisted man's diet). The chicken killing was one such detail. The regular diurnal round of reveille, barracks inspection, mealtimes, raising and lowering the colors, lights out, and so forth, was observed. This military regulation of daily rhythms was, in fact, one of the more effectively conveyed lessons of the exercise. Also, considerable time was devoted to learning basic elements of drill formations and to the use of firearms, including the manual of arms, rifle loading, firing (blanks exclusively), and cleaning, and the formal infantry maneuvers that might be used in skirmishes with the "hostiles."

Finally, two other components, somewhat marginal to the main activities, complete this cursory survey. Each evening the participants stepped out of their first persons for a group evaluation session. The day's activities were described and experiences shared. The instructors offered feedback on participant performance. Then on Friday evening a "Moonlight Tour" was conducted. Although the site was not yet open to the public for its regular operating season, this one evening was established as the time when the participants could display their reenactment skills to an outside audience. The nighttime tour was advertised regionally and the participants were assigned to occupy various posts around the fort (enlisted men's bar, laundress area, guardhouse, etc.). Visitors were led around the site and encouraged to interact with the reenactors, who were supposed to maintain their first persons. This was something of a "final exam" for the academic course.

Although my own location did not give me direct access to the daily activities of the women participants, it was apparent that the life of the laundress, even more monotonous than that of the common soldier, did not lend itself to the development of diverse living history scenarios. This was compensated to some degree by the inclusion of lectures for the female participants on various aspects of women's nineteenth-century experience, birth and midwifery for example. On the evening the male participants were away from the fort, the women were visited by an expert on frontier military living history. He discussed with them some of the intangible and even preternatural aspects of historical reenactment, a subject to which I will return.

*   *   *

As expressive forms, the jokes, legends, and literary texts I have analyzed to this point are rather concentrated manifestations of discourse. As such they lend themselves to relatively focused readings. The Fort Laramie living history exercise is of a different order. It is a many-layered event arising from an institutional and social context of considerable complexity. Its representation in an ethnographic account cannot have the same interpretive simplicity as a joke or a photograph. While the reenactment exercise is not in such a straightforward way a staging of the Western discourse of looking, nevertheless it is thoroughly informed by this visuality, and it illustrates how institutional practices and "on the ground" human behavior conform to the protocols of a visual regime.

To get more directly at how this visuality operates in the Fort Laramie exercise we can begin with the climactic scenario, the overnight bivouac away from the Fort. This occurred on the third day (Wednesday), roughly the mid-point of the program. The arrangement of the scenarios over the five days gave the exercise as a whole a kind of loose narrative shape, building in stages to the excitement (for the male participants) of this mock "campaign" into "hostile territory," and then subsiding to the concluding ceremonial events of Friday evening. The "themes" of the first half of the exercise were characterized by a vaguely domestic/romantic subtext which I will elaborate on below. The concluding day and a half, following the infantry company's return, became progressively more focused on the preparations for the high ceremony of the final retreat parade and the Moonlight Tour, both of which were directed toward a public audience.

Leaving at mid-day on Wednesday, the company marched approximately five miles across open prairie, which took us out of the historic site boundary and onto the property of a local rancher whose permission had been secured in advance. Each person carried a rifle, canteen, and overnight provisions. Tents and other camping equipment, as well as those few participants whose conditions of health prevented them from making the march in the unseasonably warm weather, were trucked out to the campsite. On our march we were admonished to keep an eye out for rattlesnakes. Outriders were posted front and back and on each flank, since we were to assume that our movements might be under the observation of "Mr. Lo," which we learned was the common soldier's derogatory term for a hostile Indian.[4]

Just prior to arrival at the bivouac we were drilled in skirmish maneuvers, adding to a growing anticipation that some sort of engagement was impending.[5] For this scenario each participant was issued six rounds of blank ammunition, a departure from the practice firings up to this point, where cartridges were dispensed one at a time. A significant minority of the participants came to the exercise out of an already developed interest in historical firearms, and the prospect of shooting in a mock engagement clearly was a key attraction. The tension that began to grow ever more palpable was premised on the largely unspoken notion that we were under surveillance. Given the build-up of the march, indirect cues from the instructors, and the whole physical context, this feeling pushed close to the edge of the exercise's fictive frame—perhaps for some, beyond it. [6]

One clue to the influences at work in this bivouac scenario occurred during a subsidiary activity after our arrival at the campsite. Various work details were assigned—setting up tents, digging firepits, and so forth. In addition to these, a small reconnaissance detachment was sent out under the command of the one officer being portrayed in the exercise. This "mapping expedition," to which I was assigned, went perhaps half a mile away from the camp, taking us to the bluffs above the North Platte River. We were, in fact, out of sight of any modern intrusions, and the late afternoon sun threw the river valley into sharp relief, creating a particularly tranquil scene. While taking a break, one of the participants commented on this peaceful prospect. In the most natural way, without the slightest shade of irony, someone actually responded with the cliché from countless frontier adventure tales: "That's what worries me, it's too quiet."

That this pop culture colonialist sentiment, mediated through who knows how many textual channels, was received apparently in the spirit in which it was spoken (at least no one, including myself, showed any sign that it seemed absurd) indicates how thoroughly a particular discourse can penetrate and organize (textualize) our behavior in actual situations. Perhaps the most remarkable effect of this five-day event, its greatest "success" as a discursive apparatus, was to produce the felt presence of an unseen, threatening watcher—one obviously marked as "different."

Whether this persistent sense of being observed by a hostile gaze was in fact a permanent condition at nineteenth-century colonial outposts is perhaps unverifiable at this remove. In any case, that is rather beside the point here, since my concern is not with the ethnographic accuracy of the exercise. What is of interest is that the raw material of the frontier military reenactment provides a symbolic context for the expression of a very modern condition—one where the complex relations of looking and being looked at *are* unquestionably central to the conditions of daily life, if typically only at low levels of intensity and often outside conscious awareness. The moment of high drama where the infantry company is out in "hostile territory" is really only the least ambiguous expression of a complexly layered structure of observation and display that "belongs" ethnographically to the advanced consumer culture of the late twentieth century.

After a tensely watchful night sleeping two to a tent, with everyone taking a turn at guard duty, the "payoff" to this main scenario occurred the next morning as the company was getting ready to leave. Several shots were fired by parties unknown from behind a nearby hill. The alarm was sounded and a skirmish line formed, allowing for some organized volleys to be fired in return. The remainder of the ammunition was then expended at the order to "fire at will." When calm was restored a reconnaissance party was sent out. It reported finding shell casings but nothing more. The official determination was that a small raiding party of Indians happening to pass by had taken the opportunity to harass the company.

For at least some of the participants, the opportunity to "shoot back" at these unseen observers clearly represented more than just another clinical moment of reenactment. It carried a considerably greater emotional load, one that cannot merely be reduced to the regressive staging of childhood fantasy, though the considerable affective charge no doubt tapped into deep sources of emotional energy for at least some of the participants.[7] However else we might want to frame it, this moment of temporary release—and that was very much its effect—involved at least a partial sense of relief from the threat of an unmastered gaze from elsewhere. It is rather to state the obvious to say that, in coding this hidden viewing location as "Indian," the Fort Laramie exercise participates in a long tradition. We encountered in *The Virginian* an important moment in the development of this trope. Based on my observations of the narrative shape of the Fort Laramie exercise and of the emotional rhythms that registered more in the participants' general demeanor than in easily quantifiable ways, I would go so far as to say that the central symbolic "function" of the Camp of Instruction was precisely to load and then purge, however temporarily, the oppressive power of a pervasive, unseen, surveillant presence that seemed to reside in the very landscape itself. That the exercise builds this presence to the point that it threatens to break the fictive frame of reenactment, and then "drives" it off in a seemingly anti-climactic episode of inconclusive, desultory engagement, only works in a system of symbolic arrangements, where apparently trivial causes can produce disproportionate effects.

And one of the effects in this case was that the central scenario—the bivouac culminating in the Indian raid—reduced the discourse of looking I am concerned with to its most basic, direct expression. The symbolic or discursive logic is as follows. Complex arrangements of visuality are expressed over the course of the reenactment period, arrangements that, as in the Lone Ranger jokes, destabilize the normally assumed locus of power and authority. However, the centerpiece of the event, at least for the male participants, is a climactic scenario in which the complexities and instabilities of modern (advanced consumer) visuality are symbolically reduced to the familiar protocol of a hostile gaze, marked as racially Other, being driven off by violent, heroic action. Thus the discursive center of gravity of the Fort Laramie exercise could be seen precisely as a reassertion of the authority that was being pilloried in those anticipatory Lone Ranger and Tonto jokes.

This said, however, we should not lose sight of the fact that the symbolic reductiveness at the heart of the five-day event was surrounded by a rather richly layered elaboration of visual discourse. Though temporarily suppressed at this symbolic center (and even then not entirely), these discursive complexities were abundantly available for observation over the course of the five days. For purposes of analysis, and recognizing that ethnographic representations entail their own forms of reductiveness, I will examine briefly three arrangements of looking and display separate from that of the central scenario. These strands interwove with one another over the course of the exercise, and they all involved in various combinations the apparatuses of spectatorship and surveillance, which, as we have begun to see in the previous analyses, stand at the foundation of the modern discourse of looking West. The first of these arrangements is one constructed in terms of gender relationships; the second is the structure of tourist spectatorship that figures in all public living history re-enactment; and the third is the surveillance apparatus that is built into this exercise as a tool of academic instruction. There is also one further arrangement of looking of interest here, and I will address it in conclusion to this ethnographic excursion. It is perhaps the most difficult to get a handle on, since it involves the spectatorship (surveillance?) conducted by the ghostly presence of the past itself, one of those seemingly marginal phenomena that turn out to have considerable symbolic importance.

After our encounter with the "hostiles," the infantry company broke camp and marched the five miles back to the Fort. Just before we got there we were allowed to fall out and make ourselves presentable, so that our arrival would make the best possible impression. We were informed that the population of the Fort (i.e., the laundresses) would turn out to witness our entry. As we marched in we were led in the singing of "When Johnny Comes Marching Home," and we had been instructed in some of the formal parade commands (e.g., eyes right), the use of which would enhance the pageantry of our return.

In short, in this small scenario the infantry company was actively constructed as an historical spectacle, with the laundresses as the spectators. In terms of the overall narrative shape of the exercise, having been threatened by a hostile surveillance that we then successfully resisted, we were rewarded (compensated?) with the opportunity to occupy the position of visual display object, which is to say, the object of fictive desire. The apparatus of spectacle, organized around a thematics of gender, displaced that of surveillance, coded in terms of race. The relationship between these two modes is crucial to our understanding of the Fort Laramie exercise as a realization of visual discourse, but before pursuing this point further we need a better sense of the fictive model of gender relationships set in place from the very beginning of the event.

What we learned in the classroom about the common soldier and the laundress in the frontier army suggested that they led lives of isolation, heavy labor, and boredom, occasionally punctuated for the soldier by moments of debauchery at "hog ranches," the bawdy houses that grew up on the periphery of western military installations. Desertion rates were remarkably high. However, from the very beginning of the exercise themes developed that might fairly be described as domestic/romantic. That a subtext about gender should inform the Fort Laramie reenactment is perhaps not too surprising, since the roles of army private and military laundress were set up as balancing, more or less equivalent categories, in keeping with our modern expectations of supposed gender balance in public higher education (cf. the discussion of ostensible gender balance in Chapter 6). As it turned out, many of the activities over the five days played out largely in terms of quasi-domestic, fictively eroticized interactions and scenarios.

Two scenarios on the first day bespoke these themes. In one the company was taught a number of period songs and then marched to the officers' quarters to perform them for the "captain," the one officer portrayed in the exercise. He in turn commissioned us to march to the laundress area and serenade the women with "The Girl I Left Behind Me," dedicating it to a particular laundress. That he was wooing this person became a running motif, though in fact such a relationship would have been a major violation of the strong class divisions of the period. Also, on this first day the laundresses were invited into the barracks for an evening of music and dancing. Though we were not expressly told how to behave at this event, the tenor was that of polite reticence, suggesting a Victorian social decorum that seemed in keeping with the period.

One thing that had been emphasized in the classroom instruction was that historically the military laundress was not a quasi-prostitute. She was in fact a respectable woman, if of low degree, and therefore deserving of proper regard. Furthermore, the laundress was a potential partner for the enlisted man, and marriages between people in these stations was not uncommon. Although this was not a theme actively developed through scenarios and no fictive liaisons were formed between participants (with the one exception already mentioned), the whole exercise was suffused with an oddly domestic quality. The Fort at times edged toward seeming a kind of bourgeois household writ large, with the laundresses occupying the position of a wife who stays home to clean and cook (they were responsible for preparing the special chicken dinner on the day of the company's return to the fort), while the soldiers provided protection and went off to "work." These qualities seemed especially prominent during the first half of the exercise.[8]

The relevant point here is that the development of a general context which models gender relations according to middle class domestic norms is not just engaged in the scholarly/recreational business of recovering a past period. It also unwittingly enacts or reflects our contemporary social agendas. Indeed, it cannot help but do so. It is exactly through the alchemy of discursive processes that what must be one of the least domestic of historical contexts, the frontier military outpost, is re-created in part through a subtext informed by modern ideals of domesticity. But against this background of a familiar and comfortable arrangement of gender relationships, an arrangement not presented in particularly visual terms, the exercise also plays out a somewhat more troubled gender drama, one in which visuality *is* central.

If we revisit the scene of the infantry company's return to the fort, we might recognize two sides to the role the laundresses played. On the one hand, they occupied the "natural" position of the wife welcoming her husband home in the quasi-domestic/romantic framework. On the other hand, they moved toward the position of a detached and distanced spectatorship. The ideal domestic relationship presumes the closeness of direct personal attachment, virtually the opposite of the commodified visual structures of spectacle. When positioned as the audience at a parade, the laundresses became consumers of the pageantry of "heroic" military performance. This spectatorial mode, with women as the visual consumers of male activity, ran throughout the exercise as a counterpoint to the implicitly domestic gender coding. In some instances the line between the two was considerably blurred, and the overall effect was a subtle dissonance, a fluctuation between comfortable familiarity and moments of "display anxiety" (at least for the male participants).

The laundresses, then, were regularly called on to serve the function of an audience, while the soldiers were positioned as objects for their spectatorship. Only one scenario, an afternoon visit to the laundress area for tea, was constructed expressly so the men could observe the women's activities. By contrast, the women were frequently—and artificially, from the perspective of historical accuracy—located so that they could observe the men's tasks and performances.

Perhaps the clearest example of the women being positioned as spectators occurred on the second day of the exercise, the highlight of which was a scenario organized around the ritual of the monthly payday. In our preparatory classroom work much was made of the wretchedness of the compensation for military service during this period, approximately thirteen dollars a month at the rank of private. The instructors cleverly used the payday scenario as a way to demonstrate some aspects of the enlisted man economy. The historical building known as Old Bedlam, which had been the unmarried officers' quarters, was set up as a pay office. The soldiers stood in formation out front and were called in individually to receive their scrip, with various deductions identified to indicate how the common enlisted man might have spent his meager salary. For example, in my case several dollars were subtracted for the bill I had supposedly run up at the Fort sutler's store. We were not informed in advance what our deductions would be. In order to observe this rather lengthy operation, the laundresses were brought into Old Bedlam and seated on the open stairways, from which vantage they could see and hear the transactions. Needless to say, this would not have happened in 1876.

Positioned as she was in the payday scenario, the laundress-as-spectator occupied a role that has become common in our current historical moment, perhaps even diagnostic of it. She sits in an ambiguous social zone where her looking at a staged display overlaps with but does not completely annul her participation in it. Her detached spectatorship, which would seem properly to belong to a viewing location outside the fictive frame of the reenactment, remains suspended in the same space as her first-person identity *as* fictive laundress. At such moments she is neither entirely inside nor outside this frame, and that inbetweenness is precisely the quality that characterizes much of contemporary visuality. Most relevant here, it is the location held open for the tourist at living history sites. The laundress, then, served in some situations as the tourist surrogate at the Fort Laramie exercise, enacting in this capacity the ambiguous relationships of looking and display endemic to advanced consumer spectatorship.

As an example of how this arrangement operates in the regular interpretive program at Fort Laramie, we might consider the scene of the post store. One of the official living history characters portrayed at the Fort is the sutler, the merchant who held the lucrative commercial contract to sell what goods might be desired by soldiers at the post, by passing wagon trains, or by local settlers. When the tourist visitor to Fort Laramie enters the store, he or she is treated as an Oregon Trail emigrant by the sutler, a fiction maintained throughout the interaction. The interpretive strategy is to disrupt the visitors' modern worldview, jarring open the possibility of historical insight. The irony, of course, is that in the process of experiencing this historically edifying effect at the level of conscious interpretation, the visitor is also actively placed in an in-between status—part spectator, part reenactment participant—that increasingly characterizes social experience in an advanced consumer culture. In mundane experience this condition is not generally felt as confusing or disconcerting, indeed does not generally reach the threshold of awareness at all. When foregrounded in living history reenactment however, it can produce a kind of discomfort, although one intended to be entertaining rather than unpleasant, part of the intangible commodity consumed in our modern tourist system.

Along with being the fictive objects of potential romantic and domestic attachments within the reenactment frame, the laundresses also, then, represent a position in a very contemporary structure of looking and display. They merge at times with the tourist spectator, agent of a whole external apparatus of infrastructures, institutions, and social formations. While I will not examine it in detail, the Moonlight Tour that concluded the Fort Laramie exercise was the one occasion when this larger system was directly present. This event was built up as the point where all aspects of the exercise were supposed to come together in the fullest realization. That a relatively small number of visitors actually took the tour does not diminish its importance as the culmination of display, and preparations for it were characterized by a considerable amount of anxiety. This was also true of the penultimate scenario, the high ceremony of the formal retreat parade on Friday evening. The message was conveyed that this event, marked by "precision" formations and the solemn ritual of lowering the colors, would be for most participants the moment of greatest emotional involvement, the point at which we would get most deeply into persona and period.

These concluding events point up another aspect of the visual discourse underlying the exercise—a quality I have referred to in passing as "display anxiety." If the laundresses in some instances shifted into an ambiguously spectatorial role, the male participants served as the primary objects of display, or, as I have already said, objects of a certain kind of optical desire. But this role, too, is double-edged and ambiguous. As at least quasi-heroic in some contexts, such as the triumphal parade into the Fort after campaigning, the fiction of being the object of the admiring gaze is the expected, "comfortable" position for the male participants, the one long since firmly established in mass media depictions of western frontier life, not to mention through a host of other supporting discourses. However, as the object of looking in the modern consumer order, the primary display object is also in some respects at risk.

For one thing, pre-established images and expectations must be met. A minimum adequacy as display is required, and in the activities where display was foregrounded a great deal of pressure to get it right was brought to bear. But even more important, in an interesting kind of gender reversal, for the men to be objectified as display objects at all is to submit to a powerful gaze that they may not actively resist. Within the fictive frame of reenactment there is a sense in which the spectatorial gaze of the tourist must not be "returned." And not to "see" the gaze of the Other is in some sense to be subjugated to it (cf. the opening joke in Chapter 1). On those occasions where the laundresses served as tourist surrogates, the men were placed discursively in visually subordinate positions generally coded as female in our culture. Men killing chickens at the foot of a hill while women spectate from above may be a ludicrously trivial instance, but it is a remarkably literal realization of the structural relationships I am getting at here.

The operative point in all this is that both the male and the female participants in the Fort Laramie exercise occupied shifting positions over the course of the five days. Both laundresses and soldiers were implicated in a regime of visual discourse characterized by the ambiguities and subtle anxieties of advanced consumer culture. If the climactic scenario of the Indian attack provided the occasion for symbolic resistance to the threatening gaze of an archetypal Other, it could not permanently dismantle the modern apparatuses of looking that are part of the very fabric of living history reenactment. What got played out in that central scenario through familiar textual representations of race and gender might be read as the alibi for a deeper, more complex cultural text. In this latter text resolutions are not so clear, and the modern apparatus of commodified looking and display retains a persistent note of insta- bility, indeterminacy, and dis-ease. The temporary recuperation of white male authority through heroic resistance to a hostile gaze, placed in this wider context of modern visuality, takes on the quality of symbolic wish- fulfillment.

And in this wider context, for which modern tourism is emblematic, the conventional gender and racial coding cannot capture the full range of visually discursive relationships. The narratives of men looking at women, women looking at men, Indians looking at whites, and so on, all constitute merely partial realizations of an immensely complex and fluid commodification of visuality. In my view, the most significant feature of the Fort Laramie exercise was not the set of these conventional themes and narratives. Rather, it was the way participants moved into and out of the fictive frame of re-enactment, and into and out of positions of looking and display, positions structured by the modern apparatuses of spectatorship and surveillance.

If the gendered arrangements of looking within the frame of the re- enactment merge in various ways with the commodifying apparatus of modern tourism, that massive institution for which the Fort Laramie National Historic Site exists in the first place, then it is also true that the academic frame of the exercise frequently collapses into the gen- eral process of visual commodification. I will not dwell on this aspect of the optical arrangements at the Camp of Instruction, but I need at least to acknowledge that the educational frame is not independent of these other structures. To state the obvious, surveillance is a pervasive feature of modern systems of education, civilian as well as military (Mitchell 1988:34–94; Foucault 1977 [1975]:135–94 passim). In a very direct way, by transforming the instructors into noncommissioned officers the exer- cise makes the taken-for-granted procedures of military surveillance a kind of metaphor for the relationships of looking in education, where it is less acceptable to acknowledge openly the hierarchy of authority. And, like the arrangements of gender, both the military and the aca- demic systems merge with the processes of touristic commodification. For example, throughout the exercise the instructors documented our activities by taking photographs. Although they did so as unobtrusively as possible, the general practice of evaluation and documentation was a felt presence throughout. The "fictive" activity of military observation and discipline (e.g., in the daily inspections and drills), the "real" world activity of academic observation and evaluation, and the processes of tourist observation and consumption all blended together, reinforcing those qualities of slippage, ambiguity, and vague anxiety that were the definitive features of this living history exercise.

*   *   *

The last turn we will take in this ethnographic excursion is prompted by a feature of living history reenactment that, as far as I know, has not gotten much analytical commentary, namely, its occult aspects. As I mentioned above, on the evening the infantry company was away from the Fort the laundresses were visited by a prominent figure in frontier living history reenactment. A special interest of his was the undeniable frequency of reports about paranormal phenomena associated with historic sites and with the process of historical reenactment itself.

In a recent collection of ghost stories from Wyoming locales, Debra D. Munn offers the observation that Fort Laramie "may very well be the most haunted spot in the state, judging from the number of eerie happenings that have been reported there" (Munn 1989:53). Not a few of her extensive examples have to do with tourist experiences at the Fort and with the very exercise I have been documenting here. The evidence for a supernatural presence falls into familiar patterns: inexplicable noises, lights shining in the windows of empty, locked rooms, a sense of being touched or restrained from behind when no one is there, and so on.

But the nature of these manifestations or opinions about the reality of the supernatural are not my concern here. What does seem relevant is the theory, apparently shared by some serious, scholarly reenactors, that "the 'living history' experience may actually encourage spirits from the past to reach out to those who have symbolically stepped back in to their time period. By dressing as they dressed, by acting as they acted, and by generally entering into the essence of their bygone age, we may seem reassuringly familiar to these earlier inhabitants of the fort, so that they want to make their presence known to us" (Munn 1989:64).

Whatever one thinks about the reality of supernatural visitation, one implication of this idea is that the living history exercise as a whole is subject to a kind of ultimate surveillance, observation by the most "other" of Others. That the past itself is somehow there invisibly watching itself being recreated strikes me as a limiting case in the discourse of looking West. Not only is the past out there watching, but its ghostly representatives reveal their desire to participate in the reenactment, breaking down the fictive frame in the most radical way possible. Needless to say, this notion that an all-encompassing surveillance is being conducted by a pervasive but absolutely intangible presence can be a source of extreme anxiety. But, as presented in the living history context, it is also something to be desired. When this spectral surveillant force makes itself known it may be taken as a sign of the reenactment's success. In keeping with the line of analysis I have been pursuing, this look of an unseen Other that is simultaneously dreaded and desired constitutes an altogether apt metaphor for a central paradox of advanced consumer relations, wherein a troubled sense of being invisibly monitored, even to the point of profound paranoia, goes hand in hand with the desire to become the acceptable object of a supreme, abstract Gaze.

I have not finished with this phenomenon of the ghostly apparition as a metaphoric structure in the modern discourse of Western looking. However, I hope by now to have provided enough concrete analyses to sketch the broad outlines of this discursive formation, fluid though its borders may be. Before undertaking a few case study excursions to western display environments though, a quick detour into some history and theory might help us get our bearings more firmly.

Chapter Four
Looking at Looking
A Theoretical and Historical Excursion

To this point I have been using rather promiscuously such terms as "discourse of looking," "optical regime," and "mode of visuality." While I will not presume to tease apart all the many strands of what has become a very large body of theoretical literature on the nature of "visuality,"[1] I do need to be more explicit about the conceptual background of this study. To begin with, I mean to indicate by the term "discourse of looking" (and its equivalents) *the particular historical constellation of components, both material and intangible, through which human visual experience becomes organized at a given moment in collective social life.*[2]

It has no doubt become apparent that there is a certain ambiguity to the term "Western discourse of looking." The doubleness of reference, a possible source of confusion, actually captures an important feature of discursive formations in general, namely, their embeddedness or their nested levels of specificity. In its most immediate sense, "Western" refers to a particular region of the North American continent: that large district west of the hundredth meridian from which I have selected as a convenient sample the rectilinear patch identified on maps as the state of Wyoming. I have found that this frame encloses ample material (verbal texts, sites, images, etc.) to accomplish an adequate analysis of the discourse in question. As I have acknowledged in my Introduction, this selection, both the overall box of Wyoming and the particular items I pull out of it for closer inspection, is in one respect artificial, since it was made largely on the basis of my own contingent location. However, one of my premises is that the mode of visuality I am interested in pervades the whole "modern text of the West," and so can be expected to show up wherever particular stagings of this textual West occur.

In other words, virtually an infinite variety of "representative" samples of the discourse of looking West are available to us, though subregional and local variations could no doubt be identified. For example, a "desert

Southwest" version probably exists and has features that differentiate it from the high plains, central Rockies version that my Wyoming sampler exemplifies. Nevertheless, I believe that at a reasonable level of abstraction there is a common genus of modern Western visuality, of which these are species variations.

But having raised the possibility of levels of integration, or nested boxes of specificity/abstraction, where does this layering stop? Or, to put it more directly, at what point does the term "Western discourse of looking" cease to specify a distinct regional phenomenon, in the sense of trans-Mississippi American West, and become indistinguishable from the epochal discursive formations of *the* West, that is, the whole post-Renaissance heritage of European culture, including its New World and latter-day colonial extensions? The Western regime of visuality I have attempted to illustrate in the previous chapters and that I associate with a particular regional identity is but one moment in the much larger "scopic regime" (Metz 1982:61) that coalesced over the course of the nineteenth century in Euro-American culture generally.

Such acknowledgment of different levels of integration, however, does not diminish at all the need to examine as concretely as possible the more localized and historically specifiable manifestations of this larger, world-historical system. The American West as both a tangible region and a textual construction does have its own distinct history of visuality, with special nuances, themes, images, narratives, symbolic markers, and icons, even if these can be shown to resonate with national, indeed trans-national developments. The readings of specific texts in the previous chapters are intended to isolate through concrete example some of these distinctive features. If nothing else, I hope these readings demonstrate that an operative discourse is not a fixed body of pre-set elements, but rather an actively generative system, a form of production with the capacity to colonize new cultural domains and to create new spaces for realization. As a result, a fully functioning discursive formation is hard to reduce to a simple descriptive formula. Always somewhat fugitive, opportunistic, incorporative of elements outside itself, and adaptable to new contexts, a discourse is liable to be somewhat vague and shifting, certainly at its boundaries, but often even at its core.

As things of history, discourses arise and decline, hold sway and are contested. Any one we might attempt to isolate for analysis really only exists as a dispersed flavor within the immensely complex discursive gumbo of a given historical moment. And of course, most fundamentally of all, discourses are the medium in which lines of power organize and propagate themselves. A full account of the discursive practices in a given historical moment, were it possible at all, would require not just the isolation and analysis of individual elements, but also an account of how they overlap, interweave, and interfere with one another. This study presumes no more than to attempt the more realistic task of following one discursive set artificially isolated from the larger cultural/historical context.

Two further general properties of discourses are worth mentioning, one I have already made much of and the other a feature that will bear importantly on the discussion to follow. First, discourses are never fully present in any single, isolated text. The readings I have offered so far illustrate that certain features of a discursive formation may be hyperbolically displayed in a given location, while others are only hinted at indirectly, or ignored, or even actively suppressed for all sorts of subtle reasons related to the immediate context of expression. Therefore, only by gathering together a collection of texts and allowing them to vibrate against one another can we gain some purchase not just on the specifiable elements and pathways of a discourse, but also on its overall "structure of feeling" (Williams 1977:128–35).

Second, the historical development of a discourse is also an immensely complex issue. Discursive studies in the Foucauldian tradition have tended to emphasize points of clear rupture, relatively specific moments (though rarely, if ever, precise dates) at which discursive procedures clearly shift, with new arrangements of knowledge and power appearing rather suddenly to displace older ones. But of course this is not always how historical changes in discourse occur. Processes of slow accretion, piecemeal cannibalization or retooling of already existing elements, and the simultaneous operation of different, even contradictory discursive formations may be more typical than sudden breaks and wholesale displacements. Attempts at easy periodization are doomed therefore to failure.

Furthermore, the subtle persistence and sometimes surprising reappearance of discursive elements that had seemed to be completely defunct is something to be expected. Some vestige of an "old" discourse lurking within the body of a "new" mode may suddenly undergo an unexpected efflorescence. And that is only one of the possible scenarios of "interference" that may occur within discursive processes. It is certainly the case that the procedures of visuality emerging in the late nineteenth century and exemplified in the Wister moment did not simply replace preexisting modes. Nor was their emergence a matter of the sudden appearance of completely unprecedented visual practices. Rather it involved, along with "new" elements, the refashioning and rearrangement of features ready to hand. And although I will argue that this discursive coalescence occurring around the turn of the century has come to dominate at least some spheres of our current visual practice in an advanced consumer culture, it has not simply eliminated ways of seeing that are traceable to the Renaissance invention of the "humanist eye." In fact, one might even argue that the mode of visuality of concern to me in this study exists precisely in a kind of symbiotic tension with this older, deeply rooted paradigm of seeing which is still very much with us.

*   *   *

With that as a rather abstract preamble, we may now turn to a more concrete consideration of the historical context in which the discourse of Western (in both senses) looking spins out. And we might begin with the mode of Western (in the larger, epochal sense) visuality Martin Jay succinctly characterizes as "Cartesian perspectivalism" (Jay 1988:4–7). This is his name for that combination of an objective, scientific rationality and an empirically accessible material world that was embodied in the visual field of Renaissance painting.[3] The rationalized optics of single-point linear perspective is its defining structure. In his elaboration of this Cartesian "way of seeing" (Berger 1972),[4] Jay enumerates a number of features that will bear upon the discussion that follows. Paramount among these is the assumption of visual objectivity—the transparent or unmediated retinal recording of a stable outside reality that is, in spatial terms, "geometrically isotropic, rectilinear, abstract, and uniform" (Jay 1988:6):

Cartesian perspectivalism was . . . in league with a scientific world view that no longer hermeneutically read the world as a divine text, but rather saw it as situated in a mathematically regular spatio-temporal order filled with natural objects that could only be observed from without by the dispassionate eye of the neutral researcher. (1988:9)

Perhaps most important for my purposes here, this visual order is premised on the mechanism of a single eye that is "understood to be, static, unblinking, and fixated" (7). This monocular model of vision is the optical analogue to the stable, monadic subject of Renaissance humanism, that sovereign figure who stands over against an empirically knowable, rationally manipulable reality. It is a discourse of looking that renders objects of the external world morally neutral, measurable with a new kind of precision, and, perhaps most important, appropriable with unprecedented firmness and finality. For future reference we should also notice the rather obvious fact that this visual mode takes for granted the simplest possible subject/object relationship of looking: one eye trained on one unseeing world, neither of which "moves." Following the historians of optical regimes, I will adopt as a premise that this Cartesian visuality, with all its attendant humanist and empiricist associations, is something of a master discourse, an epochal formation that constitutes one kind of horizon of the visual. In many respects late twentieth-century participants in Euro-American culture continue to operate within this Renaissance/humanist visual field, at least in terms of commonsense experience.

At a more modest scale, one might identify a whole panoply of localized visual discourses that in one way or another derive from or take for granted some of the deepest principles of Cartesian perspectivalism, though each with features that set it apart as an identifiably distinct structure of looking. Especially relevant here are those forms that were applied most consistently to the American far West in the years leading up to the turn of century. Fortunately, there is available to us a body of historical writing concerned with the cultural conventions of Euro-American visual experience in the West during this period. We can use these historians' accounts of the dominant nineteenth-century traditions of Western looking as a foil against which to see more clearly the alternative visual mode reflected in the texts I have assembled in the previous chapters.

One of the most lucid and comprehensive examinations of the main thoroughfare through the visual discourse of the nineteenth-century American West is to be found in Anne Farrar Hyde's book, *An American Vision: Far Western Landscape and National Culture, 1820–1920* (1990). Drawing on the evidence of explorers' accounts, travelers' journals, railroad promotional literature, scientific survey reports, tourist advertising, and even the architectural styles of early western resorts, she demonstrates how a language develops through which the landscape of the West becomes visible in new ways during, roughly, the last quarter of the nineteenth century. Before that time, she argues, Americans had relied on a visual "vocabulary" inherited largely from European aesthetic traditions. The two categories of looking from this heritage most frequently applied to the western landscape were the *picturesque* and the *sublime*.

As the word itself indicates, the picturesque refers to the visual construction of nature as something "artfully designed so that it [can] be read like a picture" (Hyde 1990:14). Vegetation-framed, garden-like scenes, bucolic serenity, and genteel appreciation of nature's artfulness characterize this mode of looking. Most important, the viewing position it assumes is explicitly detached from the object being observed. It is a visual mode that experiences landscape as a series of views apprehended through the apparatus of an intervening picture frame, that transparent "window on the world" of objective external reality that is at the heart of the Cartesian model. Implicitly at least, the viewer stands outside the space in which the object of looking is located.

The nineteenth-century tourist industry catered to this visual mode by extending into the far West the network, already well established in the East, of luxury travel. The Raymond and Whitcomb Company in particular specialized in deluxe packaged tours for the genteel tourist used to first class rail and hotel accommodations and for whom views of the western landscape from the glassed-in porches of European-inspired resorts were consistent with the romantic tradition of refined appreciation of nature (in addition to Hyde, see Pomeroy 1957:3–30). We have already encountered reflections of this tourist mode in Wister's journals and fiction.

Alongside this picturesque mode, the language of the sublime was applied early to the more impressive sights in the western landscape. Although sublimity need not be an exclusively visual phenomenon, most characteristically it applies to scenes in nature that are so overwhelming as to exceed the limits of human comprehension, both logical and emotional. Contact with the sublime induces feelings of awe and even terror at one's insignificance in the face of immense and transcendent forces. In nineteenth-century America, Niagara Falls is the paragon of sublime sights. Not surprisingly, the sublime in nature was frequently adduced as evidence of a divine presence in the phenomenal world (Sears 1989:13–16).

Americans were well prepared to apply the discourses of the picturesque and the sublime to the landscape of the far West, having at least a half century of experience in using them to comprehend and organize conceptually (and often materially) the natural world they knew east of the Mississippi. What Donald A. Ringe refers to as "the pictorial mode," the inclination to place "a strong emphasis on the visual" (Ringe 1971:1), was second nature to nineteenth-century American artists:

As heirs of the aesthetic views of the eighteenth century, they were well aware of the relation of vast space to the theories of the sublime developed by eighteenth-century writers and critics, and much of the American practice in both literature and painting during the early nineteenth century derives, in part at least, from that source. (Ringe 1971:18)

Much the same could be said of the picturesque mode, which we might think of as the side opposite the sublime on the coin of romantic visual aesthetics. In fact, these two conventions of seeing were clearly structured together in a contrastive relationship that operated within a larger visual discourse.[5] This encompassing system was, according to Hyde, the only one available to Euro-Americans experiencing the West up until the 1870s, and it remained operative well after that (in some respects even up to today). It was certainly the mode of visuality that dictated the "viewing position" of such figures as the genteel female tourist we encountered in "Bad Medicine."

The historical problem with this visual regime, Hyde argues, was its complete inadequacy to the physical qualities of vast sections of the western landscape. It was hard to find anything picturesque or sublime in the seemingly endless stretches of sage-covered prairie on the high plateaus of Wyoming or the alkali wastes of the Great Basin, or at first even in the deserts of the Southwest. The only way European-derived aesthetic discourse could deal with such western environments was to revile them as hideous, monotonous, and dangerous. In short, the received conventions could only "see" these spaces as the uniformly repugnant wastelands one must endure in order to reach the locales that were worth a look.

In the decades after the Civil War, however, more and more Americans experienced the far West first-hand. The transcontinental railroad links were, of course, the most important facilitator of this process. The great scientific surveys of King, Wheeler, Hayden, and Powell in the post-bellum decades opened new regions of the West to national view, especially through the publication of popularized, well illustrated reports designed for the lay public. Most important, these reports provided the elements of a new language, empirical and practical rather than romantic, more capable of capturing the variety of visual experiences the West had to offer. The western tourist industry discovered a middle class audience increasingly interested in a less expensive, but also "truer" experience of the West than that offered through the system of railroad palace cars and elite resorts that catered to an upper class clientele. By the 1880s, according to Hyde's argument, these and other forces had come together to produce a new, more self-confident, and more distinctively American discourse of looking, through which the West could be seen in much greater variety and complexity than was possible through the older, European-derived visual categories.

Ultimately, this newly visualized West, this formerly "strange landscape became *the* American landscape. . . . A set of new words, images, and styles—based on American realities—gave observers, promoters, and tourists the tools and the power to recognize the value of the far western environment" (Hyde 1990:302, emphasis added). The value referred to here is primarily imaginative value. With the shift in discourse Hyde identifies, the West becomes America's "epitome region" (Clay 1973:38–50), the primary symbolic landscape through which the nation defines itself and the face by which it is most readily recognized throughout the rest of the world.

Hyde's historical scenario of sequential displacement, one set of visual conventions being supplanted by newer, more adequate procedures for "seeing" the West, is by no means the only story available to us. William Goetzmann, for instance, in his masterful *Exploration and Empire*, offers a commentary on visual representations of the West that suggests a less progressive, more devolutionary trajectory (Goetzmann 1966:199–228). Proposing a different alignment of aesthetic categories, he sees a shift after the Civil War from the conventions of the romantic pastoral to "the sublime, picturesque aesthetic of Ruskin" (Goetzmann 1966:224). He equates this shift with the movement toward a touristic, that is to say less authentic, way of seeing the West, one that purveyed limited, pre-scripted forms of experience (cf. Chapter 2 for Wister's comparable opinions about early western tourism).

Also in this devolutionary mode is Peter Bacon Hales's definitive account of William Henry Jackson's career as perhaps the premier nineteenth-century photographer of the western landscape. Hales sees in Jackson's work a shift from "views" to picturesque images, from representations of "the infinite space of the West" to "the consoling, engrossing shallow space of the picture" (Hales 1988:150). As in Goetzmann's scenario, this change is diagnostic of a whole cultural trajectory in which the West of adventurers, explorers, and scientists, a West of "views," is supplanted by a packaged and marketed West of touristic experiences, including visual experiences that did not have to occur first hand. One could merely sit in one's parlor and peruse a commercially available set of western scenes.

It is not my intention here to sort through these various constructions of nineteenth-century visual practice, with the purpose of judging among or reconciling them. I refer to them, rather, because they collectively demonstrate a way of thinking about western visual experience that conforms to traditional historiographic principles. Identifying the contrast between this general approach to Western visuality and the approach I have adopted in the present study will, I hope, help clarify my argument. Their superficial differences of plot and causality notwithstanding, all three of the historical scenarios I have mentioned, each exemplary in its management of sources and its logic of argument, play out in a common discursive field structured according to taken-for-granted assumptions about how the very act of looking works. And at the most basic level these assumptions themselves fall within the Cartesian paradigm.

I am not proposing, of course, that the pastoral, picturesque, sublime, pragmatic, and touristic ways of seeing presented in these historians' accounts can simply be equated with that all-embracing Cartesian perspectivalism identified as a master discourse by the theorists of visuality. Each mode has its distinctive features and conventions of representation, not all of which conform to Cartesian principles in the same way or to the same degree. For example, the scientifically precise alignments of Renaissance linear perspective are not necessarily emphasized in all these modes, the picturesque and the sublime in particular being romantic alternatives to Renaissance and Enlightenment empiricism. But beneath these differences in matters of iconography, style, and representational technique is a shared assumption of a self-contained viewer who registers an external reality through an unmediated and essentially unproblematic act of looking. The effect the outside world has on this viewer might be dramatic and varied, of course. The observer of a landscape might be charmed by a quaintly picturesque scene or overawed by sublime majesty. But these are to be understood as the internal emotional effects on a stable viewing subject caused by qualities that are empirically there in the objects of looking, and not as something structured into the very activity *of* looking itself. All these nineteenth-century modes of visual representation, including the category of observationally pragmatic American visuality Hyde identifies as emerging in the 1880s, presuppose a model of vision that entails a straightforward transaction between a single, coherent subject and an independent exterior world. By focusing only on the various shifts and developments in these representational modes and styles we miss the deeper processes of social and material relationships. The discursive construction of visuality itself, and historical changes therein, are not addressed in the developmental scenarios of traditional historiography.

The first principle of discourse study as I have been attempting to practice it here is that one is always implicated in the object one interprets. This is not a failing to be remedied, but an inevitable consequence of all textual production. We always participate in the discourses that we set ourselves up (or, we ourselves set up) to analyze. Acceptance of this epistemological dilemma need not be seen as a denial of the very possibility of cultural interpretation, and it should not be taken as a license to force interpretation in any imaginable direction. It does require of us a constant awareness of the provisional nature and the relatively local application of our interpretations. Where we are located discursively ourselves allows us to see some things and not others. My claim here, then, is not to provide a corrective or a truer account of the "facts" regarding nineteenth-century visual experience than the historians I have been citing. Rather my goal is to occupy a somewhat different discursive position than theirs, an alternative to, not a replacement for the classic cultural history approach. It is from this alternative analytical position that another level of looking West in the late nineteenth century comes into view. It is my contention that an understanding of this other domain of visuality gives us a valuable critical purchase on ethnographically available sites—display environments—in our own historical moment.

By adopting this other perspective I have been led to consider what falls outside the dominant discursive tradition that the western historians both chronicle and reproduce in their own historical constructions. I have been prompted to ask, what alternatives to the "normal" way of seeing can one find evidence for? The textual and ethnographic analyses in the previous chapters are intended as one kind of answer to this question. I have proposed that the texts examined there are linked discursively through their collective registering of a system of seeing characterized by visual complication, deception, misperception, lack of fixed positioning, and a nagging undecidability about what is the subject and what the object of looking—in short, a discourse of troubled or dislocated vision that entails entirely different procedures from those of Cartesian empiricism.

As we have seen, a key aspect of this Cartesian way of seeing is its *monocularity*. While it allows for the possibility that the viewer may experience some resistance from the object of observation—as in the sense expressed by many nineteenth-century travelers that they did not have a language adequate to a full appreciation of the western landscape—there is never any acknowledgment that the visual field may be occupied by other, independent gazes, perhaps ones that are competing for "control" over the same object of observation. The dominant discourse is monocular in the sense that it ascribes a self-contained, unitary coherence to the looking subject, a position from which full and untroubled mastery (and by extension, appropriation) of the object of looking is at least potentially possible.

Perhaps the clearest expression of this monocular quality is the pervasive nineteenth-century artistic convention of depicting landscape as a vista seen from a great height—what Albert Boime refers to as "the magisterial gaze." It is a convention associated particularly with the sublime:

The privileged nineteenth-century American's experience of the sublime in the landscape occurred on the heights. The characteristic viewpoint of contemporary American landscapists traced a visual trajectory from the uplands to a scenic panorama below. (Boime 1991:1)

And this convention is not only evident in landscape art:

. . . wherever one turns in the travel literature of the times, he is likely to find one or more set descriptions of a vast landscape, almost invariably seen from an eminence and suggesting not only the expansiveness of the view but, perhaps, a philosophic thought or two as well. (Ringe 1971:19)

While one cannot simply dismiss the influence of the natural landscape of North America, with its ample opportunities for expansive visual experience, neither can we rest easy with determinist explanations for the pervasiveness of this landscape convention. Nor should we succumb to the notion that "it's only natural" to view landscape from on high (Ringe 1971:20). The very idea of looking at a physical environment as scenery, and that it makes sense to climb a mountain to do so, is itself a cultural decision. The saturation of culture by this magisterial gaze, as Boime argues, is thoroughly ideological.

It might seem that the American far West is the ideal landscape for the realization of this mastering vision. Reduced to its conceptually minimal components the West is a binary landscape—mountain and plain or mountain and desert—high places on which to locate the dominating look, and beneath them seemingly unobstructed fields of pure visibility. In fact, it is a landscape of such eminent visibility that one does not even need a mountain to accomplish visual mastery. In the West of popular westerns, the mere elevation of a few hands is sufficient:

. . . when a lone horseman appears on the desert plain, he dominates it instantly, his view extends as far as the eye can see, and enemies are exposed to his gaze. . . . And the openness of the space means that domination can take place virtually through the act of opening one's eyes, through the act, even, of watching a representation on a screen. (Tompkins 1992:74)

Ironically, it is precisely in this environment that seems a kind of paradise of completion for Cartesian/magisterial visuality that a major discursive challenge to it arises, a challenge that deploys differently some of the very elements—apparently clear vistas and the seeming absence of other sets of eyes, for example—privileged in the regime of visual mastery. What characterizes this new (in the late nineteenth century) discourse of looking West is its use of such elements to reveal the elusiveness of objects of looking, the unsuspected presence of other sets of eyes in places that are not so open to view, and the uncertainty of visual mastery itself.

*   *   *

While as I have said, discourses of any sort are by definition dynamic phenomena, constantly shifting in relation both to the immediate circumstances of a particular utterance and to the larger forces of social life, still it is possible to consider in the abstract the set of interrelated features that allow us to recognize we indeed have a coherent discourse before us. To pin down a little more precisely the contrast between the two visualities of concern to me here, we might consider an admittedly crude schema of the basic elements that would seem to be the irreducible criteria of visual discourses. As a first approximation let us consider these minimal components: 1) the assumed positions *from* which looking proceeds; 2) the privileged objects and positions *toward* which looking may be directed; and 3) the apparatuses *through* which looking is mediated. Of course the relationships among these components are thoroughly dynamic, or perhaps better, each automatically implies the others and already has them structured into itself. Our separation of them is only justifiable for heuristic purposes. The concrete realization of actual discourses is in part a matter of how these components get "filled in." An identifiable repertoire of possible objects of looking, for example, may be diagnostic of a certain discursive procedure (e.g., the "organic" compositional arrangements of picturesque scenes). But even more fundamental is the way the components of a visuality are organized together. It is in this structuring that a discourse's ideological efficacy most inheres.

In terms of its most abstract structural arrangements, Cartesian visuality takes for granted the following: 1) a visual subject or agent of looking conceived as a self-contained monad; 2) a fundamentally binary visual geometry, one eye that sees over against one empirical world that is seen; 3) an assumption of absolute separation between the subject that looks and the object of that looking, that is, these positions are spatially and ontologically disjunct; and 4) the assumption that positions of looking and looked at are "pure" and stable. Finally, a hallmark of this visual mode is the notion that the apparatuses of looking are essentially transparent and epiphenomenal rather than constitutive. They are mere instrumentalities that only enhance or impede visual processes that exist independently of their application. To put this last point more simply, in the Cartesian visual regime the category of visual apparatus is understood to fall outside the fundamental processes of looking. Its paradigm is the neutral aperture metaphorically represented by the hole in the wall of the camera obscura. The apparatus in general is, thus, a primary site of mystification and suppression in this discourse. And perhaps here is the place to remind ourselves of the fundamental tenet that all discourses are in the business of both highlighting and hiding, revealing and concealing.

*   *   *

Perhaps at this point I should simply refer the reader back to the texts I have examined in the preceding chapters. Collectively they display visual procedures drastically different from those I have just been characterizing. However, a reading of one further concrete example might be helpful here. I have mentioned in passing that the opening scene of *The Virginian* is much concerned with visual transactions. The scene begins with the narrator seeing an act of seeing. Rather than just having the eastern tenderfoot look out upon the world himself, Wister has him first observe his fellow passengers gathering around the window of a railroad car that is part of a train just pulling into the town of Medicine Bow. They are looking at, according to the very first words of the novel, "some notable sight." The narrator crosses the car, abandoning the position from which he watches people watching something in order to join them in their spectatorship. What they see is a comic spectacle of cowboys in a corral trying to rope an especially wily cow pony, a procedure that is itself presented as a complex visual exchange:

> Have you ever seen a skillful boxer watch his antagonist with a quiet, steady eye? Such an eye as this did the pony keep upon whatever man took the rope. The man might pretend to look at the weather, which was fine; or he might affect earnest conversation with a bystander: it was bootless. The pony saw through it. No feint hoodwinked him. This animal was thoroughly a man of the world. His undistracted eye stayed fixed upon the dissembling foe, and the gravity of his horse-expression made the matter one of high comedy. (1)

At this point another act of looking comes into the narrator's view. He sees the as yet unidentified Virginian sitting on the fence "looking on." Like the tenderfoot crossing the car to occupy a new discursive position, the Virginian crosses the corral to participate directly in the drama of exchanged looks with the pony.

In this brief scene I count no fewer than five distinct acts of looking that are directed at other visual gestures (looks) and three "positions" that are marked simultaneously as both sites of spectatorship/observation and sites of spectacle (the tourists at the train window, the cow pony in the corral, and the Virginian on the fence). This complex circuit of looking at looking only ceases when a "failure" of vision occurs, the Virginian's hand proving quicker than the horse's (and the easterner's) eye. When the horse is finally roped the temporarily halted train proceeds, as if on cue, into the station, in effect ringing down the curtain on a scene saturated with visual exchange.

In itself the observation of an exterior scene through the window of a Pullman car conforms to the "straightforward" procedures of Cartesian visuality (but see Schivelbusch 1986 [1977]:52–69 on train travel and panoramic viewing). However, in this case the assumed stabilities are thoroughly disrupted. One is tempted to read this opening scene as the novel's inaugural invasion of one visuality—premised on the fixity and clear separation of subjects and objects of viewing and the transparency of the apparatus through which viewing occurs—by an altogether different visual discourse, key features of which would seem to be the "circulation" of the look and the collapsing together of subjects and objects of viewing.

And we might recall here that the figure of the Virginian serves as the primary nexus of visual transaction and exchange. We have seen how the assertion of his visual mastery, which we might now associate with Boime's magisterial gaze and with the epochal Cartesian regime, is undercut at key moments in the novel. Any time his visual dominance comes under observation by another gaze, especially when the source of that looking is unseen by him, the field of his visual mastery is contaminated. This opening scene illustrates the visual geometry perfectly. It is, on the one hand, our first encounter with the hero's seemingly absolute competence. The elevated position from which he coolly observes the proceedings reflects this self-possession, and his effortless roping of the vigilant pony, his domination of its eye, so to speak, confirms his mastery. But this mastery is itself observed from a distance by unseen spectators. And even though their admiring gaze would seem to confirm his authority, it simultaneously relocates his ostensibly masterful eye to a subordinate position as an object of their looking. The tourists' spectatorship here occupies the same structural position as the hostile surveillance by unseen Indians in the later scene of the novel, in the bivouac scenario of the Fort Laramie living history exercise, and, in a somewhat different way, in the Sitting Bull/Cody promotional photo.

Another key feature of this "other" visuality is its implicit acknowledgment of the constitutive role of the devices and material conditions of looking, which is to say the optical apparatus. The striking motif of the visually deceptive landscape, most notably the recurring trope of the West's magnifying atmosphere that we encountered in several folk narratives, including the fictive tall tales the Virginian tells, is one especially elegant expression of this abstract discursive feature. The very air, light, and openness of this landscape, symbols of transparent access to the empirical world in Cartesian visuality, are in these tales the cause of distortion, misreading, and confusion. They reveal the exterior world as something that is mediated, inscribed, and in need of expert interpretation (e.g., by the knowing eyes of regional insiders).

Another feature of some of the texts we have encountered elaborates on this recognition of the apparatus as constitutive of looking. We might recall that symbolic arrangement in the legend of swimming rattlesnakes whereby the position from which looking proceeds is also the site of production of the spectacle. The boat simultaneously creates the conditions of possibility for skiing and serves as the platform from which the skier is observed. Subject of looking and object of looking are thoroughly bound up with the apparatus of looking, so that they can be said to form one fully integrated ensemble. And I would invoke here as well that scene in "Hank's Woman" where the hotel spectacle seems to be the product of the workings of a tourist apparatus. The very presence of the tourist gaze, made possible by a whole assemblage of advertising, transportation, scheduling, and economic transaction, creates the very spectacle that it misperceives and reifies as having an independent prior existence.

To conclude this contrastive account of the visual discourse emerging at the end of the nineteenth century, I need to take note of the re-alignment of desire it entails. The magisterial visuality so prominent in the pictorial and literary representations of the nineteenth century has, of course, its own structure of desire. Put simply, it is a rather directly acquisitive visual mode. The mastering gaze from on high implies appropriation of land and extraction of resources, with all the attendant symbolic associations and material effects these carry with them (Boime 1991:136–58). Of course the connection between the whole regime of Cartesian perspectivalism, with its emphasis on precise quantification of a neutrally empirical reality, and the forces of capitalist accumulation is hardly a new story. The stable bourgeois subject indigenous to this visual regime is, after all, one of the indispensable conditions of possibility for private ownership and capitalist relations of production in general.

In the mode of visuality I am contrasting to this Cartesian, magisterial one desire is not so orderly and direct, for it is not merely a binary arrangement. As I have suggested in my discussion of the joke about the deluded tourists, the primary object of desire is precisely the position of visual mastery, the desire to possess the completed, knowing eye and to occupy the position of visual plenitude. It is this structure of desire that is being enacted in all the variations on the theme of "looking at other acts of looking" we have encountered.[6] The circulation of looks, the misrecognitions and visual occlusions, the layering of or alternation between spectatorship and surveillance, and the oblique lines of sight that do not exactly match up with the seemingly authoritative gaze are all stagings of this discursive structure. Minimally, it entails a trinary arrangement: a position from which some object of looking is observed, the location *of* that object, and a position from which this first act of seeing is itself seen. Without too much violence to English usage we might think of these positions as, respectively, the site of spectatorship, the site of spectacle, and the site of surveillance. Far from being a mere elaboration of elements already there in Cartesian visuality, this arrangement is a fundamentally different way of seeing in which an endless circuit of visual exchange is actively acknowledged. And as such, it is also a way of seeing that cannot avoid recognizing the inseparability of the positions of looking from the apparatuses of looking. Indeed, the discursive positionings and circulations of the gaze *are* the apparatus, which in this visual regime cannot be consigned to an epiphenomenal realm of "external" devices applied instrumentally to enhance inherently transparent acts of looking.

*   *   *

The sort of comparative account of discursive formations I have just engaged in can be helpful for purposes of theoretical clarification, but it quickly exhausts its utility when confronted with historical contexts. At this point, therefore, I want to disavow some possible implications of the preceding discussion. First, I am not at all proposing that the discourse of looking West I have been insisting upon arose at the end of the nineteenth century as a kind of counter-hegemonic response to Cartesian visuality. There do seem to be sites, Wister's moment being my prime example, where these discourses are structured together such that the emergent one lurks in the shadows, constantly calling into question the magisterial visuality that seems to be almost desperately or defensively insisted upon at the narrative's illuminated surface (most emphatically in the person of the romanticized cowboy hero). However, I by no means intend to suggest that the one discourse constitutes a radical critique, much less a replacement for the other. Merely by coming into coherent shape, this new discourse does displace all preexisting ones, since it creates a new discursive environment for them by its very presence. But that does not necessarily diminish their force.

Cartesian visuality is still very much with us in all sorts of ways at the level of our commonsense experience. My larger historical point is that if Cartesian visuality is an important enabling discourse for one phase of the capitalist formation, a visuality of the circulating look participates in the extension of the capitalist project into the modern consumer order. It is precisely the disruptions of the visual, the conflations of looking and looked at, the uncertainty of the gaze, and the circulating displacements of visual authority that correspond to a new mode of consumption, one that has perhaps only reached complete fruition in our own historical moment. It is a mode of consumption in which the private accumulation of goods and economic capital is inseparable from the ceaseless desire to mark semiotic differences and to engage in the endlessly renewable display of identity (Dorst 1989:164–69).

In more specific historical terms, it is my belief that we find in the discourse of looking West a perhaps surprising enactment of a visual mode pervasive in the advanced consumer culture of *the* West (the global hegemony) today. Surprising because, if my case for the importance of the Wister moment is at all convincing, this discourse was emerging in the textualized West (the imaginary region) already by the end of the nine-teenth century, making that development both anticipatory and para-digmatic. And surprising, too, because the American far West is not a region, physical or textual, that one immediately associates with the mechanisms of advanced consumer culture. When the state of Wyoming adopted a number of years ago the motto "Wyoming is what American used to be," it was expressing a certain pride in its resistance to the blan-dishments, and by implication the ill effects, of the twentieth century. The notion among many of its residents that the "true" West somehow preserves older, better values than the rest of the country (especially the East) is an ethos that we already see active in Wister's romantic nostal-gia.[7] Ironically, it may be that the American West, at least as a textual construction, is an important early staging ground for some of the cen-tral discursive mechanisms of the advanced consumer order we now all inhabit.

*   *   *

Having made a case for the late nineteenth-century West, this textual West as opposed to the geographic entity, as a privileged site of dis-cursive innovations with important implications for our own historical moment, I must hasten to add that we can of course point to other loca-tions where early manifestations of these trends are discernible. The rise of the modern city, above all, has come in for extensive commentary as the cradle of twentieth-century consumer capitalism. One apt example of an eastern, urban parallel to the discursive shift I have associated with the Wister moment is evident in an essay by Emily Fourmy Cutrer. She finds William James's philosophical psychology of the visual sense as presented in *The Principles of Psychology* and William Dean Howells's treatment of vision in *A Hazard of New Fortunes*, both published in 1890, to contain the traces of a new mode of visuality—what she characterizes as "a pragmatic mode of seeing" (Cutrer 1993:259–75). She explicitly contrasts this new mode with the Cartesian regime, especially in its pic-turesque form, which Howells has been accused by some of conserva-tively embracing as a response to the social and cultural turmoil of the late nineteenth century (264–65). She observes that this was a period of "markedly self-conscious and ideologically charged" constructions of visual discourse, a period that saw the emergence of new visual practices that "acknowledged, even embraced the 'slipperiness' of vision" (260–61).[8]

Along with addressing the struggle between visual discourses as it emerged in the urban context of the late nineteenth-century American city, Cutrer's essay points us to an issue that demands more direct attention than I have given it so far. In her discussion of *A Hazard of New Fortunes* she describes how Basil March has an experience which disrupts his complacently detached spectatorship. She characterizes the effect this has on him as "a curious and revealing reversal" in which "March no longer possesses the male gaze but becomes himself the 'penetrated' object of desire" (270). The most compelling insight of Cutrer's essay is that the shifts in visuality she identifies are bound up with a gender politics. She argues that both James and Howells are tentative in their treatment of the new, destabilizing visuality because it entails a certain confusion of gender positions, of the male gaze and the female object of male looking. It will have become obvious from a number of the excursions we have taken, especially our visit to Fort Laramie, that the discourse of looking West is highly elaborated in terms of gender. As an ideological force, this visual practice is pervaded by gender codings.[9] As we will see, these are especially explicit in the display environment on our itinerary in Chapter 6. While the richly elaborated body of feminist theory devoted to visual experience is relevant at many points in this study, I will only take the time here to highlight one key issue: the nexus of visuality, consumption, and women's social experience.

In her study of the cultural antecedents and the pre-existing visual procedures that shaped the film viewing experience, Anne Friedberg offers us a useful entree to this issue. She is particularly concerned with the social formations and technologies that contributed to the development of the dual qualities she most associates with film: the mobility of the gaze and its "virtuality." I am especially interested in the first of these. Building on the classic work of Walter Benjamin in his unfinished study of the commercial arcades in nineteenth-century Paris (Buck-Morss 1989), Friedberg has much of interest to say about the gendering of consumption. Elaborating on Benjamin's category of *flâneur*, the casual, directionless wanderer and observer of the city who appeared in response to the new conditions of modern urban experience, she points out that spaces appeared in this new environment that allowed for a new female social position that was neither the "*fille publique* (woman of the streets)" nor the "*femme honnête* (the respectable housewife)" (Friedberg 1993:36). The arcade, the department store, the amusement park, the world exhibition, the packaged tour, the museum (these last two especially relevant to the present study), and eventually the cinema were all spaces open to a relatively free female observer, the female *flâneur* or "*flâneuse*" (32–94). And shopping in particular was this figure's métier, shopping, that is, in the sense we now take for granted as built around the visual procedures of commodity display, advertising, casual, mobilized perusal (window shopping), image identification, and so on. "As consumers," Friedberg suggests, "women had a new set of social prerogatives in which their social powerlessness was crossed with new paradoxes of subjective power" (35). And this "power" is in no small measure a function of the circulation of identity built into the modern commodity-experience. The constant repositioning of the gaze and the endless circulation of image identifications are sine qua nons of the modern consumer order.

It might seem, then, that we are left with a paradox. It is hard to dispute that in its dominant, late nineteenth- and twentieth-century form, the text of the American West is masculine and patriarchal to its bones (Tompkins 1992). The discursive formation I have been exploring, however, seems intimately bound up with a consumer order commentators like Friedberg associate with an expansion of the social orbit of women. The view I have been taking in this study is that the play of differences itself, the movement into and out of "other" positions, is the crucial and definitive feature of this discourse of Western looking. That such differences are sometimes coded in terms of gender, sometimes of race, sometimes of region, and often in complex combinations of these and other categories, is a function of the local contexts of enactment. The larger issue is the circulation of the gaze across boundaries of difference in general, for it is this abstract process that constitutes the discursive staging of the modern consumer order as a mode of visual experience.

Of course how this staging is realized locally in terms of gender and race, not to mention other dimensions of difference, is of considerable analytical interest. These features need to be acknowledged ethnographically and examined in their discursive variability. Anglo men are sometimes presented in the position of the spectator, sometimes as the spectacle; Indian men are often constructed in the position of surveillance, but also as objects of tourist spectatorship; Anglo women may be positioned as objects of visual desire, but also sometimes as desiring observers of (Anglo and Indian) male display, to mention only a few of the variations. It is my contention that such variability calls into question any simple identification of a privileged category of visual authority. It is the disembodied process of sign exchange and "dematerialized" consumption itself that is modeled and promoted in the particular discourse of looking West that is my subject here. At the end of the nineteenth century, in the moment of its emergence, this discourse was no doubt subordinate to longstanding visual regimes and ideological dominants previously in place. Over the course of the twentieth century, however, its fundamental procedures, if not the western regional accouterments that are its surface manifestation, have come to penetrate ever more completely virtually all spheres of our late-capitalist cultural life.

*   *   *

Before concluding this brief excursion into historical/theoretical territory, there is one last ideological issue that needs to be acknowledged
overtly, though it too has no doubt become obvious through the preceding analyses. In her observation, cited above, that James and Howells
were quite tentative in their acknowledgment of the new, destabilized
visual practices of the late nineteenth century, Emily Cutrer identifies
a quality that is especially prominent in the western manifestations of
this discourse.[10] Both during the "crisis" of its emergence and still in
our latter day enactments, a haze of male anxiety hovers over the landscape of Western visuality. I have suggested that the bivouac scenario in
the Fort Laramie living history exercise constitutes a kind of compensatory assertion of stabilized, heroic male authority amid a context of
visual slippage and display anxiety. Likewise, *The Virginian* could almost
be read as an obsessively replayed drama of alternating assertions and
subversions of authoritative, magisterial (i.e., male) looking.[11] As we will
see, very much the same elements are encoded in the physical spaces of
the prison museum we will visit in Chapter 6.

But with these specificities of gender ideology acknowledged, I would
assert again that the unfixing and the ceaseless circulation of the act
of looking itself is the foundational armature of the advanced capitalist
consumer ideology that underlies the discursive procedures of Western visuality. The codings in terms of gender and race are two common
ways our culture hangs visible shapes on that irreducible framework.
The truly distinctive quality of the discursive procedures I have been
focusing on is the constant inclination to display, if only symbolically
and often with paranoid inflections, the triangulations of a visual field in
which spectators, their objects of looking (spectacles), and acts of visual
surveillance (a seeing presence that cannot itself be seen) all exist in a
play of exchange and displacement.[12]

In actively revealing its dynamic optics, this system of visuality makes
the apparatuses of seeing themselves visible and part of the display. This
is where it most differs from the Cartesian/magisterial modes, which
rely for their ideological force on the concealment of their procedures
and mechanisms.[13] We have come to inhabit a world full of visual discourses and devices that constantly acknowledge and enact, even if not
consciously intending to do so, the absolute centrality of their own
operations *as* apparatuses for constructing the visual field. Or to put this
slightly differently, we have on every hand a technics of the circulating
visual subject, that circulation in itself constituting the operation of an
apparatus. What one finds in the sort of modern display environments
we will visit in the second part of this study are precisely material, in-

stitutional apparatuses of seeing that enact in the most concrete and physical ways the discourse of looking West I have attempted to corral in the preceding chapters. It is time, then, to embark on a few excursions to representative sites where we may look at this discourse in full, late twentieth-century flower.

Part II

Chapter Five
Machines and Gardens
Two Cases of Vernacular Display

As I have said in the Introduction, to follow the winding paths of a discursive formation inevitably entails the transgression of many fencelines. In our excursions so far we have crossed boundaries between current and past historical moments, between oral/vernacular and formally literary modes, between verbal and visual expressive media, and between fictional representation and dramatic (re)enactment. The stoutest fence, though, and the one I am most intent on violating, is the one that separates texts from things, words (and images) from objects and their physical manipulation, language from material practice. At this late date it hardly seems necessary to invoke the Foucauldian doctrine that ways of speaking, recording, and categorizing are inseparable from ways of acting, producing, and institutionalizing. I am attempting in what follows to realize this indispensable idea of a unified discourse/practice by treating texts and artifacts, expressive forms and physical sites, narrative patterns and institutional entities all as part and parcel of that larger thing I have been calling a modern discourse of looking West. Under current cultural conditions one of the most logical places to examine this collective visuality is the domain of the "display environment," and in these three remaining chapters we will be making excursions to several such locations.

By *display environment* I mean nothing more than a physical space in which material elements have been selected and arranged primarily for the purpose of being looked at. While these elements might be intended as something more than objects of looking—as objects for private appropriation, for example—and the display space might have other purposes—marketing, for example—visual apprehension is paramount to display environments, as I am using the term. This loosely defined category covers a great many of the spaces that make up our material world today: most domestic front yards and other facade spaces, most retail commercial spaces (though in varying degrees), artifact containers of bewildering variety (e.g., private curio cabinets and trophy rooms), zoos, theme parks, fairgrounds, sports arenas, theaters, art galleries, and of course museums, to mention only some of the most immediately familiar examples. In fact, our world is so full of spaces where viewing things is the dominant activity that the category of display environment quickly approaches the limit of utility. Perhaps it will be helpful to identify a sub-category that covers most of the particular sites I will be examining here. What they all (with one exception) have in common is the display of discrete, mainly static artifacts that are not themselves available for purchase, though of course this does not mean that economic functions and the commodity form do not apply to them (far from it). To put it another way, most of the sites I will consider are fundamentally museum-like, though the category of museum itself covers considerable ground.

In this chapter I will look at two examples of "vernacular" display: environments where objects are formally organized for viewing, but largely as the result of personal, non-institutionalized, and non-professional agency. They are examples, in other words, of what some might call folk art environments, or "outsider" arts, or idiosyncratic assemblages, or "found" art, or recycled arts, or manifestations of the folk aesthetic of *bricolage*. A comparative look at these two environments, both of which are explicitly western in their thematic programs, will illustrate something of the range of display procedures through which artifacts may evoke certain modes of viewing and thereby construct viewing subjects and viewing positions of certain sorts. They also are "closest to the ground" of all the display environments I will consider, in the sense that they are very direct, personal responses to the western landscape.

Chapter 6 is devoted to a museum/history park complex that constitutes my fullest example of the material expression of the discourse of looking West. More than any other site, the Wyoming Territorial Prison and Old West Park, with the restored territorial penitentiary as its centerpiece, embodies the circulation of viewing positions and the layering of spectacle and surveillance that I have argued is central to the visual discourse of the modern text of the West. Of all the sites I will examine, it is the most complete laboratory for observing how viewing positions become fully integrated into the material fabric of the artifacts that are the ostensible objects of that looking.

Finally, Chapter 7 will bring us to Devils Tower National Monument in northeast Wyoming. We will see how this fantastic rock formation— a massive igneous monolith that seems a remarkably pure realization of the "forces of nature"—is thoroughly constructed as a display, but one that has in recent years been the subject of different and conflicting ways of seeing. It will provide us an occasion to consider how a regime of visuality structures the institutional management of contested social space. Thus our excursion to this display environment may serve as an object lesson in the inseparability of discourse (in the sense of language, text, image, etc.) from on the ground practice.

*   *   *

The two vernacular display environments we are about to visit have a great deal in common. Most obviously, the basic medium of both is welded and painted metal. I suspect most students of material culture would consider them to belong to a single genre. The folk or outsider art environment is one, typically, that results from the productive efforts of people who have little or no formal art training, whose creative endeavors are not connected, at least initially, to the institutionalized art market, and who produce their works not as a primary occupation but as a hobby in a leisure context, though obsessive commitment to such production seems rather common. By the time I began looking at these two display environments their producers had reached retirement age. One difference, however, is that Mr. Dellos's yard display has been developed during the time *of* his retirement, while Mrs. Young's fence was constructed by her and her husband, Mr. Floyd Young, over a number of years while they were still engaged in active occupational life.[1]

There are a great many ways one might examine vernacular displays such as Mr. Dellos's and Mrs. Young's. A typical approach is to relate them to the personal histories and aesthetics of their producers (Greenfield 1986; Jones 1989), that is, to view them as the individual expressions of "unusual" people who are particularly gifted, energetic, nonconformist, obsessive, etc. Other approaches entail locating such folk art environments in the larger cultural terms of life cycle pursuits and memory arts, or placing them in broad social context (Hufford, Hunt, and Zeitlin 1987). While I will consider each of these sites briefly in ethnographic terms of this sort, my main concern will be to "read" them for their discursive procedures. It is my assumption that, while these environments are obviously the products of individual creativity, personal history and predilection, and other psychological and social factors, they also may be viewed as passages in the larger text of the modern West we have been exploring, and as such they participate in the order of Western visuality. As purposeful, aggressively visible, and even perhaps idiosyncratically excessive display spaces, both sites actively offer themselves for viewing, and they do so in terms of particular visual practices. They are, one might say, especially notable outcroppings of the discourse of looking West, being display environments located *in* the West, made of artifacts *from* the West, and alluding consciously to the history and traditions *of* the West. What their specifiable visual practices are is my focus here, and I will be reading them to some degree "against" one another, for our understanding of their discursive procedures will be sharpened by noting how they differ, even while operating within the same visual regime.

Mrs. Young's Fence

It is something of an understatement to say that Edna Young's remarkable open-work fence (Figure 2) stands out dramatically in its quiet neighborhood of trim homes, shade trees, and well-tended yards. In contrast to the conventional middleclass accouterments of decorative yard display—ornamental plantings, rock gardens, commercially produced "accents"—the fence consists of a bewildering array of collected artifacts—tools, utensils, and specialized occupational gear—many of the items associated with the history of western settlement and industrialization. These objects have been welded together to form flat panels that run continuously around three sides of the house, marking the boundary between the sidewalk and small, slightly raised sections of lawn. The fence is painted in a pattern of alternating silver and black exterior enamel, each artifact uniformly covered in one of these colors. Some exceptions occur where certain details, lettering stamped in the metal for example, are picked out with the contrasting paint.

A total of twenty separate sections, each framed in a rectangle of steel pipe, run continuously, end to end, around the perimeter of the house. Although one's first impression is that the fence is of a piece, in fact each panel is a distinct entity, the pipes at each end set down into holes in a concrete border. Even more important, each of these sections, examined up close, constitutes a unique, separately designed and executed compositional unit. Among these twenty elements there are four gates, two curved corner sections, and thirteen flat panels. All the panels are 29 inches high and range from 5 feet 5 inches to 14 feet 2 inches in length, most of them falling between eight and ten feet long. In addition to this main fence, there is a separate run of two panels at the back of the house. These stand on either side of a tall gate. Finally, there is a separate gate at the front of the house. A large bell hangs at its top. In addition to these fence elements, various sections of the small lawn contain free-standing artifacts, most notably railroad switches and semaphores in one area and antique ore cars in another.

Before investigating this decorative display first hand, I encountered several versions of what appeared to be the dominant folk explanation of its origin. A common local assumption about this community landmark was that it had been constructed by a man who worked as a welder in the Union Pacific Railroad shops located in Laramie. This seemed cred-

Figure 2. Welded open-work fence, Edna and Floyd Young.

ible, since railroad paraphernalia are prominent in both the fence and the yard displays, and one panel, the "first" section in order of construction, has mounted conspicuously atop it the word RAILROAD, spelled out in bent rebar. The kernel of truth in this account turns out to be that Mr. Young *had* worked for the railroad, but as an engineer on a line running through Laramie. He was not a welder at all, even as a hobbyist. In fact, an initial interview with Mrs. Young (February 1, 1986) revealed that she was the one primarily responsible for the construction of the fence, but as its designer rather than its welder. The physical manufacture of the fence panels is actually of minimal importance to a reading of this display environment. The collection of the artifacts, the initial conceptualization of the fence, the determination of panel designs, the overall plan, and the surface treatment are the aspects most relevant to its place in a visual discourse.

In my conversations with Mrs. Young she was somewhat vague on the dates of the fence's production. I believe this is at least in part due to the fact that the actual design and assembly of the display was inextricably bound up with the activity of collecting the artifacts. For the most part the objects in the fence were actually gathered by Mr. and Mrs. Young during their rambles along railroad rights-of-way and on the ranches of friends in the area. In other words, many of the items in the fence are the cast off remnants of earlier phases of industrial production in the West.

Though unable to attach the fence to a timeline more precise than "the 60s," Mrs. Young was clear on how it was conceived in the first place. The industrial implements she and her husband collected over a period of years could not be conveniently displayed by conventional means — on shelves, framed and mounted on the wall, etc.[2] For one thing, the objects were quite varied: wrenches of different types, cogs, spoked wheels, plow parts, clamps, tongs, ladles, horseshoes, railroad gear, an antique sewing machine treadle, bits from horse bridles, and movable hitching posts, to mention only a fraction of the pieces included. Along with this variety, the sheer unwieldy bulk of the material was not suited to indoor display spaces. As a result, their collecting efforts left the Youngs with a considerable pile of rusting metal sitting in their yard. Mrs. Young was responsible for the idea of an exterior fence. "I dreamed it up one night and talked it over with my husband," she explained. When I pressed her on this point she said that she "visioned it out," presumably while asleep. Although I was unable to get her to elaborate at any length on this experience, it seems that there is at least a touch of the visionary influence to this fence, a feature that one finds quite commonly in the work of so-called outsider artists.[3]

To see whether her idea was feasible, the Youngs tried constructing one panel. This is now located behind the house, largely hidden from passersby, indicating its status as a not entirely satisfactory experiment. But with this serving as a kind of preliminary sketch, the individual panels of the main fence began to take shape. The basic procedure was that Mrs. Young would select artifacts for a panel and lay them out on the ground to generate a design. She would consult Mr. Young on the proposed pattern and when they were satisfied with the plan they would make a drawing. They then turned over the actual welding to vocational classes where this skill was being taught. The actual workmanship of assembly, it seems, was of little importance to them compared to the collecting and design. In this way the fence developed panel by panel. By the time it extended from one front corner of their property to the other they had pretty much used up their stock of collected artifacts. At this point they undertook to collect more items expressly for inclusion in the display, with the goal of encircling their lot. This seems to me an interesting moment in the history of this display environment. Whereas the fence had been at the service of the collection — its display vehicle — now the process of collecting became subordinate to the process of display itself.

I will return to this important "turning point," literal and figurative, in the history of the fence, but it is not the only relevant temporal feature of this vernacular display. Although no doubt a feature that is invisible to the casual observer, the fence panels are not merely random selections of objects. There is a conscious thematic program. The fence is organized roughly in terms of classic western industries. The railroad comes first, an apt convergence of Mr. Young's occupational background and the historical sequence of industrial development in the West, in which the arrival of the railroad is the standard inaugural marker. The first panel, the one with "railroad" spelled out atop it, consists of three rail car wheels mounted on an actual section of rail. In the yard behind this panel one sees a collection of devices used for train switching and signaling.

Although the progression may not be absolutely precise, in following the panels around from the front to the back of the house one traverses the industrial domains of railroad transportation, mining, ranching, and farming, these last two represented by artifacts from the pre-World War II era of agricultural mechanization. In fact the whole display hearkens back somewhat nostalgically to an earlier industrial era, one in which corporate ownership was not fully established in the agricultural sector, much less the major multinational conglomeration we are familiar with today. The implements welded into the fence suggest relatively small scale industrial production. The railroad is perhaps an exception, but even in this sphere the display emphasizes implements that require manual manipulation and the application of personally directed human force.

If this thematic progression through the panels of the fence was quite intentional as an organizing principle, it is unlikely that a development in formal design was so consciously planned. Nevertheless, what one sees when moving from the early to the later panels is an overall increase in formal regularity and redundancy, especially in terms of those familiar patterns of folk design common in Euro-American tradition. Although none of the panels is purely a welded hodgepodge of artifacts, they move progressively toward ever more insistent symmetries. A combination of radial elements (the fence contains more than forty spoked wheels of various sizes) with bilateral tripartition (Glassie 1972: 272–73) becomes increasingly evident. The recurring trinary pattern of the panels is made up in many cases from a central radial element with two congruent flanking sections or, even more emphatically, of three radial elements, the central one distinguished in some way from the outer two, which mirror each other. One of the earliest panels consists of no more than a central wheel flanked on each side by a helter-skelter selection of rather densely packet artifacts (Figure 3). By the time one gets to the late panels there are fewer artifacts and strikingly formal, highly symmetrical tripartite arrangements dominate (Figure 4). It is as if classic principles

Figure 3. Early fence panel.

of formal design are working themselves out as one moves around the fence, with an impressive series of improvisatory changes being rung on the basic pattern.

For present purposes one further feature of the fence needs comment —the treatment of its surfaces. Initially, Mr. and Mrs. Young intended to paint the whole thing black. This they immediately found unsatisfactory. It would seem that this simple scheme obscured the individuality of the artifacts too completely. No doubt what one would see with a solid color was the abstract design of the whole panel rather than the separate objects. As the display of an artifactual collection, where one is supposed to see the individual items, this was unacceptable. The solution was to paint the artifacts in an alternating pattern of contrasting surfaces—silver against black. The effect is quite striking. That this vivid "visibility" of the individual elements in the fence is vitally important to its discursive significance is indicated by the labor intensive maintenance required to preserve the desired decorative effect.[4] Considerable care has to be taken in each repainting. Mrs. Young's domestic environment reflects a similar rage for clarity and order. Although densely packed, the spaces of her house and yard are by no means cluttered. The collector's commitment to the orderly, coherent arrangement of artifacts is pervasive,

Figure 4. Late fence panel.

and the painstaking differentiation of the items in the fence through the alternating silver and black color scheme is entirely consistent with the rest of the domestic scene.

The sensibility reflected in Mrs. Young's collections and displays is one place where the larger discursive formation I have been pursuing manifests itself through everyday vernacular behavior. To sharpen our understanding of her aesthetic inclination we might note how it contrasts with another decorative sensibility found widely in the West. A yard display (Figure 5) located alongside a ranch house in the Little Laramie River valley exemplifies the salient features of this second decorative mode. Typically, such displays include bleached bones, dried or petrified wood, antlers, crystalline mineral forms of various sorts, and wrought iron and steel artifacts, usually in the form of fragmentary or cast off implements and utensils. The treatment of surfaces in such displays is left entirely to the elements. Desiccated, sun bleached, wind eroded, and rusting away, these surfaces express the effects of time and decay in the western environment. They speak of hardship, harshness, and dissolution. The arrangement of artifacts in this "entropic" display tradition, studiously random and tableau-like, emphasizes historical contingency and accident. The objects in this particular example, most of them fragmen-

Figure 5. Ranch house yard display, Little Laramie Valley, Albany County, Wyoming.

tary, are presented as if time had scattered them randomly and as if the area within the display frame (note the border of split poles and petrified wood) were simply a piece of the prairie that had been scooped up and deposited next to the house. Of course the artifacts in the display *are* in fact things casually gathered from just such an environment, things lost, broken, dead, and decaying, brought together as a kind of concentrated "vignette" (Dorst 1989: 119–26) and "in situ" exhibit (Kirshenblatt-Gimblett 1990:388–90) of the high plains landscape.

Mrs. Young's fence seems to operate on virtually an opposite set of principles—anti-entropic, fixed, and in some respects even monumental. Resistance to or denial of decay is enacted in the uniform and uncorrupted surfaces of the objects, an effect achieved only through considerable investment of labor. One might say that the forces of human productivity vs. the entropic effects of a harsh environment is a kind of implicit material culture dialogue going on between the two display modes. And this dialogue being conducted on artifactual surfaces may be associated with more general aspects of visuality in these two display styles. The most obvious of these is, simply, "clarity" itself. Entropic displays emphasize precisely the dissolution of artifactual integrity. The objects are fragmentary, often jumbled, sometimes positioned as half buried in the ground, and often decayed to the point that their internal segmentation, and perhaps even their very identities have become indistinct. In short, the basic act of visual apprehension, of being clear about what one is seeing, becomes at least slightly obscured. And by extension, the sense of appropriability of the artifacts in such displays is diminished. It is a central if implicit point of this mode of display that materiality is always in the process of slipping away from the grasp of human control.

Mrs. Young's fence, on the other hand, is thoroughly informed by the impulse to make *things* clear, which is to say, visibly present and permanently fixed for viewing. This is apparent both in the differentiating binary color scheme I have already mentioned and in the rigorous frontality of the fence. That the assemblage of objects is presented as much as possible as a flat surface, rather than in oblique arrangements that would emphasize three-dimensionality, gives the fence a graphic, visually apprehensible quality. One might say the fence renders the objects of which it is made coherently legible. In doing so, however, it also reduces the physical tangibility of the these artifacts. The fence's hypervisibility is inseparable from, indeed the basic condition for a kind of material inappropriability. There is a certain congruence here, I think, between the material/visual qualities of this display environment and the structure of visual experience we have encountered in the narrative motifs of a deceptive western landscape in which physically distant, perhaps unattainable things seem vividly present and even preternaturally clear to the eye.

One thing a consideration of vernacular display environments such as Mrs. Young's fence can help us understand more fully is the "economy" of the discourse of looking West. Entropic displays imply the inappropriable nature of artifacts due to the material processes of dissolution, desiccation, and petrifaction, all of which lead to the rather direct disappearance of material (use) value. Displays such as the fence also enact a removal of artifacts from their place in the material economy of utility, in which the ladle could be used to dip out liquid or the wrench to tighten a bolt. In this case, though, what the display represents is not the mere disappearance of value, but the substitution or displacement of one form of value by another.[5] In fact, to appreciate the full complexity of Mrs. Young's fence in terms of its visual economy, we must take into consideration at least three sources of value either implied or enacted by it. One of these, which I have just been referring to, is the direct utility of the artifacts for the purposes they were manufactured to serve. As mainly obsolete and discarded items, the loss of this form of value is already mostly accomplished prior to their inclusion in the fence, a loss only symbolized and ratified by their being rendered completely immobile and literally unusable. The second form of value is that invested in these artifacts as items in a collection. The labor of finding, identifying, categorizing, and physically ordering the objects invests them with this "taxonomic" value, the primary condition of which is precisely that they *are* obsolete, that is, old, antique, objects of nostalgia (Stewart 1984: 151–69). It is as collectibles that the artifacts were originally of interest to Mr. and Mrs. Young, whose thematic arrangement of them in terms of emblematic western industries is an expression of the taxonomic coherence this type of value depends on.

Both these first two systems of value, though apparently mutually exclusive of one another, entail economic exchange. They both exist in the context of commercial markets, monetary quantification, and, most important, straightforward ownership. The third type of value, which we might think of as "display value," is ambiguous in terms of economic exchange. I have suggested above that the point at which Mrs. Young's fence literally "turns a corner" is a conceptual turning point as well. Initially, the Youngs built the fence to solve the problem of how to exhibit their collection of found industrial artifacts. But having finished the panels along the front of the house, they had exhausted their stockpile, at which point they set about gathering objects expressly to allow them to continue the fence. Here the function of display itself supersedes the economy of the collection. It is the symbolic moment at which the fence undergoes an "invisible" material transformation from taxonomic value to display value.[6] The goal becomes not the completion of a collection, but the formal closure of a coherent display accomplished by fully encircling the house.

There is within the panels of the fence itself a rather nice material analogue to this conceptual shift. At first the Youngs were stumped about how to negotiate the curve at the corner of their yard, since the fence is composed of flat sections. The problem was solved when they discovered the motif of the "frozen chain," a widely familiar version of which is found in mailbox supports formed from logging chains welded into curved shapes. The Youngs designed a smoothly bent corner section composed of curving chains crossed in a centralized X pattern. This "trick" is of interest mainly for its arresting visual quality rather than as a way of "storing" and arranging items as part of a collection. The comic optical ambiguity of suppleness and rigidity, the slight disruption of visual expectations that draws looks (as of course does the whole display), is at the heart of display value.

As I have said, this third form of value is not so straightforwardly economic as the other two. When fixed in the fence, the exchange value of the artifacts as a collection is annihilated along with their simple use value. But in place of these an unlocalized, unquantifiable, unaccumulated value is invested in the fence through the very process of looking. It is a form of value in which straightforward ownership and control does not obtain. The intense clarity of the individual artifacts, combined with their rigid inappropriability, the figure/ground confusions between the specific items and the formal patterns of the individual panels, and the larger figure/ground alternation between the visual coherence of these panels and the overall "chaos" of the fence as a whole—these are the qualities of display through which the ceaseless movement of visual desire (and unlocalized, circulating value) is generated. It is a version, constructed through an apparatus of contemporary display, of that circulating look we see operating throughout the texts we have encountered.

And there is one other way that Mrs. Young's fence may be located within the same discursive terrain as these texts. I have suggested that the swimming rattlesnakes legend discussed in Chapter 1 entails a symbolic confrontation of modes of production. The humanly engineered, large-scale landscape transformations of dams and reservoirs most obviously, but the more fleeting motif of barbed wire as well, bespeak the order of industrialized production in the West, especially agricultural commodity production. Water-skiing, however, belongs to the order of recreation and spectacular display, elements in quite a different productive regime. I have suggested that the tale enacts symbolically a disastrous collision between these contrasting modes. Much more benignly, Mrs. Young's fence enacts a similar confrontation. In this case, however, it takes the form of an archaic phase of industrial production being contained by and subordinated to the demands of spectacle, as materially realized in a vernacular display.

* * *

While it may be possible to make this sort of thematic connection between texts (in the narrow sense) and artifacts, there are obviously great differences in the expressive resources available to each of these cultural domains. The verbal texts we have visited so far, and in its way the visual text of the Cody/Sitting Bull photograph as well, occupy themselves thematically and narratively with dramas of looking. Some express quite explicitly, and others through symbolic implication, the structures and procedures of a distinct visuality. Mrs. Young's fence does not so clearly articulate this optical regime through its content. But while narratives may depict explicitly or express symbolically relations of visuality, the fence "enacts" those relations. As a display environment it requires our actual and active visual engagement. One might say it *performs* the Western discourse of looking through its management of our visual experience. In this regard it demonstrates a key characteristic of display environments in general, namely, that they are simultaneously objects of looking *and* apparatuses of looking. How Mrs. Young's fence and the other display environments we will visit organize visual experience is of vital concern.[7] Before moving on to our next excursion in the landscape of Western visuality, a brief consideration of the fence as an optical apparatus is in order.

It is perhaps not too much of a generalization to say that no matter what other functions it might serve or effects it might produce (magnification, clarification, projection, inscription) an optical apparatus is fundamentally defined by the fact that it "positions" the eye in some way. This might be quite literal, as in those devices that require us to look through an eye piece, or it might be a more general or conceptual sort of positioning. Display environments such as Mrs. Young's fence can be said to organize our looking by presenting themselves to be seen in certain ways and not others. A minimal description of the fence's visual protocol would include such basic features as frontality (it is best seen face on), exteriority (it is meant to be seen from "outside"), sequentiality (it cannot be seen in a single comprehensive view), and visual "slippage" (it requires a fluctuation of focus), about which more in a moment. Of course display environments vary widely in the degree of constraint they place on the eye. Some are quite draconian in how they position the act of viewing, while others allow much more visual play. The sites we will visit in following chapters provide some sense of the range of possibilities in this regard, but for something to constitute a display at all, at least as I am using the term, means that it constrains and organizes vision in some fashion.

To examine Mrs. Young's fence as a visual apparatus let us consider three distinct ranges or scales at which our looking occurs. The first of these is the range of "overview," that is, the distance at which the display environment as a whole impresses itself upon us. This is the point where the display occupies much of our field of vision but does not significantly exceed it. In concretely physical terms, this is roughly the view one gets of Mrs. Young's fence when standing diagonally across the intersection from her house (Figure 2). As is often the case in vernacular displays, at this range of viewing the dominant impression one gets is of a profuse jumble of artifacts, a visual confusion which is both arresting and seemingly without coherence. The complaints that accretive vernacular displays such as the fence often elicit are usually a function of this first viewing position. At this scale they appear disruptive of the "order" surrounding them. Of course the perception of disorderly profusion is itself a discursive convention. For one thing, it is read as a marker of vernacular production in general in that it is associated with an absence of professional training, lack of coherent overall design, idio-syncrasy, obsessiveness, and so on. At this viewing range the individual artifacts in the fence are for the most part obscure, both literally too far away to identify clearly or "missed" because the whole view is over-whelming. Nevertheless, a general impression of the artifacts collectively might well be conveyed at this distance. A sense of rigidity or flexibility, hardness or softness, dullness or brightness, density or sparseness, recti-linearity or sinuousness can be perceived, if only vaguely, a rather long way away. The metallic rigidity of the industrial material from which the fence is made is a quality one can "feel" at this first position.

The second general viewing position is that at which formal patterns in the arrangement of elements become visible. Of course displays may vary widely in terms of the distance at which the internal components and their structural relationships come into view. In some cases this point of pattern resolution is not significantly closer than the range at which the whole display is experienced. Given its graphic and two-dimensional character, Mrs. Young's fence is relatively straightforward in its internal patterning. At some point while crossing the street in ap-proach to the fence it becomes clear that it is composed of separate panels. In other words, at this range the fence reveals itself to be not just a continuous flow of artifacts, but a series of formally distinct units punc-tuated by gates and corner pieces. And it becomes possible to see that the panels are not mere jumbles of frozen shapes, but rather coherent designs that follow some basic principles (the bilateral and radial sym-metries, tripartition, and color alternation I have described above). As I have already suggested, if one follows the fence around at this range of observation, one might also discover that the overall formality and sym-metrical precision of the panels increases, as does the degree of design "integration." The patterns of balance and centrality are increasingly conceived in terms of whole panels, rather than as a series of subsets or modules added end to end to produce a panel's overall design.

Finally, the third and most intimate degree of viewing is that range at which the formal patterns and gross shapes of the display resolve them-selves into the individual artifacts that are the fence's minimal units (Figure 6). It is the point at which one begins to see that the fence is constructed out of spoons, pliers, horseshoes, chains, spoked wheels, pulleys, cogs, and so on. This is also the range at which artifact bound-aries, surface textures, verbal and iconic elements (e.g., embossed letter-ing), and detailing of various sorts become noticeable. It is the zone of viewing at which optical perception enters the haptic range. One could reach out and touch the objects.

I have proposed this somewhat arbitrary three-fold division in the geography of looking because it gives us some purchase on what for my

Figure 6. Fence detail.

purposes is the most significant aspect of Mrs. Young's fence as a visual apparatus. This display environment's most distinctive optical procedure is to set in motion a slippage or fluctuation between the last two viewing ranges I have just described. I have already made much of the fact that in its painting scheme the fence clarifies artifact boundaries so as to foreground the identities of the objects out of which the formal designs are made. There is something of a paradox here, of the familiar figure/ground variety. Seeing the abstract design of the panels depends to some degree on *not* seeing the separate elements. On the other hand, one can only examine the distinct artifacts by losing the larger patterns. The silver/black color scheme has the odd, mediating effect of serving as a kind of compromise between these opposed impulses. It makes the individual artifacts visible at a considerable range, but in its uniform alternation it does not unduly disrupt the larger design. This visual accommodation the fence establishes between an emphasis on the discreteness of the individual artifacts and the force of larger patterns points us back to the regime of visuality I have attempted to tease out of the texts examined in previous chapters.

In bestowing special significance on this dynamic boundary zone of viewing, where overall forms and discrete pieces engage in a play of mutual displacement, the fence activates the appropriate conceptual position for a visual subject that is in a constant state of fluctuating motion. One of the clearest threads running through this study is what we might think of as the destabilized circulation of looking. Fueled by the desire to achieve visual control and authority, but dogged by the sense that a more comprehensive visual field surrounds one's own contingent vantage point, the discursive formation I have been exploring is fraught with such fluctuating motion and is characterized by constant displacements of one viewing position by another. Arising at first out of the impulse to impose order on an unruly collection of artifacts, and then taking on a life of its own as the abstract expression of the very principles of orderliness and closure, the fence can legitimately be taken as a material realization of the idea of mastery over the visual field. However, straining against this inclination toward formal, abstract mastery is the emphatic inscription of the individual artifacts as discrete identities. Recognized as distinct items with productive functions, material histories, potentially appropriable shapes, in short, contingent existence in a social/historical world, the objects of which the fence is made are material embodiments of socially situated looking. In their seemingly accessible discreteness they contradict the ungraspable abstraction of the formal design. As soon as one reaches out (conceptually) to appropriate one of these items, however, its fixity in the fence asserts itself. It "disappears," one might say, back into the pattern. I have already suggested how this dual quality of the fence expresses the "dematerialized" commodity form so characteristic of our historical moment. The definitive procedure of consumption in this advanced consumer order is to occupy a position in which one is suspended between vivid visual apprehension and infinitely deferred material appropriation. The circulation of the look is the embodiment of this principle in the domain of visual discourse. Mrs. Young's fence is a vernacular material culture display that stages this commodity optics with the same kind of parsimonious elegance that we saw in the joke about deluded tourists at the beginning of Chapter 1.

Mr. Dellos's Yard

In 1981 Jake Dellos (Figure 7) and his wife retired from more than thirty years of ranching on eight hundred acres along Gooseberry Creek, a stream that runs through north central Wyoming's Big Horn Basin. They moved to a three-acre tract just south of the Basin town of Worland, primarily an agricultural center.[8] Mr. Dellos came to this area as a small boy and he has extensive family connections in the vicinity. His people have mostly been farmers, as was the case with Mr. Dellos himself, until

Figure 7. Mr. Jake Dellos.

he and his wife took up the small livestock operation. The ranch was economically diversified, with a small herd of about seventy-five head of cattle, some sheep, and a large egg business. With several hundred chickens, Mrs. Dellos marketed many dozens of eggs weekly around the Worland area. In addition to these aspects of the ranch, the Delloses raised grain and produced more hay than they could use on their own place, the pastures along Gooseberry Creek being excellent hay ground. Success of course, as in the West generally, was tied to water, and no doubt the task of getting adequate moisture to the land (mainly through flood irrigation) was a constant concern. The amount of work required to

Figure 8. Dellos yard display—overview.

maintain such a diversified ranch, run mainly as a two person operation, is beyond the ken of most of us today. "It was a struggle," was Mr. Dellos's characteristically understated comment about their years on Gooseberry Creek. For the most part their efforts seem to have paid off in the end. Although not rich, the Delloses apparently did well in the sale of their property. Land prices were good in 1981 and Mrs. Dellos reports that they were lucky in the sale of their cattle. Although advised to hold onto the herd until spring (their auction was in winter), she insisted that they get rid of "the buggers" with the rest of the property. They sold on a Thursday. The next Monday the bottom dropped out of the beef market.

The remarkable energy the Delloses invested in their ranch has been carried over to their three-acre retirement property, so much so that "retirement" hardly seems the appropriate word. A new orchard now occupies a large section at the front of their lot, and a very well-tended vegetable garden sits behind the house. A patch of dark green, weedless front lawn reflects considerable effort in this semi-arid environment. But these and the other "normal" markers of industrious homeownership are easily missed when one first encounters the Dellos place, for the artifactual display one finds there is quite overwhelming (Figure 8).

Beginning a couple of years after they moved to their new home, Mr. Dellos undertook the project of transforming his domestic land-

Figure 9. Orchard border with umbrella "trees."

scape, tirelessly applying his cutting torch and welder to produce decorative metal sculptures, some of them one-of-a-kind pieces or paired
objects, others generated in series. Setting them out around his property, he has produced over the years an increasingly elaborate folk art
display. Unlike Mrs. Young's fence, the immediate process of manufacture is an important part of Mr. Dellos's work. As so often in avocational
folk art production, he has applied skills developed in his working life
to the sphere of personal, aesthetic expression.

He began by mounting spoked metal wheels in frames welded together from sections of pipe, not unlike, if much less elaborate, than
some of the panels in Mrs. Young's fence. He painted these wheels, a
whole wagonload of which had come from the Gooseberry ranch itself,
in bold, simple colors and added visual interest by surmounting each
frame with a unique "finial" made from other pieces of ranch equipment
or cast-off iron. At first his productions were distributed so as to mark
internal boundaries on his property. But as time went on, he began to
fill in some of the "interiors" as well.

Over the years Mr. Dellos has developed a growing repertoire of sculptural motifs. The most prominent of these is the representation of organic growth, especially flowers and trees. His orchard, for instance, is

Figure 10. "Sunflowers," etc.

surrounded by sixteen "umbrellas," as Mr. Dellos callls them (Figure 9). Formed from a series of curving iron rods that spring from a central, vertical pipe, the impression they give is of a cross between a cafe table umbrella and an ornamental tree. This latter quality is enhanced by the fact that suspended from loops at the end of each arm (branch) is a small metal "pendant" of some sort, different in both form and color for each umbrella/tree. Whether consciously intended or not, they strike one as being like blossoms at the end of branches. Other evidence of this organic impulse can be seen in the driveway border. This consists of a series of small spoked wheels alternating with bunches of plastic flowers, both set down in the holes of cinder blocks. Mr. Dellos fabricated the "wheels" from pipes and metal rods. Their radial symmetry, the dominant formal principle of the whole display, is decidedly floral, and their juxtaposition to the artificial flowers is an intentional redundancy.

Most clearly, however, the floral/organic theme is embodied in the large "sunflowers" that appear prominently in the display (Figure 10). As of my last visit, Mr. Dellos had produced three separate versions of this form. In calling them sunflowers he is referring not to the familiar large-blossomed plants grown decoratively and for their seeds, but rather to a small, roadside wildflower common in the Big Horn Basin and elsewhere

Figure 11. Irrigating shovel (vernacular minimalism).

in the semi-arid West. The sculptures are magnified versions of this modest, yellow-blossomed plant.[9] This sort of exaggerated, literally enlarged "florality" is an important element of this display, and I shall return to it.

The other main theme of Mr. Dellos's display environment is agriculture/ranching, as embodied in his sculptural representations of implements associated with these pursuits. The most striking examples of this are the two gigantic spurs mounted atop poles on opposite sides of his driveway. Mr. Dellos jokes that if a cowboy comes along who can wear them, they are his. One also finds a pair of decoratively painted, full-sized plows of the sort that would be drawn by horses or mules. These are not actual plows, but rather plow sculptures that Mr. Dellos has fabricated from old plow parts, pipe, and other cast-off pieces. Each is topped with a small cowboy figure made from horseshoes, an item Mr. Dellos has produced separately and profusely, with the intention of selling them as souvenirs. The most blatant and literal expressions of this agricultural implement theme are the small Ford tractor and the sickle bar that the Delloses had actually used to cut hay on the Gooseberry Creek ranch. Mr. Dellos has painted these in bright primary colors (the sickle bar a striking blue) and set them out as part of the overall display. My favorite example of this theme, though, is the small "throwaway" piece I found sitting behind Mr. Dellos's workshop. He had painted his old irrigating shovel entirely silver and stuck it, handle down, in the middle of a cast-off wheel rim, producing a kind of minimalist gloss on the general theme of devices related to ranching/agricultural production (Figure 11).

I have already mentioned that the radial symmetry of the small spoked wheels along the driveway are decidedly floral. This point might be extended to the dominant wheel motif in general. That Mr. Dellos paints his wheels in vivid colors is perhaps an acknowledgment of this connection. In one of the most interesting and impressive pieces, the mechanized wheel motif is explicitly juxtaposed to floral elements. On either side of the driveway as one enters the Dellos property, and forming a kind of gateway, stand two imposing, brightly painted "medallions" enclosed in frames of pipe (Figure 12). Mounted atop each frame are three yellow "flowers," with sharp-pointed petals radiating from central disks. The large, red, mandala-like components, floral themselves in a rather monstrously mechanical, hard-edged way, turn out to be rear wheels from an antique Oliver tractor, the serrated outer rims functioning in place of rubber tires. Inspecting closely, one discovers that the petals on one of the surmounted yellow blossoms are teeth from exactly the sort of tractor-drawn sickle bar that Mr. Dellos has painted and set out elsewhere in his yard.

This merging of the mechanical, industrially produced implement with the motif of decorative organic growth pervades Mr. Dellos's folk art environment. The series of umbrella trees and sunflowers are fabricated out of components that originate in the mass production of uniform artifacts. Especially relevant is the fact that many of the implements Mr. Dellos has cut up and reassembled in his sculptures are *obsolete* devices from the sphere of primary agricultural production, and most especially from the process of hay making that was so vital to the Delloses in their own ranching life. In addition to the sickle bar teeth, which show up as elements in several sculptures, various pieces from mechanized hay rakes also figure prominently. The arms/branches of the umbrella trees are ribs from an outmoded device known as a dump

Figure 12. Organic/industrial hybrid.

rake. Perhaps most ironically, the blossoms in one version of Mr. Dellos's sunflowers are the cutting disks from a weed mowing machine formerly used by farmers and ranchers in this area. Thus this fabricated folk art sunflower is made from pieces of a device that might well have been used to mow the very plants that inspired its production. These sorts of ironies are thickly layered in this display environment.

The last element of Mr. Dellos's display that I need to mention is something that seems out of place. It does not immediately fit with the other components, being neither a mass produced mechanical device related to agricultural production nor a form meant to evoke organic growth. As so often in the reading of discourses, however, its very anomaly turns out to be useful for purposes of interpretation. Sitting in the middle of

Figure 13. Cannon/post-puller (visual practical joke).

one display area is the object shown in Figure 13. Mr. Dellos delights in the fact that its appearance is deceiving. He says that most people, especially if only driving by on the highway, think it is a small cannon, presumably of the sort that might be placed memorially on a court-house lawn. When I first visited he asked me whether I knew what it was. I was stumped. He gleefully revealed that it is a fencepost puller of his own design and manufacture—a tool he had made out of old pipe and other metal detritus and that he had used on the ranch. One rotates the pipe around the axle so that the "cannon mouth" is at ground level. The sharpened plate attached to this end is then rolled up against the post and the chain is wrapped around and pulled tight. When one heaves down on the other end of the pipe few fenceposts can resist the force. I will suggest in a moment that this artifactual practical joke may be read as an especially concentrated expression of the tone that characterizes this display environment overall.

*   *   *

Obviously, Mr. Dellos's yard has a number of features in common with Mrs. Young's fence. Along with sharing the *bricolage* aesthetic of found object assemblage and the medium of welded metal, both these display environments project an ethos devoted to the orderly stability of the material world. This is most apparent, perhaps, in their treatments of surfaces.[10] In both cases the careful application of enamel paint is an important part of the visual effect. Complete coverage and uniformity of surface is an imperative of both displays. As we have seen, Mrs. Young's fence is coherently organized in a carefully designed alternation of silver and black. Mr. Dellos's sculptures display considerable color variety, but he starts out by applying a complete coat of silver enamel to each piece before deciding what other colors to use and what parts should be elaborated. Nothing goes unpainted. In fact Mr. Dellos extends the application of his own color schemes to his extensive collection of hand tools. One finds in his shop, for example, wrenches he has painted silver and then detailed with green or red. Here again, the silvered irrigating shovel seems a kind of pure expression of Mr. Dellos's aesthetic, his compulsion to cover and make smooth, to "neaten" the artifactual world around him. This principle of orderliness certainly characterizes his whole exterior environment, with its small patch of well tended front lawn, its carefully cultivated vegetable garden, and its sharp delineation of distinct yard spaces.

The individual items in Mr. Dellos's yard display, like those in Mrs. Young's fence, have a vivid clarity about them. They are discrete entities in themselves, and they are placed so as to "clarify" one another and to reveal the coherent overall plan of yard arrangement. Thus, as we have seen, the driveway is emphatically bordered along one side by a line of small floral wheels alternating with bunches of artificial plastic flowers. The impulse to "line things up" and to mark boundaries is evident in the series of framed wheels and in the sequence of umbrella trees running around the perimeter of the orchard. Both in its inclination to neaten all surfaces with paint and in its impulse to arrange objects so that they make explicit the conceptual geography of the yard, Mr. Dellos's display shares the anti-entropic sensibility expressed in Mrs. Young's fence.

But if this imperative to impose order on a landscape and to make artifacts coherently legible is one quality these vernacular displays have in common, they also both enact the sort of optical slippage we have encountered throughout the comprehensive text of the modern West. It is exactly this combination of apparent visual control and order with a subtle, "contaminating" destabilization of the viewing experience that justifies locating both these display environments within the twentieth-century discourse of looking West that I have attempted to track in Part I. But to complicate the relationship between these displays a bit, we should be aware that they stage this visual discourse through quite different means. As optical apparatuses they use different procedures and they produce quite different tonal effects. The fact that they differ in these ways demonstrates that the discursive formation in question is by no means a simple set of rules to be followed. It is, to invoke my earlier metaphor, a landscape of meandering pathways, not all of them heading in the same direction.

We have seen in Mrs. Young's fence a certain kind of play of visibility, a figure/ground ambiguity at a certain range of viewing that stages the contradictory impulses of advanced consumer desire. A timeless order of visual stability reflected in the abstract patterns of the panel designs struggles against the seemingly appropriable, vividly discrete artifacts: visual plenitude and closure versus multiple, contingent acts of socially motivated looking. In Mr. Dellos's yard, by contrast, the point of optical slippage is located differently, and it is also more "intentional" than in the fence. Unlike the constituent elements of the latter, which retain the integrity of their original boundaries as tools, implements, machine parts, and so on, the minimal units of Mr. Dellos's display, the individual sculptures, are fabricated by violating the boundaries of preceding artifacts. They purposely "hide" the old objects in the new forms. Whereas the alternating paint scheme of Mrs. Young's fence serves in part to emphasize artifact identities, Mr. Dellos uses paint to mask the sutures in his Frankenstein-like productions, or in some cases to create the impression of seams where none had existed in the artifactual raw material.

These literal boundary confusions are the concrete material analogues to the larger, conceptual boundary confusion that stands at the heart of Mr. Dellos's display. I mean, of course, his imaginative dismemberment and reassembly of the devices of mechanized agriculture to produce artificial icons of organic growth, or at least allusions to organicism. One important thing to note about this display is that the hard, sharp-edged quality of its industrial raw material and the precise uniformity of mechanized production are never fully submerged in the organic forms of the sculptures. In fact, the dominant quality overall is precisely the playfully undecideable conflation of the utilitarian mechanical and the decoratively organic. Is it a mechanized garden or an organic apparatus, the machine in the garden or the garden in the machine?

This physical, artifactual ambivalence is accompanied by a significant economic ambivalence. To look at them collectively, Mr. Dellos's sculptures seem to "belong" to the space of his yard. They are neither haphazardly placed nor arrayed as a detachable collection. Rather, they embroider the "natural" divisions and spaces of the yard's conceptual geography. On closer examination, however, one finds that most of the individual pieces are not fixed. Rather, they are mounted in wheel rims so that they may be moved, and by implication, alienated. Mr. Dellos takes pride in the fact that "tourists" [his word] regularly stop out on the highway to take pictures of his display. Sometimes they turn in, and he is quite happy to sell them at least some of his decorative pieces. He has even developed a set of small, easily portable souvenir items that he can produce in large numbers and sell cheaply. These include a miniature rocking chair made of horseshoes, his horseshoe cowboy, and a whimsical "dune buggy" made out of small elements taken from haying equipment.

Mr. Dellos's sculptures, then, and their overtly commercial extension into souvenirs connect his display environment to the tourist economy of the contemporary West, albeit rather marginally. This gives his artifacts a kind of value ambivalence we do not see in Mrs. Young's fence. The artifacts there are unavailable for physical appropriation, though the vividness of their presentation sets them forth as potential objects of appropriating desire. The artifacts in Mr. Dellos's display are more visually ambiguous in terms of the boundary confusions I have just mentioned, and likewise they are more mixed in terms of how they structure value. For one thing, the raw material of his display is not an artifact collection, as is the case with the fence. Rather it is a stockpile generated from various sources and assembled expressly to be transformed into imaginative sculptures. One of these sources, as we have seen, is the agricultural machinery the Delloses actually used in their own ranching operation. In addition to this, much of his raw material Mr. Dellos has simply purchased, but mainly at auctions and estate sales rather than through retail commerce. In other words, his display environment participates in the economy of recycling and reuse so important to rural, agricultural communities. And finally, some of his stockpile of raw material has come as gift or through informal barter. A friend who knows about his hobby might, for example, drop off a load of pipe he has come across. Eggs from the Dellos chickens or potatoes from their garden would be a typical counter-gift, with no formal calculation of or significant concern for precise economic equivalence.

The underlying economy of Mr. Dellos's display is, then, quite different from that of Mrs. Young's fence. The taxonomic value of the collection does not figure into it. Whereas the fence embodies an ambivalent transformation of collection value into that evanescent, unquantifiable form of value I am associating with inappropriable display, Mr. Dellos's yard transforms the simple use value of his stockpiled "scrap" into a kind of marginally appropriable display value, in that it has the potential of activating the commercial tourist economy of the souvenir and "folk art." By cutting up his industrially produced raw material and reassembling it into decorative sculptures, or in some cases merely repainting it and setting it out as part of the display, Mr. Dellos annuls both its basic use value and any potential it might have for collection value. But in their place he invests the material with a kind of amalgam of the "pure" display we see in the fence and the commercial display typical of a tourist site.

*　*　*

As I have already pointed out, one of the key features of the yard, perhaps its dominant quality, is its undecidable conflation of mechanized agricultural production (with a distinctly western inflection) and decorative organic growth (also with regional associations in its floral motifs). It is hard not to see in it a kind of playful commentary on the relation between industrial production applied to organic growth (e.g., raising and harvesting a hay crop) and organic decorative display (e.g., cultivating a flower garden). It is important to notice that the form of mechanization embodied in the display is one that is both imposed on the western landscape and somewhat archaic in its historical associations. For the most part the machinery Mr. Dellos has cut up to produce his display is from an era of western agriculture that has been largely superseded. It "refers" to a period in which farming and ranching, though increasingly mechanized, operated on a fairly small scale, as opposed to the corporate and conglomerated system that characterizes the great majority of agriculture today. In this way the yard commemorates the agricultural mode the Delloses themselves participated in.

The mechanical devices associated with this phase of modern agriculture, although industrial both in their own production and in their use, are still essentially tool-like. That is, they are extensions of their users' own labor power and remain under his or her ownership and control, as opposed to being apparatuses in which humans participate as components of an overall mechanism. The small tractor with sickle bar attachment Mr. Dellos used to cut his hay crop is really only one step up from horse-drawn machinery, and it stands in marked contrast to the large swathers, bailers, stackers, and other modern equipment that turn hayfields into automated factories and require a level of capital investment well beyond what the typical small-scale "family" rancher or farmer can muster. One might say, then, that the underlying material source of Mr. Dellos's display is a historical moment in which mechanized ordering of the western landscape is underway, but still at the scale of individual human endeavor. Even though the landscape might be resistant and its productive control still a "struggle," to recall Mr. Dellos's characterization of his own experience, industrial mechanization is the fundamental condition required to master it. At the same time, however, this process of industrialization has not yet progressed to the point that the human producer has entirely disappeared into the apparatus.

I would propose that these conditions, deeply embedded in the very fabric of Mr. Dellos's display, are consonant with that magisterial visuality that has been such a powerful influence in shaping the way Euro-Americans experience landscape. As we have seen, the magisterial gaze is one that implies a coherent, individualized viewing subject whose look marks the territory it surveys as being under control and available for productive exploitation. The raw material for Mr. Dellos's display comes from the classic phase of the economic/productive system which undertook to put that magisterial visuality into practice on the ground. We must consider, then, what it means that in this display environment the representative artifacts of a residual mode of industrial production devoted to landscape mastery have been submerged in a whimsical material culture fantasy that centers around the motif of floral growth.

Perhaps the most obvious thing to say is that Mr. Dellos's yard privileges decoration, an inherently visual quality of material things, over utilitarian devices of economic production. Flowers are the explicit theme, while hay is only indirectly implied through the display's raw material. The "non-productive" visuality of display displaces the tangible substance of primary production agriculture. It is as if in retirement Mr. Dellos has shifted from this older system of production, with its attendant assumption of magisterial visuality, into a new one where an advanced consumer optics devoted to the play and circulation of looking holds sway. This new system has as one of its institutional anchors the modern tourism into which Mr. Dellos has attempted to insert his vernacular productions. Viewed one way, his display could be read as a kind of critique, or at least a slyly comic "dismemberment" of the seemingly substantial and productive mastery of the landscape by a mode of visuality that constantly calls into question the stabilities this older system took for granted.

As a visual apparatus, then, Mr. Dellos's yard works quite differently from Mrs. Young's fence. One might say that the fence takes the discourse of Western visuality in the direction of classicism, while the yard tends more toward the comic, or carnivalesque register. The optical play in the former is between the stable symmetries of abstract design and the discrete integrity of constituent artifacts, while in the latter it appears as an ambiguous hybridization between organic and mechanistic elements accomplished through boundary violations and reconfigurations of pre-existing objects. Also, I have suggested that in the fence a zone of visual instability exists somewhere in the middle range of viewing. It is at this distance that the undecideable play between stable pattern and contingent artifact, or more abstractly, between static visual plenitude and the desire driven possibility of material appropriation is activated. Mr. Dellos's yard plays out the same scenario of destabilized looking, but in this case the visual apparatus emphasizes the tension between the other two ranges of looking I have proposed above, the position of general overview and the position of tight close-up.

When contemplated from the elevated vantage point of the highway embankment, the location from which most "tourists" take their pictures of the display, Mr. Dellos's yard strikes one as a miniaturized study in landscape mastery. His sculptures order and rationalize the yard, making it seem a material realization of the magisterial gaze. The orchard, the vegetable garden, and the manicured front lawn, among other things, have quite literally made this space fruitfully productive. The view at this range bespeaks complete control over material conditions. However, when one crosses the middle ground and draws close to the display, a kind of comic, artifactual "subterfuge" suddenly becomes visible, and the sense of surprise it evokes is vital to the display's discursive procedure. It is at this minimal distance that one realizes the sunflower is an assemblage of painted pipes, sickle bar teeth, and hay rake or mower disks. The elements in this display environment seem to do everything they can to hide—until the last moment, so to speak—the artifacts out of which they are formed. The surprise comes from discovering that their parts are fragments of other things, indeed, things that seem particularly incongruous: the machinery of mechanized agricultural production dismembered and stitched back together in patterns that express the theme of decorative organic growth. And here we might recall Mr. Dellos's post puller, taking it now as the paradigm of this principle of incongruity. It displays, in fact, several layers of ironic ambiguity. It is an agricultural hand tool assembled from fragments of industrial artifacts, but it has been painted and displayed so as to invite associations of industrialized warfare. The "point" is in the humor of discovering its hidden self, and for most visitors even a close-up view will not reveal its secret. It requires the assistance of an expert interpreter. And it is in such gestures that this display environment brings home to us, in this case as a kind of comic surprise, that the material world is not so ordered and under control as we might have thought. Once again, a western material apparatus has produced a version of the destabilized visuality that, I have been arguing, characterizes the whole discourse of looking West.

Chapter Six
Over Prison Walls
Display and Ideology at the Wyoming Territorial Park

In the summer of 1992, a year after it opened as an historic site, Wyoming's restored and museumized territorial penitentiary had its first official apparition. An Iowa couple was taking the tour, which had reached the point where guides call attention to the large photo of Julius Greenwald (Figure 14), the only inmate in the thirty-one-year history of the prison to have died on the premises. Suddenly, the man from Iowa felt a chill. Looking over his shoulder, he saw "a shadowy figure in prison stripes standing in the doorway. The prisoner was reaching out his hand, palm up." The tourist turned to his wife momentarily, and when he turned back around, the figure had vanished. Concerned by his sudden pallor, the wife asked her husband if he was feeling ill. "He told her he had just seen a ghost. The guy next to the couple turned and said, 'Oh good. You saw it too' "(*Laramie Daily Boomerang* 9/13/92).

It was, it seems, none other than Julius Greenwald who had made this ectoplasmic debut. At least that is the story the Wyoming Territorial Park (WTP) settled on as it eagerly incorporated the figure of "Julius, the prison ghost" into its relentlessly upbeat promotional and programming scheme (a Halloween Haunted Prison Tour is now one of the Park's most popular events).

According to the newspaper report, staff members at the Territorial Prison have experienced a variety of familiar preternatural signs—cold spots, locked gates swinging open, the sense of a presence close by when no one is visibly there, an unfamiliar face reflected in a windowpane. But this is the low level, background haunting against which a full-fledged, public apparition stands out. I will take the first official appearance of a ghost at the Territorial Prison museum to be a telling moment in the history of this institution, and as the emblematic entree to the reading that follows.

Figure 14. Julius Greenwald, the "prison ghost."

The Wyoming Territorial Prison and Old West Park, as this site is now called,[1] is itself a richly elaborated example of the discursive procedures I have been tracking through all the previous sites and texts. That its optical system is virtually a perfect material and institutional realization of this visual regime seems almost inevitable, given that the Park's centerpiece, the Territorial Pen, involves the superimposition of one system of visual management, museological/spectatorial, on top of another, carceral/surveillant.[2] It is in the odd, often ironic effects of this overlapping, many of which are evident in specific and sometimes minute material features of the site, that the discourse of looking West manifests itself. The trope of the ghostly apparition captures quite well the definitive feature of this discourse, the unfixing of positions of spectatorship and surveillance, with constant, seemingly free slippage between them. The ghost is both a manifestation, an arresting spectacle, and the felt presence of unseen observation. Crossing the boundary between visibility and invisibility, it is the very (dis)embodiment of unfixed visuality.

Taking the Prison Ghost as my mascot for this analysis allows me to reinvoke the issue of historical representation. The ghosts at Fort Laramie, you will recall, are explicitly associated by some with the evocative recovery of the past as spectacle, the spirit of the past raised by the alchemy of modern display and spectatorship, the specter as spectator. But this process is equally the evaporation of the past. When Julius the Prison Ghost is raised as a feature of the museum display, he blocks out Julius Greenwald, the Jewish cigarmaker from Poland, who on September 29, 1897 murdered his wife, Jennie, in a house of ill-fame in Evanston, Wyoming, and who died in 1901 of congestive heart failure. And, as we will see, the most ironically appropriate historical suppression is the lack of attention paid to the fact that while an inmate the enterprising Mr. Greenwald was allowed to start a cigarmaking business and market his product to the other prisoners (Frye 1990:183). Part of my argument here is that entrepreneurship is an important "ghost theme" at the Territorial Park, only spectrally present, but nevertheless central to the ideological program.

The Institution

The Wyoming Territorial Prison and Old West Park, a state historic site, is located in Laramie, Wyoming. The prison itself is a rather impressive ashlar block, sandstone building (Figure 15), especially imposing in the nineteenth-century photographs that convey its gloomy isolation on the treeless flats above the Laramie River. Today, the elevated four lanes of U.S. Interstate 80 run noisily along the Park's west boundary, and a combination of truck stops, budget motels, gas stations, an animal disease research facility, and West Laramie residential neighborhoods form its physical context. The sign of the Golden Arches that floats high above the new, westside McDonald's appears to hover over the restored Penitentiary as one approaches it from the center of town, which lies to the east across the river and the Union Pacific tracks.

That misguided nineteenth-century visitor to Laramie (see Chapter 1), visually deluded by the rather featureless landscape and the clear air at 7,200 feet above sea level, would presumably have passed near the Prison on his ill-advised morning stroll out to the Snowy Range. Today, expansive views are blocked and a mundane scale is imposed by all the material paraphernalia of the modern small town. However, I will be

Figure 15. Restored Wyoming Territorial Penitentiary.

suggesting that many features of the visuality we have observed being played out in terms of the western landscape are evident as well in the material and interpretive program of this regional historic site. They are, one might say, brought indoors—museumized, concentrated, and vividly put on display. Thus, if I have invoked a number of emblematic instances as embodiments of one feature or another of this visuality, the site in question here can serve as the contemporary master icon, the almost perfect material realization of this discourse of looking in the form of a display environment. I present it as a modern, institutional counterpart to Owen Wister's visual moment.

The grounds of the Territorial Prison and Old West Park cover about 180 acres of state owned land, roughly a quarter of which has undergone development as the actively operating facility. A core of seven acres that encompasses a number of historic structures, including a warden's house and various outbuildings, has been designated a state historic district. The premier artifact and anchor of the site is the restored penitentiary building itself, constructed in two stages, beginning in 1872.[3] The prison operated until 1903, having shifted from federal to state jurisdiction with the coming of Wyoming statehood in 1890. Transferred to the University of Wyoming's College of Agriculture in 1903, the prison building spent the next seventy years, ignominiously from some people's point of view, as a barn for the experimental stock farm. Almost all the internal prison elements were eventually removed, and two ceramic brick silos went up beside the main entrance.

Condemned and vacated in 1977, the deteriorating prison structure was placed on the National Register of Historic Places in 1978. In 1983 a committee was established through the Laramie Chamber of Commerce to look into the possibility of developing the derelict prison cum stock barn into a tourist attraction. From the beginning the idea of western heritage tourism was wedded to the goals of economic development, and that has been the guiding principle, the sine qua non of the project throughout its history. Given the cultural/political/economic context, that is not at all surprising.

Although home to the state's only four-year institution of higher education, Laramie does not have a substantial economic base in other respects. It is one of only two incorporated municipalities in Albany County. Without significant mineral extraction or a substantial manufacturing sector, Albany County has relied historically on ranching/agriculture and the infusion of state funds that support the university. Like so many other small towns in the "New West" (Riebsame and Robb 1997), Laramie has begun to turn to tourism as a potential addition to its portfolio. It has followed the familiar pattern of sprucing up the old downtown in vaguely Victorian fashion and it promotes western heritage in such things as its summer Jubilee Days Celebration.

Although the site is not ideally situated to capture a national tourist clientele (more northerly and more southerly routes being the stronger tourist conduits), the idea of developing a major heritage park at the Territorial Prison got up a head of steam through the 1980s and began to barrel forward. Perhaps it is not too far-fetched to place this process in the context of the bonanza economics and can-do boosterism that is so much a part of western history. Much like the late nineteenth-century British aristocrat who, disregarding the short growing season and semi-aridity, envisioned an agricultural empire of prosperous, peasant-like smallholders in the Laramie Basin (Lawrence 1995), the promoters of the Territorial Prison as a tourist site had grand visions. One milestone along the way toward the realization of these dreams was the legislative designation of the 180 acres as a state park, with its seven-acre core historic zone. This was accomplished in 1986, and it was followed up by the commissioning of a professional feasibility study. Sixty thousand dollars of state funds were allocated for this purpose, and a contract was let to the Wood Bay Consulting Group, Limited, of Edmonton, Canada, which was to develop a master plan.

With the state park designation and the feasibility study commissioned, a Wyoming Territorial Prison Corporation (WTPC) was established under Section 501(c)(3) of the Internal Revenue Code, which grants tax free status to institutions devoted exclusively to charitable or educational purposes. The Corporation Board is the chief governing body for the Park, responsible for setting fiscal policy, hiring the professional staff, and in general determining the philosophy and direction of the site. Although officially a state property, the WTP was committed to the stewardship of this locally constituted board rather than to the state's Division of Parks and Cultural Resources, which manages all other state sites. Apart from several mandated positions to represent governmental and educational entities,[4] the Board is occupied mainly by citizens from the Laramie community: small businesspeople, local bankers, lawyers, political figures and civic activists, retirees, and people with an interest in local history. The Chamber of Commerce origins of the project are clearly evident in the makeup and operation of the Board.

The WTP's unique governance structure is consistent with its unique (in Wyoming), if not always explicit mission, namely, to use public historical/cultural resources for the purpose of economic development. This is not to say, of course, that other state sites are unconcerned with boosting tourist visitation nor that many of those in state government do not view them mainly as an economic resource.[5] But no other site has been established with attention so completely fixed on the tourist market nor at such a scale (again, by Wyoming standards). And no other site so clearly mixes the elements of entertainment oriented theme park with historical education. The WTP is, in short, Wyoming's first attempt to use publicly owned cultural resources to tap into the mass, heritage tourism network, a formula well established in many other parts of the country.[6] The clearest indicator of this is the way a sudden infusion of capital funding allowed a quite photogenic tourist site to spring up almost overnight out of little more than a gutted, crumbling building encrusted with manure.[7]

The Wood Bay study was submitted in 1988. An executive summary identifies its main objective as the investigation of "the market, concept, site conditions and financial feasibility for development of a major new theme park in the City of Laramie." The planning process included a review of the existing site and its physical resources, "program requirements and user needs" based on a review of North American theme parks and heritage sites, a market assessment to determine "potential target markets and their characteristics as well as . . . future market trends," and a survey of interstate travelers "to confirm the most appealing type of park development." Three "development options" were proposed and vetted to the WTPC, public officials, and the general public through a series of open meetings. "Throughout the site development process, historical themes and sub-themes were evaluated regarding their development costs, revenue projections and appropriateness to an 1860's–1900 theme park" (Woodbay Project Summary).

The basic recommendation of the study may fairly be taken as the inaugural moment in establishing the fundamental and largely uncontested principles that have guided the Park's development and operation:

Based upon the market analysis, and the evaluation of the three alternative development concepts, a theme park having a broad western theme is considered most desirable for attracting people of all ages and backgrounds. Research indicated that the most appealing type of park would include such attractions as a historical theme street depicting the 1860's-1900 era, railroad development, steam train rides, special events, street entertainment, and a U.S. Marshals Museum developed in concert with the Territorial Prison. Market research results also stressed the importance of authenticity and educational displays in the overall site development. The plan develops a broad range of living history, wild west, recreation, leisure attractions and commercial facilities to help support traditional interpretive non-profit facilities. (Wood Bay Project Summary)

It is by no means the case that the plan set forth here has met universal endorsement. In fact, development of the Park has been controversial and divisive from the beginning. But the basic terms of discussion and debate, the conceptual horizon within which the Park was and is viewed, found its codification in this planning study. In simplest terms, the binary opposition between historical authenticity and economic development is the irreducible dichotomy at the core of the prevailing public ideology. Historic site versus theme park, regional identity versus touristic expectation, local culture versus mass culture, education versus entertainment, reality versus myth: these are some of the rhetorical variations through which the basic structure is expressed. In them one finds the very familiar lineaments of many public culture debates and policies in our late capitalist moment.

The preferred alternative that emerged from the Wood Bay study certainly promoted the idea that the WTP had major potential as a world class attraction. It proposed an ambitious $46,000,000 theme park organized around the idea of Wyoming's western frontier heritage. With the restored prison as its historical anchor, the Park's ancillary attractions would combine a core theme of frontier law and justice with exhibits and living history environments devoted to familiar Wild West set pieces: "End-of-Tracks" frontier town, early ranch life, fur trappers' rendezvous, Plains Indian encampment, mining, logging, and frontier military post. Along with such presentations of regional history in the period 1860 to 1900, natural history interpretation and a "Wild West Land" amusement park were part of the proposal.

With a three-year phase-in of the capital investment, the plan projected attendance by the third year of over half a million visitors, with
expected annual attendance ranging between five hundred and six hundred thousand. Its most optimistic projection was that the Park could
see by year ten attendance exceeding one million during a one-hundred-
twenty-day operating season. The primary market was identified as high
education level, moderate to higher income household parties of "50+
couples and younger couples with young families." At these levels, the
Park would turn a profit in its second year of operation (1991 by the
projected schedule) of $985,000, and over $2,000,000 by a decade later
(*Casper Star Tribune* 3/17/96).

While the basic principles of the Wood Bay plan and its underlying
conception of the site have become firmly established, the scale at which
they have been carried through is quite a different matter. Funding for
the necessary restorations, improvements, and additions at the Park was
developed cooperatively among the state, Albany County, and the City
of Laramie. Fifteen million dollars in local taxes and a ten-million-dollar
loan from the state capitalized the project at a level considerably below
that proposed in the master plan. These funds allowed for the expensive stabilization of the Prison building and its interior restorations and
exhibitry, basic restoration of the warden's house and other ancillary
structures (admissions booth, offices, storage, etc.), and refurbishing of
a large horsebarn as, on its upper level, a western-theme dinner theater
and, on the main floor, a space for "America's Star," the official museum
of the U.S. Marshals Service.[8]

In addition to these restorations and adaptations of existing elements,
the public funds were used for total construction of a high stockade wall
around the prison yard (an element visible in historic photographs), an
open air amphitheater with sound system, an extensive playground for
small children, a food booth, fencing, signage, and other infrastructural
elements, and, most important, an "end-of-tracks town" main street, with
colorfully decorated falsefront buildings and tents housing a saloon, a
mercantile, a printshop, an old time photography studio, a livery stable,
and so on (Figure 16). This somewhat miniaturized, patently imaginary
western townscape (Starr 1992:19–21) is, along with the dinner theater
and amphitheater, the clearest embodiment of the theme park idea,
their functions being overtly commercial (most of the structures are
"points of purchase") and entertainment oriented.

It was with these elements in place that the Wyoming Territorial Park
opened its doors on July 1, 1991. The grand opening had been scheduled
for the previous summer, to coincide with the one-hundredth anniver-
sary of Wyoming statehood. This had not proved possible, and in lieu
of the full-scale christening, funds were allocated for installation of a

Figure 16. "End of tracks" town.

"preview center" in one of the downstairs spaces of the prison. It consisted of an impressive diorama of the Park in its projected complete
form and an overhead promotional video entitled "This Proud Land"
(see below). These displays were produced by Wood Bay with the intention of developing interest and local support for the future Park and to
have something to offer taxpayers when it became obvious there would
not be a centennial year opening. Wood Bay received $830,000 for its
work on the preview center.

The optimistic visions of the Wyoming Territorial Park's future have
not yet been realized. In its considerably scaled back form the attendance projections have turned out to be off by approximately a factor of
ten. Annual attendance has typically fallen below 50,000 rather than exceeding 500,000, with annual deficits rather than windfall profits as the
result. Under these conditions it is not surprising that the Park Board
and staff have considered or attempted a variety of management alternatives to reverse the dire fiscal prospects. These have ranged from attempts to introduce a more substantial living history component based
on sound scholarly principles (short-lived) to a proposal to establish a
large-scale water park and I-MAX type theater on the WTP grounds.
These shifts in approach to management are part of an internal insti-

tutional history, a "ghost history" only superficially visible to the public in such evanescent materializations as changes in admission fees or the disappearance of the living history characters.

This story of the WTP must include, along with its institutional narrative, some account of the presiding "structure of feeling" at the Park (Williams 1977:128–35), that is, its tone and style as a public display environment. In comparison to the rather frantic shifts in institutional management, this aspect of the WTP has remained fairly consistent throughout, though with some "disruptions" here and there. One detail of the Park's design history is a good indicator of the display style that has characterized this site from the beginning. Among its master plan recommendations, Wood Bay proposed that the Park hire an established design firm specializing in the production of public display and spectacle. One of the firms mentioned was Jack Rouse Associates, now Rouse Wyatt, of Cincinnati, Ohio, and the WTP did subsequently engage its services as consultant. Rouse Wyatt is a major player in the field of image production. According to its World Wide Web site (<http://www.rousewyatt.com>), it is organized in three main divisions: public relations and corporate image management (trade show and conference design, business-related exhibitry, speech scripting and coaching for corporate officers, etc.); theme parks and other entertainment environments (architectural and interior design, scripting of stage shows, etc., for such venues as Circus, Circus in Las Vegas, and the Six Flags theme parks); and museum and exhibit design, with a specialty in historical theme environments (exhibitry design, interactive programming, integration of educational and commercial components, etc.).

The last of these categories is of course the most relevant here, but the whole array of Rouse Wyatt's services is an indication of their involvement in the amalgamation of private, corporate interests, entertainment and image production, and public historical/educational display that has become such a pervasive feature of our current cultural environment. Central to their corporate philosophy is that history can be presented in ways that are engaging and entertaining rather than dull and pedantic. What they refer to in their self-presentation as "edutainment" guides their approach to historic theme design in such places as South Street Seaport in New York. Through presentation of "strong storylines and immersive environments," combining interactive exhibitry and visually engaging interpretive programming, cultural and historical subjects can be made compelling for mass audiences. On a rather modest scale compared to many of Rouse Wyatt's projects,[9] these principles inform the overall "feel" of the Wyoming Territorial Park. My point here is not that Rouse Wyatt imposed these qualities on the WTP, but rather that its very involvement with the project is entirely consistent with and a confirmation of the general cultural logic that was already at work to determine what species of display environment this Park would become.

With the abiding goal of making the site's relevant history entertaining and appealing to a broad tourist audience, the WTP might seem to have a built in interpretive dilemma. How can one present a prison, seemingly emblematic of social ills and human depravity, through positive themes and with a light enough touch to leave an upbeat impression? To emphasize too strongly the negative aspects of regional history, like frontier lawlessness, vigilantism, or the true nature of criminality in the late nineteenth century, would seem to cut against an important promotional function of the institution, as well as possibly putting people out of the mood to hang around and spend their vacation dollars. And perhaps even more important than the actively negative associations attached to penal institutions is their fundamental inertness. By design prisons are characterized by restricted motion and monotonous routine. The historical realities of tedium, bleak prospects, and drudgery do not lend themselves very well to "edutainment" programming (Schlereth 1990:362).

The overall dilemma, then, is how to make a prison seem historically exciting and have it serve as a vehicle for the positive themes and comfortably domesticated images suitable for the PG audiences that sites of this sort seek to address. The solution to this problem was not far to find, and it was already stitched into the fabric of the site by the time the physical restorations and re-creations began. The strategy[10] was to combine a core historical theme of the coming of law, order, and justice to the frontier with a pervasive, lightly humorous invocation of a rootin', tootin' Old West readily familiar from countless mass cultural enactments.[11] As we will see, these two aspects of the WTP image are thoroughly interwoven.

At present the Prison is interpreted mainly in the form of a static display. Staff guided and self-guided tours provide narrative elaboration's of the information presented in exhibits and wall text. Accounts of prison breaks, living conditions, daily regimen, notable inmates, and so on present the sort of "memorable facts" that serve as the mental souvenirs without which the museum experience seems wanting. In concert with the displays at the U.S. Marshals Museum, the dominant message at the Prison has to do with progressive reform at the end of the nineteenth century and the taming of the West, an issue to which I will return.

Surrounding this interpretive core, and infringing upon it in several ways, is a domain epitomized by the slogan on one of the WTP's highway billboards: "Come See How the West Was Fun." Recreation, entertainment, and commercial exchange dominate the Old West main street

in the end-of-tracks frontier town, which we may view as the complementary environment to the Prison in the overall morphology of the
Wyoming Territorial Park. Costumed summer staff members occupy
the various Old West establishments: storekeeper, bartender, dancehall
girls, printer, volunteer crafts demonstrators, a roving U.S. Marshal, and
the like. Covered wagon and stagecoach rides may be taken, and in
some seasons a circular pony ride for small children has been included.
In recent years a miniature "steam train" (actually pulled by a small tractor) has been added. Presentations in the outdoor amphitheater run
through the summer and range from country music performances to old
time fashion shows. And most lucrative of all, the dinner theater shows
represent the high end of professional entertainment at the Park.[12] In
addition to these more or less continuous features, Park programming
includes special events.[13] A temporary "mountain man rendezvous" has
been held at the WTP for a number of years. This is an extremely popular genre of living history reenactment in the intermountain West. Also,
a Colorado group that reenacts nineteenth-century baseball has held
exhibition games at the Park.

In keeping with the philosophy of interactive programming, some
audience participation scenarios are a regular feature of the daily schedule. In one of these children are invited to join a "prison break posse."
They are issued toy rifles and sent to round up an escaped convict, whom
they escort back to the prison. In another preset drama a group of Park
visitors are selected to serve as the jury at a frontier trial reenactment
held in the Belle of the West Saloon. The scenario here derives loosely
from a notable local event. A murder case in Laramie in 1870 was the
first instance of women being included officially as jurors at a criminal
court proceedings.[14] If the defendant is found guilty in the mock trial,
off he goes to a prison cell.

Finally, perhaps the most tellingly familiar marker of Old West theme
park "fun" is the shoot-out on main street. The legacy of Owen Wister's
romantic man-to-man duel in the public, commercial display space of
the town center, played and replayed in the countless variations of
twentieth-century popular culture, flourishes in gunfight reenactment
groups and staged spectacles at western themed sites. The WTP is no
exception. It has hosted quickdraw competitions and regional reenactment groups have held demonstrations and staged shutouts against the
photogenic backdrop of the frontier town falsefronts. By all accounts
these presentations are immensely popular with visitors, confirming for
some that the success of the Park depends on "giving tourists what they
want," which is the same as saying "what they expect" based on their
shared, if tacit knowledge of mass cultural conventions.

The emphasis in all of these display activities is on light-hearted fun.

The actual effects of small arms weapons are invisible, of course. Incarceration is depicted as a kind of joke, and audience involvement is managed with a tone of wry humor derived from the mild embarrassment of the good sports who are willing to participate in the jocose proceedings. Unlike fully developed living history sites, where in many cases the interpretive technique is to give visitors the feeling that they have just happened upon normal, everyday activities, the events at the WTP are overtly spectatorial. That is, they hew to a formal schedule; they are highly scripted and "frontal" in their address to the audience; and many of them are in one sense or another enacted "on stage," whether overtly as at the amphitheater, or implicitly, as against the movie set background of the frontier main street, which only has buildings along one side.

While there are elements of local reference in some of these spectacles, for the most part the WTP takes a generic approach to the broad theme of the Old West. I will conclude this overview of the Park's history and mode of operations with the two most notable exceptions to the generic format, for taken together they constitute the most explicit embodiment of a more subtle ideological agenda that will lead us to the real subject of this chapter—the way the WTP works as a visual apparatus that reproduces the patterns of visuality we have been attending to throughout this study.

* * *

Easily the most famous inmate to have spent time in the Wyoming Prison is Robert Leroy Parker, alias George "Butch" Cassidy. A horsethief, train and bank robber, and member of the notorious Hole in the Wall Gang, Cassidy spent a year and a half in the pen, between 1894 and 1896, on a grand larceny charge (cattle theft). By this time the facility had become a state institution, and Cassidy was pardoned by Governor William A. Richards (Frye 1990: 153). It is of course George Roy Hill's 1969 film *Butch Cassidy and the Sundance Kid* that made this ne'er-do-well an icon in the popular consciousness. Paul Newman's portrayal cemented Butch's image as a handsome, roguishly appealing outlaw hero with a ready wit and a cheerful (late 60s) disregard for authority. Lest this image be forgotten, a picture of Newman as the congenial law breaker hangs in one of the Prison museum galleries. Needless to say, it goes unremarked that Cassidy's first arrest in Wyoming was for rolling a drunk in an alley (Frye 1990: 153).

Not surprisingly, this historical figure has become the *genius loci* of the Wyoming Territorial Park. His prison mugshot, which conveys a boyish, square-jawed frankness, is perfect for Park advertising and it graces most of the promotional materials (Figure 17). That Cassidy was not

Figure 17. Butch Cassidy, prison mugshot.

a murderer and died a mysterious death in South America make him especially available for incorporation into the sanitized edutainment format that characterizes the WTP. Every summer a seasonal staff member takes on the role of Butch, circulating through the grounds to provide character interest. As we will see, Cassidy's presence in the Prison itself is important to the deeper ideological program.

The other figure who has come to occupy the status of icon at the Territorial Park is Martha Jane Canary, Calamity Jane. Like Cassidy, this colorful historical character holds a firm place in American popular consciousness. Media representations have depicted her as a spunky, rough-around-the-edges frontier woman who was up to the challenges that had to be faced at the raw edge of civilization, a predominantly

Figure 18. Calamity Jane, as portrayed by her great-great-grand-niece (WTP billboard).

masculine environment.[15] Unlike Butch Cassidy, Calamity Jane has no specific connection to the Wyoming Territorial Prison. Her historical relevance is regional. She has emerged, however, as an important figure at this site because her great-great-grand-niece lives in the community and has undertaken the professional portrayal of her famous ancestor. She is employed at the Park each summer to entertain visitors by riding her horse through the grounds, giving scheduled performances in which she sings western songs and tells jokes and stories, and demonstrating the use of the bullwhip (Calamity Jane had worked as a bullwhacker). She carries rifle and pistol, dresses in fringed buckskins, and sports a beaded vest that is the exact replica of one her ancestor wore. A running theme in these performances is Jane's love for Wild Bill Hickok.

If Butch Cassidy is the emblematic human guarantor of the historical significance of the Prison, Calamity Jane as portrayed by her direct descendant is the flesh-and-blood expression of historical continuity between today's West and the Old West that the WTP claims as its object. That this portrayal is very much in keeping with the popular image of Calamity Jane as a lively, picturesque embodiment of such frontier virtues as independence, competence, directness, and trueness of heart makes her one of the most appealing attractions at the Park. Visitor responses confirm her great popularity. It is not surprising, then, that she should have become an increasingly prominent figure in WTP promotions. She has taken on a role something like public emissary for the Park, greeting visiting celebrities, being in attendance at major events, and so on. Like Butch, she is the subject of one of the Park's billboard ads along I-80 (Figure 18).

Although they moved in entirely different spheres in their lifetimes, Butch and Calamity have come together at the Wyoming Territorial Park to form a complementary pair.[16] They both straddle the boundary between historical authentication and themed entertainment, thus mediating the basic institutional division. And of particular significance for the discussion to follow is the fact that their pairing is organized by gender. As we will see, binary divisions and a thematics of gender are important organizing principles in the material discourse of the Prison as a museum, which is to say, as an apparatus of vision and display.

The Display Ideologies

In his essay on "Panopticism," that inescapable master text of modern visuality, Michel Foucault invokes a distinction between Antiquity as a civilization of spectacle, with its public culture of temples, theaters, circuses, and imperial pomp, and a modern world characterized by a regime of social discipline dependent upon pervasive systems of surveillance (Foucault 1977 [1975]:216–17).[17] Prisons, asylums, schools, the modern army, the shop floor—such are the hallmark panoptic institutions of the modern age. The distinction is between social mechanisms that "render accessible to a multitude of men the inspection of a small number of objects," and those that "procure for a small number, or even for a single individual, the instantaneous view of a great multitude" (216).

Without in the least disputing the pervasiveness of disciplinary regimes and their relation to the social distribution of power, it has been my argument throughout this study that a body of western sites and texts enacts a visual mode in which spectatorship and surveillance are not so clearly separated. In fact, its definitive feature is precisely the play of uncertainty between these two visual mechanisms (cf. Crary 1990:17–19). The hidden, panoptic Gaze establishes its presence, only to disperse into multiple spectatorial looks. Or one such incarnate look becomes positioned to perform the office of surveillance in regard to other locations of looking. This visuality is characterized by its very instability. It is an eye always in the process of moving elsewhere, and its premier material embodiments are institutions of advanced consumer display— museums, theme parks, sites of historical reenactment, and the like.

A prison museum/theme park, then, seems about as perfect a laboratory as one could hope for to investigate the material expression of this visuality.[18] One of the circumstances that makes the WTP especially interesting for considering how material forms enact cultural discourses is the seemingly inverse relationship that exists between the boundary issues at work in prisons as penal institutions and those that inform historical display sites. The panoptic prison closes off public view from the outside, but internally it is premised on potentially ceaseless observation from a central point that is itself invisible. Commodified display sites, by contrast, would seem to be premised on the principle of making everything visible to outside inspection, with no surveillant gaze constraining the free play of spectatorship. We will see, however, that this apparent visual structure is in fact much more complex and ideologically murky. And one of the ways this becomes visible is precisely through the odd juxtapositions that result when a penal institution *becomes* a tourist site. This unusual circumstance constitutes a built-in reflexivity, a kind of doubling back on itself that makes such a place especially prone to certain ironies that are themselves a kind of self-analysis.[19]

One of my premises in reading this prison museum, hardly controversial in the context of cultural studies theory but for the most part invisible in the public discussion of institutions like the WTP, is that historic sites always encode through their imagery and scenarios a host of messages that pertain to the historical moment of their own production as displays. I do not mean here that attractions like the WTP purvey bad history because of an unfortunate inclination toward presentism in their interpretations and a lack of scholarly rigor, both remediable problems. This would be to suggest only that a more seriously educational, less touristic approach to the historical themes, not merely giving visitors "what they want," could make the site a fully legitimate and accurate representation of life in an earlier period. These are exactly the terms in which the WTP's relation to history has been addressed in the public controversies over the site and in the management deliberations of the WTP Corporation Board.[20]

Of course it is possible for such sites to convey more rather than less complexity in their interpretive programs and thereby ask more rather than less from their audiences. But my point here is that, no matter what level of historical expertise is brought to bear and no matter how richly the past is interpreted, such sites will also always "be about" the conditions of cultural production out of which they arise. The primary goal of my analytical reading, then, is not to "correct" the faulty history presented at the WTP, but to discover the subtle and complex ways in which this site stages the conditions of production in our own historical moment. Of central concern in this analysis, as in my discussions of the other western display environments, is how the physical features of the Prison and Park locate the visitor in certain ways—ways that will make some things visible and "of interest," others obscure, and still others so obvious as to be hardly worth comment. The ethnographic and analytical task is to step back a little and see how the site operates both as a thing to be looked at—a display object—and also as a discursive apparatus that *produces* certain ways of looking.

* * *

As I have said, what the WTP does most overtly and self-consciously to solve the dilemma of making a prison museum ideologically acceptable is to identify its dominant motif, not as the wild and woolly story of crime and punishment on the frontier, but as the progressive image of order and justice in an emerging and increasingly civilized society. This note was sounded very concisely and emphatically in an early promotional display at the Prison. I have already referred to the expensive "preview center" produced by the Wood Bay Company. This was removed once it became obvious that the optimistic projections for the WTP would not be realized in the near term. The center consisted of a large diorama of the Park in its fully developed form and, hanging above it, a pair of TV monitors, activated by push-button, that displayed the boosterish video "This Proud Land." The video consisted of birds-eye tracking shots of spectacular scenery, close-ups of Wyoming wildlife, and vignettes of costumed figures in historical settings, all against the background of ersatz western hoe-down music and rhymed voiceover commentary. The two monitors were set at an angle to each another so that simultaneous projection created a visually stimulating mirror-image effect. At one point in the voiceover the narrator identifies a binary symmetry that we might take as a thematic analogue to the visual pairing of the monitors:

We're proud that justice tamed the West—in this very place.
Proud that women too got justice—in this great state.
For here's where Butch and the gang came to the end of the line,
And women got to vote for the very first time.[21]

There in nutshell summary is one of the WTP's dominant messages, in both thematic and structural terms. As we will see, it is recapitulated in the physical program of the Prison itself. Butch Cassidy is front and center, though the requirements of the rhyme scheme seem to have overridden the basic fact that he and his gang did not actually "come to the end of the line" at this site. That detail aside, his incarceration serves as the symbolic marker of the imposition of the rule of law and a civilized system of justice.

The reference to justice for women invokes Wyoming's claim to being the first place to grant the full rights of citizenship to women—most notably, the right to vote. Wyoming, along with its self-identification as the "Cowboy State," has as an official designation the "Equality State." While all such promotional simplifications need to be qualified by attention to the fuller historical record, it is true that Wyoming did, during its campaign to enter the Union as the forty-fourth state, grant women the right to vote in general elections. And along with this came various attendant rights of citizenship that led to a series of "women's firsts" for Wyoming: first woman justice of the peace, first woman governor, first woman bailiff.

Bringing criminals to justice and taming the West, constructed as a thoroughly male enterprise, is balanced, then, by social justice for women. And the rhetoric of this second element emphasizes the active role women took in winning their own privileges. Thus men won the West from lawlessness and women won their rights in this newly tamed environment. The distillation of what we might call "display binaries" is, I believe, a common feature of sites such as the WTP. They constitute the minimal units of identity through which these institutionalized, commodified display environments present themselves to the public, serving as kernels for the "strong storylines" emphasized by Rouse Wyatt. And once in place they quickly become the critically inaccessible, invisible blueprints for interpretive and programming strategies. In the case of the WTP, the key display binary is strongly gendered. The coming of law and order is presented as a male transaction between evildoers and lawmen, a manly game of hunt, capture, and incarceration. Balancing this is the civil justice women achieved through their own agency and the force of their moral will. While the issue of women's rights has nothing directly to do with the Prison, its presence is justified structurally by the satisfying symmetry it provides when paired with the male theme of law and order.

There are two rather obvious redundancies at the Park that resonate with this basic symmetry. One of these is the binary pair I have already introduced—Butch and Calamity Jane. Although not an emblem of civil rights for women, Calamity Jane does represent the parity of women in traditionally male contexts. Her mastery of the horse, the gun, and the bullwhip are the markers of her equality. The implicit pairing of Butch and Calamity Jane, which has emerged "naturally" in the years after the Park opened, might be seen as a kind of "frontier fun" variation on

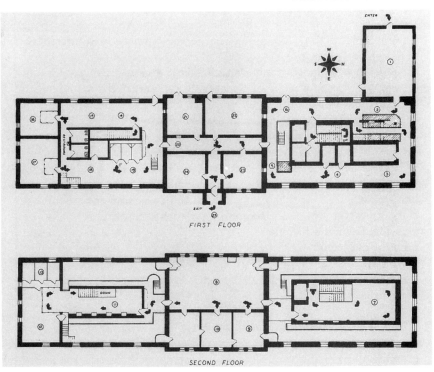

Figure 19. Floor plans, Wyoming Territorial Prison Museum brochure. Arrows indicate appropriate tourist pathway.

the somewhat more serious theme of male justice balanced by women's rights that was built into the Park's original program.

When I say "built into," I do not only mean this metaphorically. The physical arrangement of the museum galleries at the Prison offers a very tangible expression of the display binary I am proposing. While I will have much more to say about the physical characteristitcs of the gallery spaces and displays, it is worth noting here how the architectural symmetry of the prison building was put in service of the thematic and gender dichotomy. In overall morphology the Prison structure is divided internally into six main sections, roughly, the first and second levels in each of the three blocks of the building: the central gable-roofed element and the balancing north and south wings (Figure 19). The second floor galleries in the two symmetrical wings (nos. 7 and 11 on the plan) are unlike the rest of the rooms in that they are constructed as enclosed, "modern" museum spaces rather than as restored or recreated areas of the historical Prison. They are, then, foregrounded as thematic display "interludes" in one's tour of the historic artifact. And the themes they present are, precisely, law and order (north gallery) and women's rights in Wyoming (south gallery).

In the law and order gallery, balancing display cases are devoted to, on one side of the room, frontier crime and outlaws, and on the other, frontier lawmen. Two video kiosks, also located on opposite sides of the room, give push-button access to recorded "living history" addresses from, of course, Butch Cassidy,[22] the most famous inmate, and his counterpart, N. K. Boswell, a prominent local sheriff, first warden at the Prison and subsequently its lessee (see below). In the balancing gallery of the south wing most of the wall exhibits and text are devoted to the women's "firsts" of Wyoming. The presiding character here is Esther Hobart Morris, who has become the historical figure most associated with achievement of women's suffrage in the state. While we will have to revisit these balancing museum spaces to see how they function in the more complex developments of the Prison's display program, for now they can serve as a physical, artifactual confirmation of the core display binary that the WTP "begins with" in constructing its ideological program.

This structural starting point, however, is only the underlying armature for narrative elaboration. A binary pairing such as this one provides the easily consumable nut inside the artifactual shell, but it is not in itself sufficiently elaborated or dramatic to capture effectively the mass cultural imagination. It is not a "strong" storyline. Without a great deal of effort we can see how the Prison museum offers us just such a story, one that is never explicitly stated but rather expressed through the physical sequencing of galleries and displays. It turns out to be quite a familiar cultural narrative and one that is ironically appropriate in a number of ways.[23]

In my examination of vernacular display environments in the last chapter I paid considerable attention to how they offer themselves to be seen; or to put it another way, how they position us to see them. One useful question to ask about any display environment is how sternly draconian or liberally permissive it is in its management of visual positioning. The folk art displays allow relative freedom in this regard, though they do structure certain aspects of viewing through their "control" of viewing distance. The Territorial Prison museum, by contrast, is virtually inflexible in its control of the visitor's movement and visual positioning.[24] As indicated on the self-guided tour map, there is only one acceptable route to take. Barriers and signage are placed to enforce this pathway. This absolutely directional constraint serves to enforce the sequence of a defining narrative. The Prison is an artifact with one main ideological story to tell, though it is a rather subtle storyteller.

Our easiest access to this narrative is through a sequence of five moments of heightened display arranged along the path visitors are enjoined to follow. Together, they symbolically constitute a familiar story of moral progress, and this tale is reinforced by the physical contexts of their gallery locations. These five moments consist of video presentations by costumed "living history" characters. Monitors are mounted in video stations located at strategic points along the designated pathway, and the addresses are push-button activated.[25] Employing the living history convention of first-person interpretation, the video reenactors address the viewer directly as if she or he were a historical visitor to the prison (not an unheard-of activity in the nineteenth century). In their materialization at the touch of the viewer's finger perhaps we see the technologized analogue to both the touristic raising of Julius the Prison Ghost and the arrival of the tourist stage that Owen Wister observed suddenly activating the dormant scene at the Mammoth Hot Springs hotel. And this phenomenon of visual activation in general may be taken as the subtle acknowledgment that a hidden presence, an unseen viewer, is there watching, waiting to be conjured up as a spectacle.[26] But, prior to elaborating these arrangements in the visual apparatus of the Prison, I need to identify more clearly the narrative strand they enact.

The first of the video monitors is located at the end of the lower level gallery of the north wing (no. 4). What one sees in this section of the museum is a reconstruction of the three tiers of brick prison cells that would have been found in the earliest cellblock. One encounters at this video station a "typical prisoner"—a young man who, speaking with a vaguely southern drawl, addresses us through the bars of his cell. He rather pitifully laments his fate, referring to the hardships of prison life, including the risk of punishment for merely talking to us. In addition, though, he acknowledges some positive aspects of his incarceration and looks ahead longingly to freedom and return home.

After turning a corner of the gallery we ascend to the upper level of the north wing. I have already identified this area as the place where the male law and order theme is established through static displays and the videos of a representative outlaw and representative lawman. A conspiratorial Butch Cassidy, apparently just arriving for incarceration, gives some account of his career and his plans for future crimes. He concludes by inviting us to join him on a trip he has planned to South America. Across the room we meet N. K. Boswell, whom we see with pistol and rifle as he settles down beside a campfire, as if out on a manhunt. Thus it is presumably in his role as county sheriff, rather than as prison warden or lessee, that we encounter him. He concludes his address to us with a tongue-in-cheek warning that we had better stay within the law or risk becoming the object of his search.

After leaving the gallery occupied by Butch and "Bos," the next figure we encounter is May Preston Slosson. As we will see, this is an important point of transition in our progression through the galleries. Mrs. Slosson identifies herself as holder of a Cornell Ph.D., a former college professor, and currently the facilitator of polite and educated conversation in Laramie. She is also employed on Sundays as the prison chaplain, and that is how we see her here. Her direct address to the viewer is preceded and followed by her leading convicts in hymn singing. Mrs. Slosson's monitor, along with a wall text about her, is located in the upper level gallery of the Prison's central section (no. 8). Here the dining hall is recreated, with its tables set for a meal. Having served as a lecture hall and chapel, the room is also furnished with a pump organ. Along one side are several small rooms that had served as the guards' quarters (nos. 9 and 10). They are supplied with beds, dressers, and other residential paraphernalia. Upon leaving this area one enters the upper level southern gallery, which I have already identified as the location where the themes of women's rights and Wyoming firsts for women are presented.

One encounters the last of the character videos at the foot of the stairs descending to the first level of the south wing (no.14). Here we meet N. D. McDonald, warden of the prison from 1896 to 1900. He addresses us as if we were brick manufacturers come to the prison to contract for convict labor.[27] This provides him the opportunity to discuss the various production activities undertaken by prison authorities through the lessee system that prevailed in the period after Wyoming statehood. Although this section of the prison consists of another recreation of the cell block (in this case reflecting more advanced penal technology), the dominant display and textual theme is the history of prison industries. As our tour comes to an end and just before we depart the building through its main front entrance, we pass the last of the re-created display spaces, the warden's office (no. 24), with its elaborate vintage wallpaper, substantial bookshelves, and rolltop desk, hardly distinguishable from the many restored law or business offices one might see at Victorian era sites all around the country.

What I would propose here is that these video displays are not just a series of isolated encounters with representative living history figures. Taken together they constitute a coherent and familiar narrative progression. We proceed from an encounter with a generic prisoner paying his debt to society and lamenting his fate, to juxtaposed encounters with the most notorious convict/badman and the most illustrious warden/lawman to have been associated with Wyoming penitentiary, to the enlightened and maternal redeemer, who sympathizes with prisoners and, to quote her, "with the poor women who share their fate," and finally to the figure of primary authority, who reveals the prison to be a unit of production and even an entrepreneurial enterprise.

To view it more abstractly, we move from: (1) criminality, apprehension, and punishment, treated in terms of regret and repentance (the typical prisoner), or with the sly humor of mock complicity—all of this presented as male experience; to (2) the progressive voice of redemption, civic virtue and moral rectitude—presented as a female position that is piously maternal; to, finally (3) the theme of economic productivity, represented by the most senior and authoritative of male voices.

This narrative sequence is amplified by the physical appearance and demeanor of the historical characters and by the material attributes of the spaces they occupy. The "typical prisoner," the only generic figure, appears in the form of youthful manhood. Although incarcerated, he is depicted as rather pitiful and far from a hardened criminal. He is almost childishly nostalgic for his mother's peach cobbler. His video display is located in the section of the Prison that is most unequivocally about incarceration and penology, with reconstructed cells for visitors to enter and little in the way of wall text to distract from the motif of "life in prison."

Upstairs, Butch and Boswell are depicted as mature men. Their video presentations share a tone of clubbish good humor, presenting the underlying law and order theme as more game-like than grim. To some degree Butch's characterization is influenced by the film depiction, with its quality of good-natured nefariousness. This Butch is incorrigible but by no means sinister. Boswell is shown as obviously competent, self-assured, and wryly humorous. While one could easily over interpret these fleeting texts, I do not think it is too far-fetched to see in them a reflection of the conventional idea that in the manly world of the heroic frontier there was a rather fine line between law enforcement and outlawry.

May Preston Slosson is depicted as refined and matronly, and in her address she is preoccupied with the idea of moral reform. She is clearly the representative of righteous, if somewhat priggish, middle class morality. It is in her space that subtle references to the domestic sphere first come into play. Although an institutional mess hall, this gallery focuses on the idea of nurturance for both body and soul. I have already pointed out how the adjacent guards' rooms suggest private domestic space. As we will see, this motif of domesticity is an important piece of the larger apparatus. Slosson's appearance marks a point of transition into a sphere marked as feminine and reformist (the Wyoming women's gallery is the next we enter). The high moral tone introduced by the Slosson character contrasts with the rather devil-may-care feeling of the male space we have just left, but the disciplining of male mischieviousness, whether inside or outside the law, is consistent with the overall shape of the scenario and with our mass mediated expectations.

N. D. McDonald is shown as an older man, one concerned with serious matters of business. He is obviously a person of considerable standing in the community, and our view of the re-created warden's office underscores his importance. That he addresses the viewer as a labor contractor alludes to the fact that, especially during its time as a state penitentiary, the Prison was an entrepreneurial as well as a penal institution. It was operated on a lessee system in which private contractors bid for the job of running the facility based on an amount per inmate per day. The winning contractor would receive this much in public funds and then be responsible for hiring a warden, guards, and other personnel. He could pursue profit by employing the prisoners as free labor in suitable prison industries. All the proceeds from such work went to the lessee. During roughly a decade as a state pen the Prison housed at various times such enterprises as printing, tailoring, shoemaking, blacksmithing, tanning, horsehair braiding, furniture and cabinet making, and taxidermy (Banner Assoc. 1988: 12–14). Apparently the most successful of these undertakings was broom manufacturing, for which a separate facility was built at taxpayer expense.

Amplified through these visual and physical elements, the WTP uses a selection of local historical figures associated with the site to retell that master narrative of moral progress in which the naturally wayward male youth is redeemed through the ministrations of civilized womanhood, preparing him to claim his preordained place of authority in the settled world of middle class rectitude and economic success. Ironically enough, this now deeply ingrained narrative was becoming codified as part of the modern American cultural repertoire during the very period that the Prison was actually operating as a penal institution.

We have, in fact, already encountered a western text from this period that stages the same "mythological" scenario. The youthful Virginian is something of a rakehell, not above seducing a married woman and disturbing the peace of proper townsfolk. If not brought under corrective discipline, such juvenile cowboy wildness, though endearing, can lead into the paths of crime and eventually to a vigilante noose. Such, in fact, is the fate of the hero's best friend. Of course it is the love of a civilized woman that brings out the Virginian's better nature, confirming his moral superiority and preparing him to take up his rightful station. At the end of the novel we get a glimpse of him as a prosperous ranchman and perhaps even a budding entrepreneur.

What I have been suggesting here is that the WTP's core binary pairing of male law and justice with female civil rights and moral rectitude offers a satisfying balance in terms of modern, popular gender politics, but it is in itself dramatically pallid. This static dichotomy therefore takes on life and interest through narrative elaboration in the Prison museum's sequence of galleries and displays. There it links up neatly with a master narrative that draws on deep cultural expectations most visitors are sure to bring with them, if only subliminally—positive and progressive middle class notions about failure and recovery, about male success made possible through female redemption, about women as mediators of civilization and the motive force for imposing the rule of law upon an inherently lawless frontier. The indirect evocation of such received ideas, which are uniformly uplifting and optimistic, accomplishes important ideological work for the WTP.

For one thing, it goes a long way toward addressing the original dilemma of how to make a prison museum acceptably viewable. The WTP's keynote of apparent gender balance seems progressively up to date. But the very vehicle that conveys this message is itself an unreflexive, comfortably familiar, and politically regressive cultural narrative of male authority sustained by the nurturing influence of women. And there is perhaps an even more subtle ideological implication to the display elements I have been examining. That the narrative conveyed through the sequence of Prison galleries should culminate in the motif of entrepreneurial endeavor might be taken as an unplanned acknowledgment, a ghostly manifestation of the underlying institutional identity and motives of the Wyoming Territorial Park itself.[28] Born as a Chamber of Commerce project and promoted as a tool of economic development, the Park is managed primarily in terms of capitalist business practices. Close monitoring of balance sheets, economic forecasting, promotions and advertising strategies, revenue maximization and possibilities for entrepreneurial expansion are the central concerns of the WTPC Board and staff. Perhaps there is a homology to be discerned between, on the one hand, a late nineteenth-century penal institution that combined the public mandate to incarcerate and rehabilitate with the motives of private profit and, on the other, a late twentieth-century historic park that combines public education with the goal of local economic development. If so, there was an ironic justice to the fact that when the WTP was originally incorporated its officers were designated, not as president, vice president, secretary, and so on, but as Warden, Sheriff, Undersheriff, and Bailiff.

The Visual Apparatus

To this point my discussion of visual display elements at the Wyoming Territorial Park has dealt mainly with themes, narratives, imagery, and icons—what we might think of as the ideological *product* generated by the site's visual apparatus. In the larger context of this study, even more important is the "hardware" of that apparatus itself. While this can never be a pure distinction, devices and the results of their operation always implying one another, in the remainder of this chapter I will focus on the material components of the Park as a visuality machine. This will entail a consideration of such tangible and seemingly mundane things as the barriers and screens, railings and pathways, lighting and lines of sight, vantage points and "stages" for display. We may begin by entering the Prison building once more, now for a closer look at how it physically arranges visual experience. Unlike our previous tour of ideological elements, which required that we follow the prescribed line of march, here we may jump from one point in the artifact to another. Even so, however, there is a sequential logic to the optics of the museum that we should not overlook. So it is perhaps best to begin at the beginning.

One enters the Prison through what seems the back door, that is, the west extension that was the kitchen wing in the original structure (no.1). This space serves as foyer and introductory antechamber, and there is no attempt to make it appear part of the historic artifact, with the exception of the rather small metal doorway that opens into the north cellblock. This heavily reinforced door is the first explicit marker of incarceration, and next to it hangs the list of prison rules, enforced silence being the most striking. In passing through this doorway one crosses the boundary between present and past.

In the introductory space freestanding panel displays give a thumbnail account of the history of the building, from its early existence as a prison to its transformation into the main barn for the University of Wyoming's experimental stock farm, and finally to its rehabilitation as a state historic site. The seventy-five years of the building's middle incarnation are virtually ignored in the interpretive program, except in this introductory overview. Guided tours form up in this area before making their ceremonial entrance into the historical artifact itself.

Having done so, the visitor immediately comes upon a somewhat ambiguous exhibit (no. 2). Initially confusing, one soon realizes that what appears to be an area of broken walls and crumbling mortar is in fact a display intended to reveal the internal elements of the prison's cellblock construction: brickwork, heating and ventilation systems, surface treatments, hardware, and so on (Figure 20). The sub-floor layer is an excavation of the original structure, but everything above floor level had been removed to accommodate livestock. The three fragmented cells of the exhibit are reconstructions, but reconstructions in the form of conveniently accessible ruins through which one is meant to pass without hindrance.

Figure 20. Fragmented cells gallery.

Yet to call them ruins is not quite accurate, since there is no sign of the tarnish or patina one would expect in physical decay. The visible, above-floor elements are both fragmentary and pristine, giving them a disconcertingly equivocal quality. They seem on the one hand the result of the accidental ravages of time, but on the other the product of an intentional design, one that undertakes to peel back the layers of the building to offer a three-dimensional x-ray view. This intentionality is confirmed by the fact that, as the map for self-guided tours indicates, one is shunted through this display along a precisely linear track marked out by a barrier specialized to the function of museum spectatorship. Nearly invisible, waist-high, plexiglass walls topped with polished, brass-colored metal railings determine the tourist path, which cuts right through the middle of the cells' brick walls. The ragged bricks, rough plaster, and iron of the cell reconstructions contrast sharply with the linear precision of the highly polished tourist pathway.

Though bound by physical laws, our movement through this exhibit ignores the tangible, historical reality of prison walls, transporting us into the material fabric of the artifact. The brick and plaster seem to dissolve and open the building to absolute spectatorial visibility. The very walls that had served to thwart both physical motion and visual access, or at least to structure them within a strict carceral regime, are here themselves recreated as the object of looking within a system of commodified spectatorship. In this display the prison's historical functions of containing and rendering invisible to the outside are, in an almost complete inversion, made physically penetrable and open to view.

I would propose that, in terms of the visual vocabulary I have been invoking throughout, one's first encounter with the site's primary artifact takes the form of super-spectatorship. It is about as close as the spectatorial look can come in solid, three-dimensional space to actually inhabiting its object. Here the visitor briefly becomes like the ghost who moves through and is one with the very fabric of its haunted abode. The modern plexiglass wall and decorative railing maintain some distance between the physical position of the display and the location of the viewing eye, but still this exhibit seems like a kind of triumph of spectatorship. At the least it serves as a modest allusion to the fulfillment of the spectatorial fantasy in which spectator and spectacle become one. It is, in other words, a museumized, indoors realization of the greenhorn's desire to reach those ever-receding mountains.

As we will see, in following the designated track of the Prison tour one experiences an increasing distance between spectacle and spectator after leaving this opening exhibit. Rather than taking this sequential pathway again, however, it will be more instructive to leap to the museum space that reflects another extreme in the visual arrangements of this artifact. Though not exactly the opposite of the opening exhibit, it is its logical complement in terms of the visual discourse I have been exploring. Perhaps one indicator that this second space bears a distinctly contrastive relationship to the cell construction display is its location at the farthest possible remove from the latter. Such material relationships have, it has been my assumption throughout this study, symbolic and discursive significance beyond their instrumental functions.

The cell exhibit is at the north end of the lower level gallery in the Prison's north wing. Its contrastive counterpart is at the south end of the upper level gallery in the south wing. We have already seen that one finds in this area a celebration of the attainment of women's rights in frontier Wyoming. However, there is another element to this gallery that I have not yet mentioned. Over its thirty-year history the Wyoming pen housed a total of eleven women inmates. Several cells for women were located in this area of the prison, and they have been reconstructed. On the wall opposite the displays devoted to women's rights and Wyoming firsts for women one sees a large photo of Minnie Snyder, who served approximately four years of a six-year sentence for manslaughter (Figure 21). A text panel discusses the incarceration of women at this facility.

The display arrangement in this gallery is a further example of the

Figure 21. Minnie Snyder, female inmate.

WTP's devotion to balancing structures and binary pairings. It recapitu-
lates the morphology of the male law and order gallery at the other
end of the building, where Butch and Bos are counterposed. Here it is
Esther Hobart Morris facing off against Minnie. But there is an important further complication to this women's gallery, subtly hinted at in the
choice of Mrs. Snyder's photograph as the one to represent the women
inmates. In this image she appears hardly less domestically middle class
than the upstanding matron opposite her. In her high-collared, puff-
sleeved, perhaps satin dress, her bobbed hair and generally spruce demeanor, she seems anything but a hard case.[29] This area of the museum
downplays the theme of criminality in favor of a general air of public
civic virtue and private Victorian domesticity, all depicted as part of the
female sphere. And it is in the display at the far southern end of this

Figure 22. Women's section of the prison.

gallery (no. 12), diagonally opposite to the ground-floor exhibit of fragmented cells, that one finds the domestic note being struck most clearly. The physical arrangement of this area's display is of paramount importance to our understanding of the Prison as a visual apparatus.

We encounter at this point in our tour three surrounding walls of floor-to-ceiling museum glass windows set in substantial metal casings. What we see through them are areas identified as the prison infirmary, the sewing shop, the shoemaking bench, and the women's cells, one of the three furnished with toilet facilities and a bathtub. These elements are arrayed in a continuous space, no partitions separating them. The whole area is suffused warmly with strong exterior light coming through the tall southerly windows (Figure 22).

The overall impression conveyed in this display is of a rather pleasant nineteenth-century domestic interior where comfort, industry, and hygiene are the order of the day. The furniture of the infirmary is only minimally clinical: a large bedstead covered with a bright quilt, a wooden dentist chair easily mistaken for a parlor furnishing, a glass breakfront, bolts of cloth, some quaint treadle sewing machines, appropriately enough, "Domestic" brand. Such are the material accouterments of this display. It takes one a moment to register that the cloth on the sewing tables is the coarse, broad-striped fabric of prison uniforms. And although the cells along the east wall obviously bespeak incarceration, in the overall ensemble they stand in for the private chambers of a home. The small-scale prison industries of tailoring and shoemaking blend easily with the ideas of frontier self-sufficiency and domestic cottage industry. In short, the overall image here is of prison as home, and a rather cheery, well-ordered one to boot.

If we revisit for a moment the narrative program I have found to be operating in the restored Prison, the appearance of a display space with these attributes makes perfect sense. There is an absence in the narrative ideology that, left unsupplied, might be the occasion for mild discomfort—a sense that something is not quite right. To this point I have pointed out that the themes of both male redemption and civic justice are vested in maternal figures. For the complete fulfillment of the master narrative of male moral development there needs to be some acknowledgment of the monogamous, heterosexual bond at the heart of the bourgeois ethos. We have paternal and maternal elders represented, youthful manhood, and virile masculine maturity, the latter depicted in terms of the homosocial law-and-order game. The biological and social unit of reproduction, however, has been lacking. I would propose that the infirmary/workshop/women's cellblock is the material/visual expression of this previously missing component, one it would be hard to present more directly in the context of a penitentiary. That this element is withheld until this point, the "deepest" one gets into the Prison before reversing course and heading toward conclusion and departure, gives it special prominence as a kind of climax of the tour.

And perhaps, in light of such an interpretation, the use of Minnie Snyder as the representative female inmate takes on added import. That she is isolated by architectural elements in her own section of wallspace gives her a kind of prominence that is hard to explain in personal or historical terms. That she is a wife and "housekeeper" of rather genteel appearance, rather than a prostitute or product of the "criminal classes," makes her socially acceptable in the context of the symbolic scenario. And, most important, she is in the prime of life, and thus fit for procreative union. The logic of the display sequence at the museum dictates that we imagine her as the natural inhabitant of the quasi-domestic environment in the climactic exhibit area, where presumably she awaits the arrival of her formerly wayward but now redeemed and socially productive male counterpart. And remember that it is exactly from this point that the museum visitor descends to the galleries devoted to themes of commercial enterprise, middle class professionalism, and authoritative male seniority.

But coherent as this now completed cultural narrative seems, it does not tell the whole story of this complicated display environment. The viewing apparatus itself inhabits its own ideological domain, one that is even less accessible to casual awareness than the indirect, largely material expression of the male redemption scenario. To see how this apparatus is working at the climactic moment in the museum's physical program, we need to notice literally where we stand in relation to the display space.

In an arrangement unique to this spot (with one partial exception I will discuss below), we look down through the barrier of windows into the exhibit area, which sits roughly a half-floor below our viewing position. Our level is a continuation of the windowless, modern museum gallery of the women's rights area, and as such it is a space of dark walls and reduced, indirect lighting. In this respect our viewing location contrasts strongly with the well-lit domestic space we gaze into down below us.

It is obvious, perhaps, that the elements I am pointing out here are some of the familiar markers associated with covert surveillance. A downward view, if only at an elevation of a few feet, from a position that is visually obscured, if not absolutely invisible, into a space that is open and fully lit from outside so that all can be clearly seen—such is the panoptic recipe for disciplinary surveillance (Foucault 1977 [1975]:200), if in a somewhat watered down or deflected form. While we are of course still spectators looking at a museum display, we are positioned to participate in a kind of symbolic or fictive surveillance as well. And it is at this point that we are physically farthest removed from the objects of our looking, which is in fact something like a reversal of the situation in the initial cell display. In gestures such as these the museum apparatus comes closest to enacting the sort of visual instabilities I have been identifying throughout this study with a distinct visual discourse. In particular, this apparatus seems especially engineered to reenact the indeterminate fluctuation between spectatorial looking and surveillant gaze, these visual positions overlapping and changing places in a variety of ways. With these two complementary exhibits as limiting cases, the spectatorial plenum of the burst open cells and the fictive staging of covert surveillance in the women's gallery, the visual apparatus of the Prison museum engages in a play of variations, shuffling and reshuffling the discursive deck. I will conclude this discussion by considering some of these various stagings, which carry outside the walls of the Prison itself to the landscape of the Park in general.

*   *   *

If we backtrack to the point where one emerges from the exhibit of cell construction, we find the surface of the artifact being "smoothed out" into its fully restored form. On turning the corner into the eastern aisle of the first cellblock, one sees a complete reconstruction of the facade of the three tiers of cells (nos. 3 and 4). Here the goal is to present the interior surface of the prison as it would have appeared during use. Most of this facade is merely a veneer. However, at ground level two cells have be completely recreated. Visitors may enter them and pull the iron doors closed to get a feel for the space of incarceration. The aisle running around the circumference of the centrally located tiers of cells is open all the way to the roof. In this section of the museum the tour theme is penology. Guides emphasize the smallness of the cells, their coldness in winter, and the cramped conditions during prison overcrowding. Here, too, is where one hears about attempted escapes and other interesting anecdotes (e.g., the commentary on Julius Greenwald).

Obviously, here we are positioned a step farther away from the material artifact than in the cell construction exhibit. However, it is the location where we come closest to the experience of being incarcerated. This is so not only because one may briefly occupy a cell or because the guide provides information to help us imagine the experience. Even more important for my purposes is the fact that this is the space that comes closest to reenacting carceral surveillance.

The Wyoming Territorial Prison, with its rectilinear, longitudinal plan and centralization of cell spaces, was far from being a perfect panoptic device. However, a principle of centralized surveillance was at work in its design. The upper level of the building's central section (mess hall and guards' quarters, nos. 8–10) included barred cages projecting from each of its corners out over the four main cell bays (Figure 23). From this safe and elevated, if not invisible, vantage, guards could monitor prisoner activity. Here, then, is the other place where a surveillant view from above is possible, and in this case it mimics the historical dynamics of visual observation in the actual prison. As a visitor moving on the lower level, one may become the object of someone else's looking, thereby experiencing the slight *frisson* of being under surveillance and in a subordinate position, even if this visual exchange is only being enacted fictively. And, of course, when one gets upstairs, the superior position will be available for one's own occupation. It is precisely this possibility of moving from one marked position to another in the play of visuality that makes this site such a useful moment in the discourse of looking West. One could say that the Prison museum is an apparatus devoted expressly to moving sets of eyes through the variations of visual positioning that characterize advanced consumer visuality.

One further complication to the optical arrangement of this gallery

Figure 23. Cell bay with suspended guard cage.

needs some comment. As we have already seen in the cases of Julius Greenwald, Butch Cassidy, and Minnie Snyder, blow-ups of prisoner mug shots, along with identifying text, are dispersed around the walls of the museum. In this first cell bay gallery a series of these imposing images hangs in the wall spaces between the exterior windows. These photos, taken as part of the entry processing of the prisoners, were of course themselves tools of surveillance, providing a permanent, accurate record of a prisoner's appearance that could be used for purposes of future investigation and identification. When these images, with their disconcertingly direct stares, are dramatically enlarged and hung well above visitor eye level, an interesting reversal of polarity occurs. They come to seem like the imposing and slightly disturbing watchers, and we the watched, as we move along the aisles and into the cells that they once inhabited. The ghostly appearance of Julius Greenwald strikes one as merely the logical extension of the collective gaze of these menacing gray images.

The cell bay gallery is, then, the clearest expression of discomfiture induced by the operations of the Prison as a visual device. The effect is not full blown anxiety of course, which would be out of keeping with the general lightness to which the whole site is attuned.[30] But it is perhaps a small relief to leave this section and go upstairs into a space where one's "normal" touristic identity is reinforced rather than destabilized. All the markers of "museum" are in place in the second level northern gallery: modern color scheme (dark greens and reds) and materials (the brass railings reappear), subdued lighting with spot illumination of displays, distinct exhibitry in cases and under glass, and so on. We find here a respite from direct involvement with the historical artifact itself.

When we pass back into the Prison restoration, by way of a more or less instrumental transition zone that serves as a kind of historical airlock, it is to find ourselves in May Preston Slosson's domain, the second floor of the middle section of the prison. As I have already suggested, we find here a mixing of institutional (but progressive) and domestic references. The dining hall/lecture room is the location where sustenance, physical and spiritual, is obtained, though collectively rather than privately. The guard rooms are like private domestic chambers, but the cages for institutional surveillance project from them.

Consistent with such mixing of thematic elements, this space mixes degrees of spectatorial distance. One may walk into the guards' rooms and even stand in the barred observation cages, but most of the dining hall is off limits. The standard museum device of the rope barrier denies access. This implies a spectatorial distance somewhere between the actual penetration of the artifact (or free entry to its restored spaces) and the hermetic barrier of plexiglass windows, which only allow framed and constricted visual access.

I have mentioned in passing that this area of the Prison restoration constitutes a kind of turning point in the overall museum program. I can now be more explicit about how this is so. Thematically, there is a general movement from incarceration, elaborated in terms of youthful but not vicious male criminality, toward recuperation in the domestic sphere. The socially upstanding matron who has gained a degree of authority in the public sphere is the mediating figure in this process. All of these elements are alluded to in this section of the Prison. It thus sets the stage for the narrative climax: establishment of the private, middle class domestic order that allows for a positive dénouement of entrepreneurial management and implied prosperity.

Parallel to these thematic elements, in its physical and visual arrangements the dining hall gallery points toward increasing distance and separation between spectator and display. Its rope barrier is the antecedent to the full glass walls, which appear for the first time in the infirmary display and recur at several places in the remaining galleries on the lower level (prison laundry, communal washroom, warden's office). And, as with its thematic mediation between male incarceration and female domesticity, the second floor central section constitutes the point of transition between carceral surveillance and the application of an at least quasi-surveillant gaze to the domestic sphere. The eye of the visitor is, of course, the medium through which this shift of attention occurs. As it moves from the position of prison guard overlooking a cellblock to that of "hidden" tourist (peeping tom? private detective? generalized Gaze?) looking down into a well ordered, home-like interior, the Prison museum as visual apparatus produces the most powerful of its ideological effects.

At one point in his discussion of panopticism, Foucault proposes that there should be an investigation of how discipline, in his special sense of that term, operates in the "intra-familial" setting (1977 [1975]:215–16). It is my contention here that Wyoming's restored territorial penitentiary makes the link, however coded and symbolic, between the paradigm of disciplinary practice, carceral surveillance, and the disciplinary ordering of the bourgeois domestic sphere. And touristic spectatorship is the material vehicle through which the museum's visual apparatus accomplishes this effect.

It will be patently obvious by now, I hope, that beneath a thin surface of apparent gender balance the Prison museum is rather single-mindedly devoted to a well-worn masculinist ideology. It is the drama of uncivilized male waywardness, redemption through a maternal principle devoted to civic virtue, attainment of social maturity in the domestic sphere, and achievement of full authority and material success. We might compare this familiar and reassuring cultural narrative of male dominance with some of the elements of the Fort Laramie living history exercise. You will recall that there, too, the interplay of spectatorship and surveillance coalesces around the issue of male authority, although in that case the markers of both gender and race came into play. Also, I argued that a central scenario which first invokes but then overcomes a threat to the stability of Anglo male identity did not entirely resolve the destabilizing effects of the play of visual positioning. In that regard, the Fort Laramie exercise echoes Wister's creation of a quintessential western male hero who, though seemingly a paragon of self-possession and stabilized identity, is constantly being disrupted through the operation of a modern discourse of mobile, unfixed visuality.

As another moment in the accumulated text of the modern West, the Territorial Prison undertakes to impose the strictest control over the construction of a stable and dominant male identity. In this case the greatest potential threat to that stability, the possible point of disruption in the comfortable narrative of male redemption, is precisely the early attainment of women's rights in Wyoming.[31] By deploying this regional historical motif as one pole in its original binary pairing, thereby expressing gender balance, and then fitting it into the elaborating narrative of male moral progress and dominance, the WTP has introduced a potentially pesky fly to its ideological ointment. It is quite understandable, then, that a symbolic enactment of domestic surveillance should occur at just the point where this possibly destabilizing motif is presented. One could say that the notion of female empowerment in the public sphere is immediately disciplined and symbolically brought under control by the surveillant, implicitly male gaze directed down upon the domestic space, as if that very gaze decreed its orderliness, stability, and productivity. In this way the visual apparatus of the Prison disciplines and incarcerates a potentially disruptive ideological alternative.

Coda: A Discourse of Fences

In concluding my discussion of this site I feel obliged to say I am aware some strands of my argument might seem contradictory. On the one hand I have proposed that the Prison enacts the ceaseless movement of optical positioning, spectatorship and surveillance combining and changing places in a play of visuality. And this, I have been claiming, is the distinctive feature of the modern visual discourse at work in all the texts and sites I am examining. At the same time, I have claimed that the Prison uses a coherent sequence of visual arrangements to produce a particular and rigorously enforced ideological narrative in service of a very familiar (and regressive) cultural protocol.

Contradictory though this may be, I believe such paradoxes, unresolvable in linear terms, are endemic to our cultural moment. In considering them we need to accept the principle that the analysis of discourses frequently requires us to hold in abeyance our interpretive understanding at one level in order to recognize how the discourse operates at another, and also to accept that these two (or multiple) operations might be quite disparate, even contradictory. It is my contention, then, that the Prison museum both enacts the general play of modern visuality and simultaneously uses specific arrangements of display, spectatorship, and surveillance, the elements of this visuality, to construct particular ideological packages.

Late capitalist visual apparatuses such as the Territorial Prison Museum are quite capable of enacting diverse procedures at varying levels of abstraction. At this site a rather explicit display binary, coded in terms of supposed gender balance, coexists with an implicit narrative sequence constructed out of the display elements of the galleries as one moves "appropriately" through the museum. This story told through visual and material means installs in the Prison a comfortable narrative closure, replaying an all too familiar bourgeois ideology of gender hierarchy. And both of these ideological components exist in suspension with that more abstract play of visual positioning that has been my abiding theme in this study. In moving through the Prison, the visitor at one moment almost merges with the display artifact, at another becomes the fictive (i.e., spectacle-like) object of disciplinary surveillance, and at yet others is allowed the privilege of occupying the location of the controlling, authoritative Gaze.

It is precisely the point that under late capitalist, advanced consumer conditions no one of these "sub-systems" of the general apparatus simply overrides the others. All are simultaneously in force and in play with one another. One of the reasons for thinking in terms of discourse/practice at all is that it allows for, indeed requires the application of a "split (or multiple) lens" in order to get some analytical purchase on the remarkable discursive complexity of such sites as the Wyoming Territorial Park.

The last complication I want to offer on our excursion to this display environment is to register a kind of correspondence that exists between the interior apparatus of the Prison museum and some exterior elements of the Park in general. I have paid a great deal of attention to walls, barriers, and various lines of demarcation inside the historical artifact, these being important components of the visual mechanism. A brief reading of the Park's exterior fences allows me both to extend my examination of material features as vehicles of discourse and to come full circle in a final consideration of the institutional location of the Wyoming Territorial Park.

In Figure 24, a view looking north toward the Prison from just outside the Park grounds, one can see three kinds of fences or barriers: the gray utility fence in the foreground, marking the front edge of the Park; the white picket fences in the middle distance, which define particular

Figure 24. Fence types at the Territorial Park.

spaces such as the playground and the yard around the warden's house on the right; and, in the background, the stockade enclosing the prison yard. The first two fence types have in common the property of allowing visual access, in contrast to the solid, towering wall around the prison. However, more important for this discussion is the link between the stockade and the picket fences, namely, that both are reconstructions of supposedly historical fencing and so are meant to be viewed as elements of the Park spectacle. The utilitarian gray fence is merely a barrier and not part of the display. We are not supposed to "see" it in the same sense that we view the others.

Also, the two historic fence reconstructions, the stockade and the picket fences, constitute a binary set homologous with other features we have observed. The stockade wall is of course the stark emblem, the outward face of incarceration, as physically expressed in the opacity of its raw, unadorned planks and in the massive timber supports, not to mention the surveillant guard boxes, analogues to the observation cages inside the building. By contrast, the white pickets are of course a familiar icon of Victorian domesticity and social orderliness. What we have in this pair of material features, then, is a shorthand recapitulation of the interplay between penal and domestic settings that we encountered inside the museum.

There is also a fourth type of fencing relevant to this discussion. It is intriguing as a material form and as an ideological marker, in that it seems to be a hybrid of all the other three types. In materials, general appearance, and refusal of visual access it echoes the prison stockade. However, in scale it seems closer to the picket fences, a connection supported by the fact that in both these fence types the posts are capped with similar globe finials (Figure 25). In fact, the fourth type is hardly distinguishable from common forms of residential privacy fencing. And as it turns out, this barrier encloses a number of modular housing units. What this fence type has in common with the gray utility fences is its practical function. It too is not part of the historical display. Rather, it is the "modern" fence that encloses, prevents tourist access to, and visually screens the primary backstage zone at the Park—the compound containing storage facilities and the administrative offices, which are housed in those modular units.

Even in so trivial an artifact as this screening barrier one may see a material embodiment of the WTP's mixed, complex identity. Management of such display sites is very much a matter of manipulating visibility and invisibility. The most important thing to keep hidden is the actual mechanism of site production, that is, the location and workings of management operations themselves. Therefore the pedestrian office units are clustered behind an opaque privacy screen. However, this screen itself cannot be too jarringly out of keeping with the surrounding historical spectacle, hence the vaguely domestic quality and the formal echo of both the picket fences and the prison stockade.

It is from behind this blind, which appropriately enough seems assembled out of allusions to the Park's main display elements, that the real work of surveillance is carried on. The ceaseless monitoring of visitor numbers, the flow of "financials" registering every aspect of Park commerce, the conduct of audience surveys—such are the instruments of advanced consumer disciplinary surveillance that institutions such as the WTP depend on. While the Park needs to be "seen"—from the adjacent Interstate, through its advertising promotions, in the local endorsement of tax support and donor contributions—it must also stay ideologically hidden in ways that have less to do with local management decisions and practices than with the much larger system of our advanced consumer culture.

It is the central scandal of historical tourist sites such as the WTP—something to be screened out as much as possible, even from the site's own operators—that under the conditions of advanced capitalism our relation to history is inseparable from our fully commodified social re-

Figure 25. "Historical" picket fence and modern privacy screen.

lations in the present. The ongoing struggle between the ideologies of historic authenticity and commercial development, central to public debates about this site, actually contributes to the process of screening from view, or perhaps better, of deflecting our gaze, from the actual conditions of the production and consumption of our own history. As long as we can argue over whether "authentic" history or commercial development should be the controlling principle at sites such as this, we will fail to notice that in an advanced consumer order both principles are subordinate to a generalized commodification of visual experience. The anomaly of the hybrid fence around the administration structures at the WTP, part allusion to the "real" historical reconstructions, part utility barrier, and perhaps even part residential privacy screen, could be read as a small, unintended acknowledgment that the zone it encircles is an ideologically "dangerous" space where the real game, the play of advanced consumer visuality, is most actively underway.

Chapter Seven
Monumental Optics
The Visual Management of Devils Tower

Those who have seen Stephen Spielberg's 1977 film *Close Encounters of the Third Kind* may recall that its plot turns on the idea that a number of seemingly ordinary citizens have been mysteriously implanted with visions of the remarkable landscape feature known as Devils Tower (Figure 26). Standing on the northwest edge of the Black Hills, this massive rock formation, pleated with immense vertical columns of granite, rises abruptly some 1,200 feet above the floor of the Belle Fourche River valley in northeastern Wyoming. The film's hero abandons job and family to respond to an inner compulsion that draws him toward the Tower, where, as it turns out, the first official contact with alien beings is to take place.

For my purposes here there are two moments in *Close Encounters* with particular significance. Although we see numerous replicas, images, and television views of Devils Tower, it is only near the end of the film that the characters actually experience this landmark directly. The hero and his companion, having made their way to Wyoming, drive their car up to a barbed-wire roadblock. For a moment we see them through the windshield gaping open-mouthed at something above and behind the camera position.[1] They leap from the car and scramble up a dirt embankment to another wire barrier. As they do so, the camera ascends vertically to reveal in the middle distance the uncanny monolith of the Tower. The effect of the camera movement is to give the impression that this immense object is emerging from the ground right before our eyes. That this is a major moment of revelation, a kind of monumental, ceremonial unveiling, is underscored by the soundtrack, which crescendos to symphonic climax as the Tower comes fully into view.

We have encountered several examples of a motif that epitomizes advanced consumer visual experience, namely, an act of looking that seems to create the very spectacle toward which it is directed. At this moment in the film the cinematic apparatus is deployed to construct the Tower as an artifact that materializes out of the desiring gaze itself.[2] But there is also another association we might attach to this scene. Most likely unintentionally, the cinematically produced impression that the Tower suddenly rises up from the ground echoes a number of traditional Native American narratives from several Plains tribes. These accounts report just such an emergence, explained as resulting from supernatural agency.

The other moment I want to call attention to also comes near the conclusion of the film. The hero has, against the best efforts of the authorities, managed to scramble over the rockfall at the base of the Tower to discover a scientific and military installation set up to receive the alien visitors. The climax comes with the arrival of the techno-sublime mother ship, which hovers silently over and dwarfs the Tower. But prior to that stunning arrival, an advance guard of scout ships descends, presumably to survey the site. They first become visible as distant moving lights in the night sky. For the briefest moment seven of these lights come together above the Tower and organize themselves into a formation identical to the constellation Ursa Major, the Great Bear, more commonly known as the Big Dipper.

If the visual trick of the vertical emergence of the Tower is an inadvertent echo of Plains Indian associations, this brief celestial tableau is perhaps the filmmaker's actual acknowledgment, however indirect and obscure, of Native traditions. In *The Way to Rainy Mountain*, N. Scott Momaday recounts a tale explaining the appearance of *Tsoa ai*, "Tree Rock," as the formation is known to Kiowa tradition. The brother of seven sisters is mysteriously transformed into a bear. He pursues his siblings, who seek refuge on top of a large tree stump. The tree rises miraculously, lifting the seven sisters all the way to the sky, where they become the stars of the Big Dipper. The immense stump is scored by the clawing of the bear, giving Tree Rock its distinctive appearance (recounted in Gunderson 1988:32–35). Other Plains tribes (Arapaho, Cheyenne, Lakota) have traditional narratives with similar core elements, though of course with many variations and degrees of elaboration (e.g., Pleiades instead of Ursa Major, rising rock rather than tree stump, chthonic bear rather than transformed sibling, etc.). In the historical period, the most common Plains Indian name for the formation has been "Bear Lodge," a designation that appears on early maps made by Euro-Americans.

I dwell on these scenes from Spielberg's immensely popular film because they lend themselves to a parabolic reading. They may be understood, I think, as small gaps where postcolonial relations peek through, gaps I will attempt to widen in what follows. Those decidedly marginal moments in the film where an alternative narrative presence might be

Figure 26. Devils Tower/Bear Lodge.

dimly perceived mark Devils Tower, however evanescently, as a site of cultural contestation. We might take them as examples of those "moments of truth" where a text glancingly acknowledges its own instability. A dominant message of the film is that "we" need not fear the power of mysterious alien forces (with racial difference encoded in the classic mass cultural trope of beings from another world) because they will turn out to be benign and even luminously godlike. The barely visible and perhaps even accidental traces of an actual Native American narrative presence at this site introduce a potential disruption, if only because the small incursion of a "real world" cultural element implies the existence of something outside the film's symbolic space. Read for those moments where its gears slip slightly, the film points us toward Devils Tower/Bear Lodge as a place of postcolonial encounter.[3] And in many respects this encounter is staged in visual terms.

By taking this display site as our last (save for one brief addendum) critical landing pad, examining both historical and very recent developments there, we can gain some understanding of how several vectors of power converge on this unusual feature of high plains geomorphology. In particular, I am interested in how the Tower has been constructed as an element of landscape through its various narrative incarnations and through the larger management of narrative resources. A great many stories come together to "produce" Devils Tower, not all of them mutually compatible or equally emphasized in the dominant construction of this site. Many of them are about acts of seeing, and by attending to the "narratives of looking" that swirl around the Tower like its turbulent winds, we can gain some purchase on the issues of access and ownership, which is to say issues of power, in a postcolonial context.

It has not gone unremarked that the modern Euro-American colonial project as a whole is deeply invested in the fundamental rearrangement of visual regimes that occurred over the course of the nineteenth century. Timothy Mitchell (1988), for example, has demonstrated how the colonization of Egypt depended on the visual reordering of the colonial object, both conceptually and materially, so that it conformed to European conventions of "coherent" commodity display. Early colonialism had as one of its main conditions of possibility an ideological way of seeing perhaps best exemplified by the grand nineteenth-century international exhibitions, beginning with London's Crystal Palace (1851), and by other cultural/commercial institutions (e.g., department stores, museums, theaters, zoos) devoted to a distanced mode of seeing in which the whole world takes on the quality of representative display. To colonize was to occupy a position from which the colonial object could be seen coherently as an artifact available for appropriation.

To anticipate my argument, I believe the current conflict over Bear Lodge/Devils Tower needs to be placed in the context of this colonial (and postcolonial) visuality, which is intimately bound up with the discourse of looking West. Historically, the Native American claim on this site, as symbolized by its narrative traditions, has largely been contained through the simple and familiar colonial mechanisms of selective deafness and trivialization. In recent years Indian voices have become more insistent in their call for some form of reappropriation. As a result, new forms of containment have come into play.

I will take as a premise that whoever establishes and controls the definitive view, literal and metaphorical, of a site occupies thereby a position of cultural ownership. Boime's magisterial gaze (see Chapter 4) is one version of this principle, expressed through a set of general pictorial conventions. In the concrete practices of actual sites access to the controlling vantage point is bound to be strictly policed, though under postcolonial conditions this policing is less likely to take the heavy-handed form of coercive suppression than it is to rely on subtle incorporation through the liberal discourse of inclusiveness and balance. Although in recent years subaltern voices have reached the threshold of audibility at

Devils Tower, we can see them undergoing this process of incorporation. And it is on the ground of narratives of seeing that these postcolonial cultural politics have been played out.

*   *   *

First, a few general words about this site and its history. Devils Tower is a National Monument; in fact, it was the first place so designated, approved by the presidential decree of Theodore Roosevelt in 1906 under the terms of the Federal Antiquities Act passed in June of that year. That act provides for the preservation of "historic landmarks, historic and prehistoric structures, and other objects of historic or scientific interest that are situated upon the lands owned or controlled by the Government of the United States." Important for my purposes here is the proviso that the President "may reserve as part thereof parcels of land, the limits of which in all cases shall be confined to the *smallest area* compatible with the proper care and management of the objects to be protected" (emphasis added).

As early as 1892 local and state efforts were underway to keep Devils Tower and the surrounding landscape out of private hands. An area of more than sixty square miles was placed under the category of forest reserve by the General Land Office. At about the same time Wyoming political leaders proposed the formation of a Devils Tower National Park, encompassing somewhat more than eighteen square miles. Both arrangements included the Tower and a group of related but less spectacular geological formations of the same type, the so-called Little Missouri Buttes. The National Monument established in 1906 encompasses less than two square miles of territory, just enough to include the Tower and an infrastructure for maintenance and access. Under National Monument designation, Devils Tower is managed by the National Park Service (Mattison 1973 passim).

What we see in this history is a kind of narrative act being played out both on the ground itself and at the level of a national discourse of preservation. National Monument designation is the primal act of framing (MacCannell 1989 [1976]:44–45), making the Tower an object for certain kinds of narrative and for certain kinds of seeing. Put simply, it established the Tower as an object for spectatorship, organizing it as a tightly framed and, metaphorically speaking, elevated artifact to be viewed from close proximity, but with a kind of detachment. Consistent with this, the larger geological feature of which the Tower is a part is excluded from the site. The Little Missouri Buttes are just as significant geologically, but they do not share the Tower's visual drama, its coherent "viewability," the real reason for its preservation. The positioning of

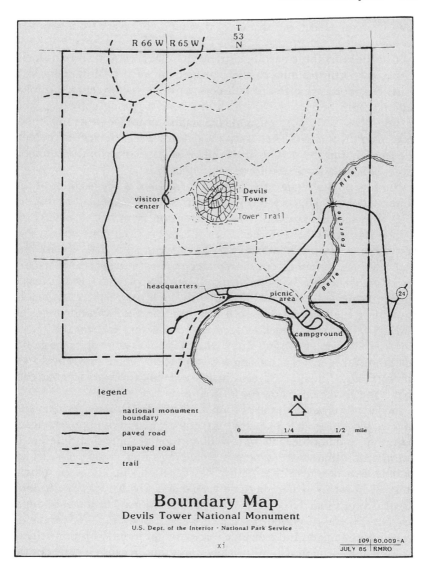

Figure 27. National Park Service site map of Devils Tower National Monument.

the visitor center and the system of roadways and hiking trails construct the Tower as a series of imposing circumference views and surprising revelations, all focused tightly on the isolated artifact (Figure 27). One might well read the unveiling scene in *Close Encounters* as a kind of paradigm text for this mode of viewing, awestruck wonder at the revelation of an uncanny object, but the act of viewing taking place from behind a barrier.

Over the years three narrative strands have been woven around Devils Tower, each contributing to the management of this Monument as a visual commodity. Expressed indirectly through visitor center exhibits, National Park Service (NPS) brochures, tourist iconography (e.g., sets of slides, postcards, posters), and NPS staff interpretive programs, these three narratives might be characterized as the *story of formation,* the *story of emergence,* and the *story of ascent.* All three participate in the common project of "stabilizing" the Tower ideologically.

The first of these tales, the story of formation, is the account of the Tower's geological history. It consists of three basic scenes—the episodes of 1) slow sedimentation; 2) violent intrusion from below; and 3) extended revelation through the forces of erosion. Over eons ancient seas laid down strata of sedimentary rock. Between sixty and seventy million years ago violent igneous forces deep beneath the earth's surface— forces associated in the popular mind, however playfully, with infernal agency[4] —pushed their way up nearly through the earth's crust before expending their energy. They left their trace in the form of congealed and striated fingers of rock wedged into cracks formed near the earth's surface by the violent assault from below. The final act involves the gentle but powerful agencies of moving wind and water, which slowly peel away the surface sedimentary layers, finally revealing the hard igneous core that is the Tower as we now see it (Robinson: n.d.).

I mean to suggest with this account of Devils Tower geology, of course, that we have here an explanatory mythology, a kind of popular science narrative, and another tale of unveiling, though somewhat different in construction than that moment in Spielberg's film. In any case, its import is as a narrative that naturalizes spectatorship. It is the official story of how this artifact became visible and why it looks like it does. Devils Tower's visual drama, framed by the National Monument boundary lines, is the displayed residue of an agonistic drama of formation in which endogenic and exogenic forces fought it out. This pop-science narrative of formation is historically important because it provides the basic alibi for federal preservation.

The second narrative formally endorsed and presented at the site has its source in the Native American cultures of the northern plains. Far from allowing it access as a fully alternative voice, however, the interpretive management of this narrative is a textbook example of the trivialization indigenous cultures are so often subjected to under colonial conditions. Relegated to the categories of the quaint, the picturesque, and the historically remote, these elements are safely cached as residual. More than twenty tribal groups have had some historical association with the Bear Lodge (Hanson and Chirinos 1991), and a number of origin myths have been recorded. One of them, a Cheyenne tale, has taken on something like official status, largely through its prominent display at the visitor center and its representation in postcard and poster form. This one tale, or more accurately its reduction to a postcard image, has come to stand for an immensely complex and long-standing history of American Indian involvement, materially and ideologically, with Bear Lodge and the surrounding region. This is perhaps an even more radical truncation than the geological one accomplished by the narrow designation of the site boundaries.

In cursory outline the Cheyenne story is about seven brothers. The wife of the eldest is abducted by a giant bear, a holy being. The youngest brother, who possesses powerful medicine and who has certain traits that perhaps associate him with the Cheyenne culture hero Sweet Medicine, uses supernatural means to recover the stolen woman. She and all the brothers flee the pursuing bear. To rescue his relatives the hero sings a song four times, causing the small rock he always carries with him to grow into the huge stone edifice of the Bear Lodge. The chthonic bear leaps higher and higher, leaving his claw marks on the rock walls. On his fourth try the hero kills the bear with the last of four arrows the brothers have made. He whistles for four eagles, each of which carries two of the humans safely to the ground. The coda to the story is that the brothers kill all the other bears in the area except two. These are warned to leave the people alone, and as emblem of their mastery, the humans cut off the bears' long ears and tails, giving them the appearance we recognize today (Gunderson 1988:45–49).

Needless to say, this narrative is much more than a mere explanation of the rock's appearance. While I will not presume to offer a cultural interpretation, some of the story's complex symbolic resonance may be intuited if we know even a little bit about Cheyenne cosmology. For example, the traditional Cheyenne world is ordered in four layers. The bottommost of these is "Deep Earth," which extends downward from the point where the roots of growing things end. It is associated with burrowing and digging animals, including the bear (the hero of the story rescues his brother's wife by transforming into a gopher and burrowing into the great bear's underground lair). This realm is also associated with the female principle, balancing the maleness of the topmost layer, the "Blue Sky Space." Deserts, cliffs, rock faces, and waste places in general are perceived in this worldview as projections of Deep Earth into the layer of the world inhabited by humans, the layer of living and growing things (Surface Dome). The Bear Lodge formation is perhaps especially loaded with significance because it not only connects Deep Earth with the human sphere, but extends through the latter into the next higher

Figure 28. Postcard representation of the Cheyenne Bear Lodge legend.

zone of the Cheyenne cosmos, the Nearer Sky Space, which is the domain of clouds, birds, and high places (Moore 1974:142–86).

Even this cursory account of a few elements of the traditional Cheyenne worldview suggests some of the symbolic richness of the Bear Lodge story. However, this narrative is positioned in the official discourse of Devils Tower as a kind of picturesque counterpart or quaint alternative to the scientific tale of origins. In fact, the "official" image of the giant bear clawing at the Tower[5] is included as one slide in a packaged set otherwise made up of cross-section representations of the stages of the Tower's geological formation. Positioned thus, which is to say trivialized virtually to the status of a cartoon, the Cheyenne tale, made emblematic of all Native American presence, becomes another easily consumable story about the Tower's appearance, both in the sense of its first emergence and in the sense of how it looks to us today. The iconography of the definitive poster identifies and freezes the moment of the bear's clawing as the climax of the tale (Figure 28). Of paramount importance in this narrative construction is, once again, the Tower's visual interest as a spectacle.

The third narrative line, the story of ascent, is most certainly the dominant one in the current construction of Devils Tower. At first glance it might seem to run contrary to the two other stories I have just identified, since it is a narrative about direct encounter with the Tower through the act of climbing it, rather than a narrative expression of distanced spectatorship. I will suggest in a moment why I think it is in fact the master narrative *of* spectatorship.

One of the earliest commentaries on the Tower by a Euro-American comes from Henry Newton, the geological assistant along on an 1875 military expedition to the region. "Its remarkable structure," he says,

its symmetry, and its prominence make it an unfailing object of wonder. . . . It is a great remarkable obelisk of trachyte, with a columnar structure, giving it a vertically striated appearance, and it rises 625 feet almost perpendicular, from its base. Its summit is so entirely inaccessible that the energetic explorer, to whom the ascent of an ordinary difficult crag is but a pleasant pastime, standing at its base could only look upward in despair of ever planting his feet on the top. (cited in Mattison 1973:6)

From the very beginning of colonial encounter with this object, the project of getting to its top was a taken-for-granted goal.

Henry Newton's despair was answered eighteen years later by William Rogers, a local rancher. On the Fourth of July in 1893, that cultural watershed year of the great Columbian Exposition in Chicago,[6] Rogers made the official, inaugural ascent of the Tower. He did so before an assembled throng of spectators numbering, by conservative estimates, at least a thousand. And this was at a time when there were no improved roads into the area and one had to ford the Belle Fourche River numerous times to reach the site.

The ascent was accomplished by means of a wooden ladder laboriously pegged to the rock by Rogers and two other local residents bent on the entrepreneurial promotion of Devils Tower and the surrounding region. At no small risk, they pounded two and a half foot rungs into a continuous crack running to within two hundred feet of the top. To the protruding ends of these pegs they nailed strips of wood for stability. A local artist sewed and painted a 7x12 foot American flag and a group from Deadwood, South Dakota provided Rogers with a handmade Uncle Sam suit to wear for his climb. In the grand nineteenth-century tradition of vernacular patriotic celebration and entrepreneurship, the event was widely publicized and served as the centerpiece of a gala Fourth of July celebration, the Tower already having been used for some years as a site for Independence Day observance.

Rogers made the exhibition climb without mishap and unfurled his flag on the large flagpole waiting there to receive it. (Obviously, a number of people had already climbed the rock in completing the ladder and making other preparations.) The violent winds that swirl around the Tower tore the flag loose later in the day and it floated down onto the dance floor that had been constructed for the festivities. The event's promoters cut up Old Glory on the spot and sold the pieces for souvenirs (Gunderson 1988:73–83).

What I am calling the story of ascent is in fact a series of small narratives or implied narratives that together constitute a cumulative tale. The Rogers ascent is merely the first in a series of "first" climbs or otherwise notable ascents: first solo ascent by a woman (Rogers's wife in 1895, again on July 4), ascent by world renowned "human fly" Babe White in 1927, first ascent (1937) by a team using alpine climbing methods and equipment rather than pre-fixed aids, first alpine ascent by a woman, and so on. Perhaps the most notable event of this sort, exclusive of Rogers's original climb, was the unauthorized parachute jump onto the top of the Tower in 1941 by daredevil George Hopkins. This stunt was particularly notable because the rope Hopkins was supposed to descend by did not land on the Tower with him. He was stranded for six days on the barren summit. His ordeal was front page news nationwide and the climb to rescue him itself became a media event (Gunderson 1988:84–91).

It should be obvious, I think, that these official narratives of ascent are, individually and collectively, just as much involved in constructing Devils Tower as a viewable artifact as the other two narrative formations I have identified. In this case, though, the focus of the spectacle is human conquest—mastery of the Tower. And to master the Tower is to achieve the ideal location for masterful viewing. These early climbs were for the most part media spectacles, or at least newsworthy special occurrences. As such, they invested the Tower with a new load of visual interest, remade it, so to speak, as an even more exciting spectacle. One might say they constitute part of a modern apparatus for making the Tower visible to a mass audience through the magnifying powers of commerce and information technologies, and in this they are continu-

Figure 29. Bear Lodge/Devils Tower, distant view.

ous with the reproductions of the Tower in tourist artifacts. Along this line of thinking, *Close Encounters* might be seen as a culmination of the mutually reinforcing narrative strands that establish the Tower as an object for spectatorial viewing.

* * *

By this point we should not have any difficulty recognizing in these narratives of seeing yet another shuffle of the deck of Western visuality. The Tower itself, having been isolated from its surroundings by, appropriately enough, the "Cowboy President" 's monumentalizing gesture, becomes an especially pure spectacle—virtually an abstract signifier *of* the Spectacular. In both its physical and ideological context there is nothing to distract our eyes from it. At the same time, though, it stands for the desired viewing location. Its naked height above the "flat plane" of the river valley offers a promise of the absolute view (Figure 29). In other words, as a visual apparatus the Tower accomplishes the seemingly

logical impossibility of merging the ideal spectacle and the ideal spectatorial position—a collapsing together of the object of seeing and the
act of seeing (cf. the discussion of the fragmentary prison cells in Chapter 6). The explanatory tales of formation and emergence are mainly
about the Tower as spectacle, with its uncanny, arresting appearance,
while the stories of ascent are about achieving the position of the authoritative viewer. One would be hard pressed to come up with another
landscape feature that approaches the simplicity and purity of Devils
Tower as a visual apparatus in the discourse of looking West.

However, in my account so far there would seem to be lacking that
contaminating element, the force of disruption that destabilizes visual
relationships. Throughout most of the twentieth century Devils Tower
seems to have held at bay that dispersal of fixed optical arrangements I
have been claiming is endemic to the modern discourse of looking West,
a discourse bound up with the thorough commodification of cultural
practice. It is, I think, exactly the narrative construction of the Tower as
simultaneously an ideal object *of* looking and a desired location *for* looking that is largely responsible for maintaining its "visual stability." These
narratives have, so to speak, frozen the dynamics of visual circulation
by constructing the Tower as a conflation of spectacle and (imaginary)
spectator. In recent years, however, this narrative machine that has so
effectively produced ideological stasis has begun to show signs, if not of
complete breakdown, at least of some slipping of cogs. And this is due in
no small measure to the introduction of "alien" ways of seeing—not the
anxiety-producing insertion of a hidden surveillant presence, but rather
the quite sudden appearance (or reassertion) of entirely other visualities
upon the very terrain of the pre-existing apparatus. And these alternative optics appear not through symbolic narrative representations, but
through concrete, material enactments and institutional practices.

Up until quite recently the three narrative constructions I have isolated have worked very well to make Devils Tower a "coherent" artifact
that fit neatly with a century of colonialist visuality. Through seemingly
innocent and "natural" ways of framing the Tower, these narratives have
participated in the long history of expulsion and containment of indigenous peoples. The kind of disruption that has been developing over the
last decade is one I am inclined to associate with distinctly postcolonial conditions of cultural production. One source of this disruption
appears to grow naturally out of the narrative thread of ascent, while
a second source might be understood as a return of cultural voices re-
pressed both by the tight framing of the site and by the second narrative
element identified above, the Native American story of emergence. That
both these new cultural forces began to make themselves felt at about

the same time, the early to mid 1980s, suggests perhaps that they are not entirely independent factors.

In 1950 two people climbed Devils Tower; in 1960 one hundred and four; in 1970 a little over two hundred. By 1980 the annual figure had jumped to almost two thousand, and in 1990 it was well over five thousand. Since 1992 the Tower has seen more than six thousand climbers each year.[7] Another change has occurred as well. Up through 1980 the majority of these climbers were making it to the top of the Tower. In no year since that time has the number of summit climbers exceeded the number who do not reach the top, and the ratio of non-summit to summit climbers has grown dramatically (FCMP/FONSI 1995:xii).

What all this means is that Devils Tower has been reconstructed, since roughly 1980, as one of the premier recreational rock climbing sites in the NPS system. Not surprisingly, the official interpretive program at the Tower incorporated this development as if it were merely a continuation of the well established ascent narrative. Among other things, a special kiosk display has been installed in the middle of the parking area. A segment of the Tower is reproduced at full scale and the methods, equipment, and types of rock climbing are explained. The brightly clad climbers who scramble up the Tower daily in the summer months are presented as an element of the spectacle. Watching the climbers was identified in a recent NPS commissioned study as the favorite activity of visitors to this National Monument (Hanson and Moore 1993:66).

The second complicating development can be dated roughly to 1984, at which time there was a public revival of the use of the Bear Lodge as a sacred ceremonial site by various tribal peoples. Since that time, prayer vigils, vision quests, and, most important, the Sundance, the premier sacred ceremonial for many Plains tribes, have been practiced again near the base of the Bear Lodge.[8]

These two major developments since 1980 present significant problems for the efficient narrative and visual operations of the site. For one thing, the Indian emergence story frozen in the icon of the giant clawing bear depends on positioning Indians as inhabitants of an absolute past, members of defunct cultures that have left their trace at the site only in the form of picturesque mythologies that can be incorporated, through a process of radical selectivity, into the dominant spectatorial program. To have actual people coming into the site, cutting trees for the Sundance or leaving prayer bundles at the base of the Tower, is a kind of implicit embarrassment to the established narrative arrangements.

The development of rock climbing as a mass sport, though *seemingly* assimilable, is also problematic. This mode of ascent is entirely different from that depicted in the historical narrative. Although they are watched by visitors, the contemporary climbers do not think of themselves as part of the display. For many, the eminently watchable act of getting to the top is not a goal. Negotiating a difficult "pitch," perfecting a crack or corner technique, exploring a new route are some of the non-spectatorial activities they pursue. The element of dare-deviltry that made many of the earlier climbs enhancements or magnifications of the Tower as a display is largely missing from the activities of the rock climbers. And for many of them the classic tourists at the site, the spectators, are merely nuisances, as reflected in such things as the personal experience narratives of "comic encounters with gullible tourists" shared among climbers.

But what would seem to be the greatest disruption of all to the narrative and visual tranquility of this site is the fact that these two "new" presences are in many respects in direct conflict with one another. For the tribal peoples who see Bear Lodge as a sacred site, the presence of large numbers of climbers assaulting its sides, many of them pounding in pitons or using permanently fixed bolts, sometimes leaving equipment, trash, and smudges of chalk, is more than an affront to religious sensibilities. It is literally destructive of spiritual power, not to mention damaging to the spiritual health of those doing the climbing. Some of the climbers, on the other hand, insist that their claim on the site is just as strong as that of Native peoples. In fact, some argue that their climbing itself has a profoundly spiritual dimension.

This is just to begin to get at the current complexities that have disrupted what has become a significantly contested site. We might fairly see the dilemma as not so much a rejection of narrative construction itself as a sudden explosion of narratives, far too many and too various for the Park Service to incorporate into the established construction of the Tower as a set of static, detached views or unique spectacles of ascent. For one thing, the narratives of both the climbers and the spiritual practitioners involve active engagement with the site in ways that are not inherently spectatorial. The most significant activities of both groups are hardly even visible to an outside audience, much less structured for mass spectatorship. Most spiritual engagement is literally hidden from spectatorial view or is by nature undetectable to sight. Oddly similar, many of the practices of modern rock climbing, its meaningful technical accomplishments, occur at a scale too small to be the object of non-participant spectatorship. Climbing of this sort is a private, small group activity, though carried out on the very public face of the Tower.

Furthermore, the visual procedures *of* these two group do not fit very well with the arrangements of the preexising apparatus. Though of course they might sometimes find occasion to enjoy the view from on high, the primary visual experience of rock climbers involves intense focus on the rock face immediately in front of their eyes, with the instrumental purpose of locating holds, routes, impediments, etc. It is a rather intimate act of close-up "reading," though a kind of reading that is inseparable from the physical experience of touching (indeed, clinging onto). At something like the other extreme, the tribal religious practices associated with Bear Lodge have much to do with "visionary" experience. Although again I will not presume to offer any kind of specific cultural interpretation, it seems safe to say that the spiritual seeing which is so much a part of Native American belief systems falls decidedly outside the mode of visuality I have been examining in this study. Whether we think of such visionary experience as a complete transcendence of the material world or a denial of the distinction between the physical and the spiritual, it certainly cannot be understood in terms of advanced capitalist commodified looking, with its triangulations of spectatorship and surveillance.[9]

The cultural forces currently at play around the site of Devils Tower/ Bear Lodge, at least the ones of concern to me here, may be summarized as follows: a well-established program involving procedures of framing and a coherent narrative apparatus has, up until quite recently, constructed the Tower as both an object and a location of spectatorship. One corollary to this construction is that it has contributed to closing out (or incorporating through trivialization) the pre-existing Native American significance of the site. In recent years the active revival of Plains Indian claims on the Bear Lodge as a sacred place and, less directly, the rise of a recreational subculture dependent on the physical properties of the Tower have disrupted the smooth operation of the dominant ideology and its attendant visual procedures. These "new" cultural factors have certain structural elements in common, but, most important, neither fits very neatly into the established program of mass spectatorship that has governed this site since well before its official establishment as a National Monument. Abstract similarities notwithstanding, however, Native American religious practices and rock climbers' recreational activity are widely perceived, especially by Native Americans, as conflicting uses of the site.

*   *   *

While this conflict is the major source of the current controversies at Devils Tower/Bear Lodge, I will conclude by suggesting that, perhaps paradoxically, it is precisely through the *incorporation* of this conflict, not its resolution, that the larger spectatorial program preserves its hegemonic place. Or to put it another way, the postcolonial conditions of possible disruption, particularly the revival of Native voices with the

potential of reclaiming the site, are in the process of being displaced
into a new containing structure engineered through the bureaucratic
procedures of "balanced" management.

Native American religious practitioners and rock climbers each make
up only about 1 per cent of the over 400,000 annual visitors to the Tower.
Their conflict, however, currently occupies a central position in the cultural management of this site. It is the main subtext of a Final Climbing
Management Plan (FCMP) recently completed by National Park Service
personnel and put into practice for the first time in the summer of 1995.
More than three years in preparation, the plan purports to have taken
into consideration all the points of view expressed during the lengthy
"scoping process" and to have come up with a balanced proposal for
use. The centerpiece of the climbing plan is a request that rock climbers
voluntarily refrain from climbing during the month of June. The period
around the summer solstice is particularly important to Plains tribes, it
being the time of the Sundance ceremony. Also, no new climbing bolts,
the permanent anchors drilled into the rock face, will be permitted, this
being the practice deemed most harmful to the Tower itself and most
offensive to Native American religious principles.

Finally, the interpretive program at the site is to be expanded to help
educate the public about the history of Native American presence at the
Tower. In this regard the NPS plan implicitly presents itself as a major departure from past practices. It is the first substantial effort to make clear
to visitors the importance of Native American cultures, both historically
and still today. What this means practically is that Native American cultural performances (e.g., drumming and dancing, craft demonstration)
are being incorporated into the official Park Service programming.[10]

While certainly a kind of improvement, the addition of these isolated Native American cultural elements is hardly a threat to the larger
and thoroughly taken-for-granted premise that spectatorship is the real
business of National Monuments. The greatest likelihood is that such
performances, with the Tower as their legitimizing backdrop, will serve
merely as "enriching" additions to the visual interest of the site. Somehow vaguely related to the issue of sacred significance, these fragmentary cultural displays will function as the symbolic stand-in for (and
deflection from) deeper political questions that cannot really be confronted in the highly managed venue of mass spectatorship. Questions
a propos of a postcolonial context—questions about cultural ownership
and control, about reappropriation, about rights of access and use remain thoroughly out of bounds.

But there is also another mechanism in play that involves a larger
"strategy" of containment, one more subtle than the familiar appeals
to compromise and inclusiveness that are the stock in trade of cultural

resource management and are operating on the surface of the Devils Tower plan. Once implemented, this plan was declared a success almost immediately (NPS News Release 95-19)—with the voluntary climbing moratorium being widely observed. It appears that tensions between climbers and Native American have lessened somewhat, the principle of voluntarism being a key factor (*High Country News* Oct. 16, 1995). The opinion has been expressed by some tribal members that there is more value to the respect shown by the active choice not to climb than would be the case if climbing were simply prohibited. Although there is still considerable ambivalence, many climbers also seem willing to accept the ban if they are given the chance to "make their own decisions." However, at this writing the legal status of the voluntary moratorium is being litigated in federal district court. Suit has been brought by an organization representing local interests, including the professional guides who take climbing parties up the Tower. Needless to say, the decline in climbing during the prime month of June has significant impact on the local economy around the Tower. The outcome of this case promises to have far-reaching significance for questions of access and use of National Park Service sites.

It would appear then that managerial policies have not yet achieved an entirely satisfactory solution to the cultural conflicts over this site. But that is only the case if we take "solution" to mean "resolution," that is, achievement of some kind of identifiable closure—in short, stability. This would mean a return to the relatively untroubled conditions that obtained at this site prior to the 1980s and that, I have argued, were effectively held in place through the symbolic management of narratives and visuality. However, in keeping with the larger argument of this book, we might consider the possibility that certain kinds of *instability* are in fact the more appropriate "solution" under our current cultural conditions. One lesson we find confirmed in the case of Devils Tower/Bear Lodge is that the postcolonial scenario of resistance and reclamation, of rights claims and repatriation, is rarely if ever straightforward. One of the directions it can take is toward subtle containment through a mechanism we might call "spectatorial conflict." Deep seated and perhaps ultimately unresolvable cultural dilemmas (Euro-American conceptions of public lands and their uses versus Native American conceptions of sacred landscape, for example) become displaced onto localized, definable conflicts (between recreational rock climbers and tribal religious practitioners, for example) that can be "managed," if not completely settled. But even more to the point, such conflicts as this one can be constructed as "watchable," as themselves objects of spectatorship. The management of cultural conflict over Devils Tower might be viewed as one more episode in a long history of the politics of display at this site.

And taking that view, we might ask how management practices serve as visual apparatuses devoted to making cultural conflicts into spectacles.

The Final Climbing Management Plan is a virtual textbook of bureaucratic procedures for conflict management and resolution. Among its more explicit guiding principles are enlistment of the fullest possible public participation; identification and representation of all relevant "interest groups" in the planning process; keeping open all lines of communication; search for compromise between conflicting interests; and devotion to democratic, middle of the road solutions, rejecting all "extreme" positions. This more or less overt ideology of liberal and rational management floats above a host of less directly acknowledged assumptions and procedures. Among these are the definition of all factors, including social and cultural ones, as "resources" subject to rational management; perception of the planning process as an attempt to balance the concerns of discrete, homogeneous interest groups; strict delimitation of the "relevant" management issue so that the more radical proposals or critiques can be ruled outside the scope of the process (i.e., little tolerance for emergent elements); and an unquestioned acceptance of positivist premises that privilege resource quantification, "objective" scientific inquiry, and narrow definition of goals.

Among other things, these "rational" bureaucratic procedures provide the mechanism for discounting certain voices, thereby reducing the terms of debate to a comprehensible level of simplicity. This is not unlike the reduction of the overt interpretive program at the Wyoming Territorial Park to the familiar binary structure of gender relationships. In some of the public meetings about management of the Tower, for example, the view was expressed that the sacred significance of the site should take precedence and all climbing should cease. This view became positioned in the planning document as one of the extreme ends of a range of management options, which meant that it would be dismissed automatically.[11] The opposite extreme was no restrictions of any kind on climbing. Placing these two positions at opposite ends of a spectrum of six possibilities makes them seem like equivalent and equally unreasonable options. This kind of flattening, in which Native American cultures and a recreational subculture are reduced to equivalence as "interest groups," is characteristic of the discursive operations of the plan as a whole.

What this process leaves us with is a condition of coherent but ultimately "undecidable" conflict that itself may be perused as a kind of spectacle. The arena of this spectatorship, however, is not so much the interpretive program at the site of the National Monument itself, where open acknowledgment of the conflict is muted at best. Rather it occurs in the much larger mass cultural venues of the news media, the legal system, and academe.[12]

A good example of this sort of "watchable undecidability" or "conflict display" is the simmering issue of the National Monument's name. One familiar gesture of postcolonial cultural politics is the recovery of pre-colonial or indigenous names. A recurring complaint about Devils Tower is that its name imposes a Euro-centric concept of evil forces on a Native American sacred site, perpetuating the long-standing colonial inclination to demonize indigenous belief systems. There have been calls to change the official name to Bear Lodge, a proposal that has met strong resistance from several quarters.

For present purposes, one of the most interesting "compromise" suggestions is to leave the National Mounument name as Devils Tower, but to call the geological formation itself Bear Lodge. This strikes me as an apt metaphor for the larger phenomenon I have been describing—suspension in a state of fluctuating, both/and undecidability. It is like the trick optics of those pictures that show one image when viewed from some angles, but then transform into an entirely different scene as we shift our perspective. From Devils Tower to Bear Lodge and back again in endless alternation—this may be taken as emblematic of the visual destabilizations I have been associating with the discourse of looking West, itself an expression of the larger cultural conditions in our late twentieth-century moment. That we should find this sort of unfixed, fluctuating suspension of conflicting perspectives being institutionalized and made visible through the late capitalist management apparatus of a National Monument seems entirely fitting.[13] As mechanisms of postcolonial containment, such displays of managed undecidability are perhaps even more effective than that comforting *Close Encounters* fantasy of a powerful threat from elsewhere that fades out in the reassuring glow of angelic aliens.

Coda: A Miniature Excursion

Having spent so much time examining the visual discourse of a nationally significant site at the western edge of the Black Hills, it might seem obtuse not at least to mention its more famous fellow Monument in the region, especially since this other display environment is so blatant, not to say absurdly literal in its expression of the act of looking West. Mount Rushmore, near Rapid City, South Dakota, is far more heavily visited than Devils Tower, and it is certainly more central to our national landmark iconography. One might also say it is an even more egregious affront to Native American religious and cultural sensibilities than rock climbing on the Bear Lodge. The Rushmore sculpture is, after all, the violent and indelible imprint of "great white father" colonialists on the sacred landscape of Paha Sapa (Boime 1991:165–66). But in terms of

my argument its explicit representation of powerful white men looking West from a great height is more in keeping with that magisterial
regime (158–66) against which I have counterposed the less stable, less
self-confident discourse of layered acts of looking and the circulating
exchange of visual positions. Therefore, it is another Rushmore I would
like to visit in a last brief excursion. And in keeping with my predilection
for marginal locales, this trip will take us to a rather out of the way spot.

Gutzon Borglum, sculptor of the Rushmore heads, was a Dane by
birth. In his homeland, on the Jutland Peninsula, one finds a second
Rushmore, at 1:10 scale. Near the town of Billund one may visit Legoland, a theme park devoted to the construction of miniature replicas
of everything from African wildlife to the architectural monuments of
the world. All these things are made from the immensely popular plastic building blocks first developed by the Lego company in 1949. The
fully integrated "Lego System," in which all the building elements are
designed to work together in a potentially infinite field of play, was marketed for the first time in 1955 (Wiencek 1987:50). Opened in 1968,
Legoland operates on a much smaller economic scale than the flagship
theme parks in the United States and Europe. At the time of my visit
in 1990, it covered only twenty-five acres (Euro-Disneyland covers 4,800
acres). Fifteen million people visited Legoland over its first twenty years
of existence (Euro-Disney prepared for eleven million visitors in its first
year alone). Legoland is, in other words, not only a theme park of miniaturized objects, it is itself a miniature theme park.

However, one might say it is this very centrality of the miniature that
makes Legoland one of the fullest realizations of theme park principles
and material practices. Miniaturization, both literal and metaphorical,
is at the very heart of the theme park concept. Disney's original idea, in
fact, growing out of his interest in model trains, was to construct a child's
miniature fantasyland of mechanically animated figures and settings. In
its own low-tech way, Legoland astonishes the visitor by demonstrating
that the simple, geometrically pure plastic block can be assembled into
convincing, scaled-down replicas of an African elephant, or the Statue
of Liberty, or a Scandinavian village. And in this central mechanism of
its display Legoland epitomizes the theme park as an apparatus devoted
to reproducing the absolute hegemony of the commodity form. Theme
parks are a paradise of the commodity in advanced consumer culture.
In them the whole world, organized into clean, manageable, packaged
units, becomes available to consumer appropriation. Legoland is literally built up out of what could be seen as nearly the limiting case commodity, the pure or empty commodity—in the form of the barely articulated plastic cube. Legos are as near as three-dimensional material
objects can come to being absolute digital signifiers, having no meaning

until combined in structures of similarity and difference (positive and negative) to produce in miniature, consumable form virtually anything in the world.[14]

The familiar idea that meaning derives from the experience of consumable differences operates, of course, at all levels of theme parks—most obviously in the process of movement from one theme area to another. The imagery of Frontierland only signifies in terms of relationships of similarity or difference with, say, Tomorrowland, which is unlike Frontierland in being about the future rather than the past, but also similar to it in being about the exploration of frontiers; or with Main Street, USA, which resembles the western frontier in being from the "olden days," but also differs from it in being genteel and civilized. The Wild West is one of the most common units of difference in theme parks, and it is to Legoland's version of this component that we now come—Legoredo.

In its very name the Old West section of Legoland enacts the basic Lego (and commodity) principle of overlapping, interlocking elements, the commodity name colonizing the emblematic Old West placename, Laredo. Legoredo rather neatly summarizes the typical theme park treatment of western iconography. All the expected paraphernalia are there—allusions to the falsefront frontier town, flattened images of Native American life, amusements that draw on the imagery of the western extractive industries (flume and ore train rides), and, most important here, a profound dislocation of scale.

If Legoland is a kind of theme park paradigm, Legoredo is its most vivid exemplar. To elaborate a previous point, it is not merely the fact of miniaturization that is at the heart of theme park seeing, but rather the pervasive phenomenon of scale dislocation. In Disneyland for example, the Victorian structures of Main Street are large enough to enter but at the same time subtly miniaturized to enhance a feeling of control, security, and, I would add, seeming appropriability. It is in fact the unfixing of our relationship, especially our visual relationship, to material reality that defines the theme park as an apparatus of advanced consumer culture. And the play with scale that produces this visual dislocation is nowhere as apparent as in the Old West sections of theme parks. Through tight control of vantage points, framing, composition of elements, and subtle sleights of scale, the Disney parks accomplish the remarkable feat of fabricating and miniaturizing the western landscape itself, while still giving an impression of its monumentality. In their treatment of the West, they enact the ultimate commodification. The vastness of its actual scale would, one might think, exempt the western landscape from direct consumer appropriation; and the extractive industries that brought the "real" West into the system of industrial production would seem to defy

Figure 30. Legoland Mount Rushmore, near Billund, Denmark.

the sort of intimate, personal appropriations definitive of the advanced consumer order. But in fact theme parks have no trouble making the West available in this way. The western industries become rides and the landscape comes under the regime of consumer desire as a set of stylistic gestures, icons, and pre-packaged "views."

Legoredo carries this dislocating miniaturization of monumentality to a kind of logical conclusion in perhaps its most arresting display, the miniature Rushmore (Figure 30), which enacts a rather dizzying play of unfixed seeing. The original Mount Rushmore is of course already a transformation of the natural western landscape into a kind of commodity, a view for tourists the subject of which is men looking (West). Its wonder as a site, and hence its value as a tourist artifact, comes from the gigantism of its enlargement. The Legoland version is a forty-six-foot-tall replica surrounded by congruently miniaturized scenery and vegetation. Its wonder comes from the fact that such a large and accurate reproduction could be assembled from the tiny unit of the Lego brick (1.5 million of them). To put it schematically, the Legoland Rushmore is an artificial monumental miniature of a gigantic enlargement that transforms a monumental natural landscape into a national monu-

ment, which is to say, a visual commodity. The circulation of visual relationships and seeing locations is endless, and it is that ceaseless motion
that bespeaks the conditions of the late consumer order.

In arriving at the Legoland Rushmore we have, it seems, come full
circle and met again our greenhorn travelers from Chapter 1. They were
caught in the discourse of looking West by the deceptive optics of the
western landscape itself, mistaking the far away for the nearby. As a
tourist in Legoredo we are at least briefly mesmerized by the artificially
manufactured sense of a far away that is *in fact* nearby. When the cars
of the ore train amusement ride pass in front of the Lego Rushmore
we experience an at least mildly dislocating optical *frisson* that is an in-
verted version of the travelers' mystification over their inability to reach
the mountains. Though these two types of visual dislocation are like
looking into opposite ends of a telescope, it is the same telescope. The
all-encompassing apparatus of late capitalist consumer culture thrives
on—depends on such unfixing of material relations, and the discourse
of looking West is one of its most subtly efficient mechanisms. The global
dispersal of this way of seeing, and its recasting in countless local forms
and specialized iconographies is something we can take for granted. But
its manifestation in the tones of the specific American region we commonly call "the West" is, I have tried to demonstrate, of particular interest, both for historical and for ethnographic reasons. The "textual" West
is interesting as one place, though by no means the only one, where this
discourse was being fashioned around the turn of the last century; and
display environments *in* the West today make for instructive viewing as
they play out the destabilization of seeing that virtually defines our own
turn-of-the-century optics.

Notes

Chapter 1

1. Although I had heard this joke before, the version reported here is my paraphrase of a telling that occurred after a public presentation I gave on material that appears in Chapter 6. I had made no reference to the uncanny visual phenomenon in my talk. That the joke was spontaneously told to me immediately afterward says something both about the astuteness of the joke teller and about the folk process as having its own wisdom. This little folk performance established for me a first link in the chain of connections presented in this chapter, and in that respect it is another in my set of "origin points" for this study.

2. It will be obvious to students of contemporary theory that I am drawing on various concepts and lines of thought in a now highly elaborated conversation about the importance of visuality in post-Renaissance culture. Some aspects of this conversation I will identify explicitly, especially in Chapter 4. Others I will leave more or less embedded, such as the Lacanian principles that lie behind what I am referring to here as "the eye that knows."

3. In further acknowledgment of the fact that as producer of this text I am also assigned my place as an effect of a larger textuality, I need to say two things about this story. One is the obvious point that in finding personal significance in it I move to the position of the tenderfoot, the foolish easterner. This role extends, I have already suggested, to the tourist, and we might aptly apply it to the ethnographer as well. These are all aspects of my positioning in relation to this text. The second point is that I have entirely lost sight of the origin of this story. I cannot recall whether I heard it in oral performance or read it. I will therefore appeal to the justification that having in some sense made this tale my own (I have told it on numerous occasions) gives me the right to consider myself a legitimate folk source for it and to consider it a useable specimen of the discourse under consideration here.

4. The motif of the visually deceptive landscape shows up in the literature of the West at least as early as Mark Twain's *Roughing It* (1985[1872]:75) and at least as recently as Larry McMurtry's *Dead Man's Walk* (1995:62). The vast openness of the landscape has been reported to induce a kind of "sickness of vision," as Robert Louis Stevenson put it while traveling the Plains by railroad (quoted in Raban 1996:63). This visual malady has its emotional counterpart in the profound loneliness experienced by many early visitors and settlers in the region, an effect the vast, seemingly empty vistas still produce in some today. On these issues generally, see Raban 1996:62–68.

5. The verb is problematic here. To say "encounters" suggests that the textual West existed somewhere prior to its "discovery" by cultural producers like Wister. There is some validity to thinking of it in this way, since many of the motifs, images, narrative elements, and so forth, that Wister brings together did already exist in Buffalo Bill's Wild West, in Wister's own earlier western sketches, in Teddy Roosevelt's political persona, in Frederick Remington's paintings, to mention only a few things. But it is also true that Wister's novel quickly became the primary conduit connecting these disparate nineteenth-century materials with the mass culture conventions of the twentieth. In that sense, Wister was very much a part of the production process. It is another advantage of making discourse/practice our primary object of investigation that it frees us from the task, in my view a futile one, of sorting out some single-stranded story of influences and effects. A focus on discursive processes allows me to locate Wister's novel as an inaugural moment in the larger text of the West without having to justify the point with an inventory of simplistic, linear, cause-and-effect connections.

6. All subsequent references to *The Virginian* are from this edition and hereafter will be indicated by page numbers only.

7. The most obvious parallel is the African native as gunbearer for the white hunter or explorer. See the reference to a classic instance, Henry M. Stanley and his "boy" Kalulu, in Torgovnik 1990:27–28.

8. I hope it is obvious that I am not arguing that the actual person Sitting Bull is consciously engaged in an act of visual subversion. Indeed, during his time on tour with Buffalo Bill he was happy to sell signed photos of himself. I am referring to the operations and manifestations of discourse, which can never be reduced entirely to the agency of individual subjects. For a discussion of another photographic construction of Sitting Bull, see Goodyear 1996:33–41.

9. A 1994 Wyoming Almanac reports observations of rattlesnakes swimming in Pathfinder and Seminoe reservoirs (Roberts, Roberts, and Roberts 1994:15). These are perhaps dim reflections of the legend. In an early episode of Larry McMurtry's immensely popular cattle drive saga, *Lonesome Dove* (1985), one of the drovers is bitten to death by swimming snakes as he is crossing a Texas river. This would seem to be a literary refashioning of the story, a common occurrence with such contemporary legends.

Chapter 2

1. To judge from his journal entry of July 13, Wister seems to have been both impressed by the Exposition and somewhat cloyed by its relentlessly grandiose spectacle.

2. All citations from Wister's western journals are taken from the transcripts of his original notebooks, which are housed at the University of Wyoming's American Heritage Center. The Wister Collection (AHC #290) contains a wealth of material in addition to the western journals, notably, the large body of Wister's western photographs. Hereafter I will cite the journals by date of entry only.

3. Wister biographer Darwin Payne identifies this person as David Robert Tisdale, owner of the TTT Ranch, located near present day Kaycee, Wyoming (Payne 1985:117). Tisdale would the next year participate as one of the "invaders" in the famous Johnson County Cattle War. Major Frank Walcott, Wister's host on his first trip West, led the "army" of cattle barons and their hired gunmen in the abortive expedition to clean out the "rustlers" and others they saw

as a threat to the open range cattle industry. These events, of course, constitute the historical background to Wister's novel.

4. For an excellent discussion of the relationship between "reading signs" in the western landscape and reading western texts, especially dime novels, see Bold 1987:24–27.

5. In her discussion of genre westerns, Jane Tompkins (1992) proposes a rather stark contrast between the nineteenth-century sentimental novel and the emotionally constricted narratives of the twentieth-century western. I find this simple dichotomy and its equally simple gendering of cultural history far too reductive. See Chapter 4 for an elaboration of related issues.

6. Wister's actual class position was, one might say, on the boundary between haute bourgeois and truly leisured. In his youth he had the financial freedom to make extended summer trips, but he was also destined for a career in law had his literary success not rescued him.

7. All subsequent citations are from this edition and will be indicated by page number only.

8. Regarding Wister's own experience as a spectacle for Yellowstone tourists, see Wister 1979 [1936]:67.

Chapter 3

1. The conventions of this living history exercise did not countenance the possibility that a historical persona could be constructed across gender lines. The transcendence of one's historical identity is the primary goal of the exercise, but other aspects of identity are tacitly understood to be fixed.

2. Although I did not have the opportunity to observe closely the social arrangements of the laundresses, I can say that in the course of the exercise a number of social groupings emerged among the male participants. For example, there were several people who were black powder enthusiasts, that is, those with a hobbyist interest in historical firearms, in most cases combined with an interest in military history, especially the "Indian wars" period. Another group, no doubt overlapping with this first one, were the hobbyist reenactors or "buffs." This group included the participants who seemed to be most interested in adopting a role and playing it to the hilt, although for many of them this mainly meant reproducing features of mass cultural representations of the "frontier period." These were the participants most likely to adopt a "frontier accent" (e.g., dropping the 'g' from 'ing' endings) and to repeat the clichés of western film and popular fiction. There were also the professional or quasi-professional reenactors, those academically trained in living history procedures and interested in exploring a past period through rigorous living history methods. Some of these participants belonged to private reenactment groups where strict rules of authenticity and persona maintenance are observed. These three groupings are not closed compartments, of course, and a much more minute observation of behavior would be necessary to give anything approaching the full picture. As a participant observer I stood in a somewhat unusual relationship to the others, especially to the instructors, one of whom was a faculty colleague and two of whom had been my students. Although I was not treated differently in any overt way, these relationships did of course have some bearing on my experience. For example, I believe I was assigned to the chicken killing detail as a kind of practical joke.

3. It should be acknowledged that at least among the male participants this living history exercise became a space for certain kinds of regressive behavior. At times the atmosphere was not unlike a summer camp. This was perhaps most evident in some of the joking behavior, which frequently turned on sexual themes, most notably teasing innuendoes about homosexuality. We also learned and performed obscene barracks genres of verbal art. Although such things were no doubt an actual part of frontier military life, it is not surprising that these aspects of reenactment were kept separate from the sphere of public display.

4. This designation is apparently a disdainful reference to sentimental poems by easterners who sympathized with the plight of the Indians. Specifically, it ridicules the opening line, "Lo, the poor Indian . . ."

5. Although never officially announced, it was generally assumed that some sort of attack would occur. I cannot at this point identify the cues, hints, or shared knowledge about prior exercises that contributed to this tacit understanding. What seems interesting to me is that part of this understanding was an unspoken agreement that the fiction of surprise be maintained. There was no speculation, as far as I was aware, about when the skirmish would occur, though everyone was anticipating it. This is a case where the living history frame, the instructional apparatus, seems to merge with the historical moment being recreated. One can imagine the nineteenth-century foot soldier out on campaign feeling the covert gaze of "hostiles." In the reenactment of such a moment it was really the covert gaze of the instructors, designers of a fictive hostile Other, that we felt, though we observed the convention that this surveillance was coming from outside rather than inside our group.

6. As part of the classroom preparation we were warned against wandering around the Fort Laramie grounds on our own during the night. Armed security patrols would be present, and we were informed that this National Park Service site had been targeted by certain militant Native American groups (unspecified) for disruptive action.

7. In the course of practice drills it became apparent that the ejection mechanism of my rifle was not working properly. For safety purposes I was prevented from participating in the climactic skirmish, being required to stand behind the firing line and watch the proceedings. I have to confess to ambivalent feelings about this development. After the fact I found myself relieved at having avoided participating in even a fictive representation of violent action toward imaginary Indians. At the moment of performance, however, I believe I felt some regret at not getting to "fire at will." At some level I resented not having the chance to enjoy the "payoff." This is one small moment in what seems to me in retrospect the very complicated and conflicted feelings I had about participating in this exercise as a whole. While one might certainly approach the historical issues critically and justify the reenactment process as a tool of objective analysis, one can never entirely escape the feeling that the reenacted activity is being dignified, if not glorified.

8. I hasten to add that I am not mounting a critique of the Fort Laramie exercise as being faulty in its observation of historical realities. It undertook the difficult task of teaching reenactment methods while at the same time teaching about the period being re-created. Artificial or somewhat "inaccurate" situations (presumably, respectable women—or any women—would never have been allowed into an enlisted men's barracks), are unavoidable if the full pedagogical mission is to be accomplished.

Chapter 4

1. The field of "visuality studies" has emerged as a subset of cultural studies taken more broadly. While its deepest roots are in art history, it now draws on a wide array of theoretical approaches to address questions of visual representation and visual experience in any number of areas—film and media studies, photography, museum studies, performance studies, and considerations of spectacles of many sorts, to mention only a few. That it has achieved a distinct academic identity is indicated by the fact that we now have book-length introductions to its history and methods, and readers devoted to visual practice broadly construed. See, for example, Walker and Chaplin 1997; Cooke and Wollen 1995; Melville and Readings, eds. 1995; Jenks, ed.1995; Bryson, Holly, and Moxley, eds. 1994; and Levin, ed. 1993.

2. As this definition suggests, I am using the less clumsy single designation "discourse" to cover what Michel Foucault means by "discourse/practice," that is, both the expressive forms of verbal and visual discourses and the material practices of institutions, including their physical, artifactual embodiments. Or to put it more crudely, I am considering texts and things as equally important, indeed inseparable discursive media.

3. The much discussed artifactual metaphor for this Renaissance and Enlightenment rational-humanist visual mode is the camera obscura. See Crary 1993:25–66.

4. John Berger's Marxist art historical studies are an important precursor to the current development of visuality studies.

5. One manifestation of this could be seen in the iconography of the theatrical panoramas and dioramas that flourished in the mid-nineteenth century. These elaborate displays were frequently organized as rhythmic alternations between tranquilly picturesque and grandly sublime scenes, and as time went on western landscapes became increasingly common subjects of such spectacles (Ringe 1971:60; Hyde 1990:43–45; Sandweiss 1992:195–96). On panoramas and dioramas as visual apparatuses in general, see Friedberg 1993:20–29.

6. The cultural significance of acts of looking directed at other acts of looking has come in for extensive theoretical commentary in relation to a posthumous work by Marcel Duchamp. *Etant donnés* is a diorama-like museum installation that requires the gallery-goer to peer through a hole broken into a door to see, or partially see, the supine body of a nude woman amid weeds and debris. Rosalind Krauss points up the connection between this work, begun by Duchamp in 1946, and Jean-Paul Sartre's seminal discussion of "the gaze" (*le regard*) in *Being and Nothingness* (1943). The museum installation seems to enact the Sartrean scenario of the peeping voyeur who is surprised from behind by a watching presence. This intruding observer contaminates and thereby disrupts the act of absorbed looking at the object of desire. Krauss discusses this work (Krauss 1993:111–19) in relation to Jean-François Lyotard's earlier commentary (Lyotard 1977), and more recently Kaja Silverman has provided another layer to this theoretical ensemble (Silverman 1996:170–73). To track this discussion is to encounter many abstract theoretical issues directly relevant to the present study. In an entirely different cultural and theoretical context, Catherine A. Lutz and Jane L. Collins raise some related questions about acts of looking at looking. In their book *Reading National Geographic* they include a chapter entitled "The Photograph as an Intersection of Gazes" (1993:187–216). Their whole discussion

of the magazine's photographic discourse is of interest here, but in particular they single out an image from 1982 in which a tourist is being photographed with an Amerindian couple. It is a photo, they argue, that reveals the apparatus of touristic image making, and as such it is implicitly disruptive of the normal visual procedures of the mass circulation magazine (211–13). The parallels between the authors' observations about this moment of looking at looking and the present discussion should be obvious. A particularly relevant spin is placed on this issue in the work of Native American photographer Zig Jackson. His series "Indian Photographing Tourist Photographing Indian" is especially apt (Jackson 1995:36–37).

7. Wister's disdain for the commercial practices of the emerging consumer order, though he was in many ways an active participant in them himself, is manifestly evident in his journals and fiction. His anti-Semitism, only one among many prejudices, is most clearly on display in relation to his views of turn-of-the-century American commercial culture. See, for example, his depiction of commercial travelers in Chapter 2 of *The Virginian*. Wister's racial and class ideologies are well addressed in Payne 1985.

8. Although there are some obvious similarities here to the elements of visual discourse I have been describing, Cutrer focuses on a reciprocal structure of exchanged gazes rather than on the minimally triangular circulation I find to be diagnostic of the new visual order.

9. Feminist theories of the gaze constitute perhaps the most advanced thinking about visuality in general, especially as they have been developed in film studies. Laura Mulvey's universally invoked analysis of the structure of visual pleasure in film viewing is an indispensable touchstone for anyone considering discourses of looking, at least in the period of concern to me here. That under patriarchal conditions maleness is associated with bearing the authoritative gaze and femaleness with objectification beneath that gaze is the ultimate horizon against which all discursive elaborations and complications must be viewed. And the recognition that visual pleasure is mobilized by an interplay of erotic desire for an other with narcissistic impulses of identification is equally fundamental (Mulvey 1989:14–39). For a discussion of the western hero as the object of the desiring gaze and its relation to patriarchal visuality, see Mitchell 1996:160–163.

10. This is perhaps the place to recall that William Dean Howells was Wister's friend and something of a literary mentor (Payne 1985:70–75). Both William and Henry James were also family friends.

11. Lee Clark Mitchell makes the interesting suggestion that *The Virginian*'s immense popularity might partly be explained by the fact that it provided one kind of "solution" to the threat to male sovereignty raised by the growth of the women's suffrage movement. This issue, he suggests, may have been especially acute for Wister as a regular visitor to Wyoming, since the constitution drafted for its statehood in 1890 extended the vote to women. The depiction of Molly Wood, the hero's sweetheart, shows her to be initially rebellious and of independent mind, but in the end she bends to the will of her "master." In this way the anxiety over loss of male prerogatives is assuaged (Mitchell 1996:113–19; see also Tompkins 1992:131–55).

12. Although I have not kept in strict accordance with its terminology, it will be obvious to students of post-structural theory that the present study is influenced by Lacan's seminal discussion of the optical structures he sees as fundamental to the formation of human subjectivity (Lacan 1981 [1973]:67–119). Building on Sartre, his categories of the look, the Gaze, the screen, the image-

ideal, the "given-to-be-seen," and so on are all reflected in this study, if not systematically applied. The joke that opens Chapter 1, for instance, is almost a perfect representation of the Lacanian distinction between look and Gaze. I find Kaja Silverman's book *The Threshold of the Visible World* (1996) to be an excellent guide to and extension of the Lacanian framework, and I have drawn upon it in thinking about the discourse of looking West.

13. I am not arguing, of course, that this "other" visuality is more liberating or ideologically desirable. It is a virtual truism that reflexivity of the sort I have been describing may serve as a powerful mechanism of ideological capture. For an historical consideration of the development of visual apparatuses in the nineteenth century, especially with regard to questions of visual reflexivity versus "phantasmagoric" concealment, see Jonathan Crary's important *Techniques of the Observer* (1993), another book that I find indispensable to the issues of concern in the present study. He demonstrates how specific optical devices developed in the nineteenth century position the body so that "it is at once a spectator, a subject of empirical research and observation, and an element of machine production" (112). Obviously, this resonates with the discourse under consideration here. For an attempt to combine Crary's historical analysis with Lacan's ahistorical theory of the subject as an optical structure, see Silverman 1996:133–37.

Chapter 5

1. Mr. Young was deceased by the time I began this research.

2. The Youngs were active collectors of many types of artifacts other than the implements in the fence: railroad memorabilia, antique bottles, commemorative ceramics, glass and ceramic insulators, and barbed wire types, to name a few. Their collection of Wyoming license plates hangs on a wall at the county courthouse. Most of these collections are displayed throughout the Youngs' home, on shelves, in cabinets, and in museum-like display cases. In fact, their basement is something of a vernacular museum. In the past they opened their displays to tour groups (e.g., Boy Scout troops) and even provided a museum-like signature book.

3. Although certainly unusual and unlike anything in the immediate vicinity, the Youngs' fence actually resembles other folk sculptural endeavors to be found all over the country, some of which have been documented by scholars. For instance Red Rosemond's "home museum" of artfully displayed ranch implements has much in common with the fence, including the importance of the "scavenger hunt" process through which the artifacts were gathered (Hufford, Hunt, and Zeitlin 1987:63–64). Even more similar is the work of Gus Rosebrook, a retired rancher who assembled a vernacular museum of occupational memorabilia. Like the Youngs, he arranged his objects into panels and welded them together into gates and fences. An example of his work held in the Hemphill Collection at the National Museum of American Art displays a striking resemblance to the Youngs' fence panels (Hartigan 1990:618–19).

4. Mrs. Young tells of many hours spent painting the fence, she on one side, Mr. Young on the other.

5. One could say, of course, that entropic displays create display value out of the "decay" of use value.

6. Of course it is possible for these forms of value to overlap, as when the completeness of a collection is itself one of the things on display.

7. As we will see in later chapters, display environments may have visual practices as part of their "content" as well. The Wyoming Territorial Park, our destination in the next chapter, is "about" acts of looking, as well as being the setting for visual enactment.

8. Since I completed my fieldwork on Mr. Dellos's yard display he has, unfortunately, been forced by ill health to move from this property into town. I will, however, observe the convention of the ethnographic present to speak about his productions at the time I was documenting them. As so often with personal vernacular expressions such as his, the fate of Mr. Dellos's display environment is decidedly uncertain.

9. There is actually a group of closely related plants belonging to the genus *Helianthus* that constitute the relevant reference here. These include *H. pumilus*, *H. annuus*, and *H. petiolaris*—the Bush Sunflower, Kansas Sunflower, and Prairie Sunflower.

10. In material culture study the analysis of surface treatment has often been subordinated to matters of formal pattern and design, materials and construction processes, and functional considerations. In the reading of display environments as embodiments of visual discourse the artifactual surface takes on a particular significance.

Chapter 6

1. The original name was simply the Wyoming Territorial Park, and this is the designation I will use to refer to the whole site. Feeling that this was not sufficiently descriptive, the operators recently made the change. The reference to the "Old West" is indicative of the Park's struggle to develop an identity consonant with categories familiar to mass tourism.

2. Though not in common parlance, the adjective "carceral" has currency in Foucault-inspired theoretical considerations of disciplinary practices in penal institutions. My use of the word is meant to invoke that context and to suggest that disciplinary discourses associated with incarceration are being drawn upon and reframed at the WTP.

3. The original construction consisted of what is now the north wing and a projection to the west for a kitchen. In 1889 the central section and south wing were added, giving the whole structure the rather monumental symmetry we see today (Banner Assoc. 1988).

4. I served in the capacity of university representative from spring 1992 until spring 1995. The present tense of my account refers mainly to that period.

5. Tellingly, a recent reorganization of Wyoming state government placed the Department of Archives, Museums and Cultural Resources under the aegis of the Commerce Department.

6. Of course the Wild West and cowboy heritage of Wyoming is heavily marketed through such things as the resort and dude ranch industry and Cheyenne's annual Frontier Days Rodeo, a major tourist event. But nothing else in the state involves the same mix of elements as the Territorial Park.

7. It was only five years from incorporation of the WTPC to the grand opening of the Park.

8. As indicated in the Wood Bay plan, the frontier law and order theme would become central to the site's image. The Park made a play for and secured the U. S. Marshals Museum, which was looking for a home. Although its exhibits

include material on marshals in the Old West, much of its space is devoted to laudatory representations of the modern U. S. Marshals Service.

9. One of their characteristic productions is the interactive show at the Aegis Theater in NAUTICUS, the National Maritime Museum located in Norfolk, Virginia. Using a combination of large-screen video, live actors, and three-dimensional design elements, the "immersive" show places the audience in the command center of a naval warship at the moment a "sneak attack" has been launched against the United States. The audience participates in making command decisions.

10. To call it a strategy may suggest a greater degree of conscious design than was actually involved. Although there was considerable discussion about not making the interpretive program too focused on negative or "inappropriate themes," the mix of elements that characterizes the Park's tone is hard to attach to a single source. Its "authorship" is dispersed along complex strands of cultural history.

11. More than a few theme parks with Old West components include stage shows that display the tone I am referring to here. The standard show at the WTP's Horsebarn Dinner Theater is a "western melodrama" that is very much in keeping with this tradition.

12. The original scripting for the dinner theater was provided by Rouse.

13. There are a number of off-season special programs at the Park—wine tasting, the Halloween Haunted Prison, etc.—but I am mainly concerned with the four months of summer programming, from early May to September.

14. In 1994 I served as the humanities scholar for a state humanities grant to develop a photo exhibit and readers' theater presentation related to this event. One might say the ghost of this project now makes regular appearances in the entertainment programming at the Park.

15. See, for example, Cecil B. deMille's *The Plainsman* (1936), where Jean Arthur portrays her as a rambunctious love interest of Gary Cooper's Wild Bill Hickok. Larry McMurtry offers a characteristically offbeat portrayal of Calamity Jane in his novel *Buffalo Girls* (1990). Gender confusion is an important theme in this text, making Jane's competence in traditionally male pursuits and her putative romance with Hickok decidedly ambiguous. It goes without saying that this motif is not invoked at the WTP. Nor is it mentioned that the nickname "Calamity" probably refers to her contribution to the spread of venereal disease while working as a prostitute.

16. Once again, it would be a mistake to see this as a planned development. The emergence of these two figures as Park icons has occurred over time through that oddly intangible but material process that seems to produce pattern redundancy without intentional agency.

17. This characterization of Antiquity might seem in conflict with Guy Debord's famous designation of *our* era as "the society of the spectacle" (Debord 1983 [1967]). However, it is the saturation of the world with commodified images, the "commodity as spectacle," that Debord finds distinctive of our historical moment, quite a different thing from the ritualized spectacles that express divine and royal authority in Antiquity.

18. A distinct field of critical museum studies, drawing heavily on cultural studies methods, has emerged and become highly elaborated over the last decade. For some examples of work in this vein, see the following: Sherman and Rogoff 1994; Hooper-Greenhill 1992; Karp, Kreamer, and Lavine 1992; Karp and Lavine 1991; and Pearce 1989.

19. The phenomenon of the consciously reflexive or "meta-museum" is, one suspects, an increasingly common feature in contemporary museology. When, for instance, the museum gallery is itself consciously presented as a work of art (Martin 1995), or when museum display is not merely an end in itself but becomes a metaphor for other things (Rugoff 1995), we have kinds of reflexive play going on. The reflexivity of the restored Territorial Prison is certainly not self-conscious in these ways, but rather arises willy-nilly out of the dissonance between the two distinct visual systems that overlap in this institution.

20. Though not a historian by training, as the representative of academe on the WTPC Board I was automatically positioned as an advocate of "authenticity" and the educational mission of the Park. In this way I was locked into the prevailing binary arrangement of management deliberations: entertainment, marketing, commerce, versus education, historical accuracy, and interpretive complexity. This conceptual dichotomy limited the Board's ability to imagine radically different ways of proceeding.

21. Although the video no longer plays at the Park, it has been used for other promotional purposes and the audio portion may be heard on a tape cassette available at the gift shop.

22. A picture of Paul Newman in his role as Butch Cassidy hangs next to this kiosk.

23. In their recent ethnographic study of Colonial Williamsburg, Richard Handler and Eric Gable reveal how that august institution persists in telling familiar, conventionalized cultural narratives, despite its infrastructure of professional historical expertise and critical sophistication (Handler and Gable 1997).

24. Here is one of those ironies of a prison turned into a museum. In a different way and to different ends, though equally disciplinary in its effects, the penal institution's tight control over movement and sight is "reenacted" in the tightly controlled museum experience. On museums as disciplinary institutions, see Hooper-Greenhill 1992:167–90, and 1989.

25. Two of the video stations, the ones already mentioned as devoted to Cassidy and Boswell, are built in and so remain in their original locations. However, at this writing the others have been moved to a common space because their use had tended to disrupt the guided tours. Even with this "editing" of the original display sequence, the story I am identifying here continues to dominate the ideological program.

26. An even more telling example is to be seen in a "hidden" technological system at the Prison museum. Wired into the building is a computer controlled network of motion sensors connected to lighting and audio speakers. This system can be programmed so that when a visitor enters a particular space a sensor will activate special illumination and a relevant audio tape.

27. This seems to be a slip. McDonald was warden during the period after Wyoming statehood, at which time the Prison was operated on a lessee system. It was during the territorial period that cheap convict labor was contracted out to local industries such as the brickyards. The proceeds from this work went to defray prison expenses. In terms of my argument, the apparent error in historical sequence is beside the point. The fact that the motif of economic and entrepreneurial motives is introduced at this juncture is the important thing.

28. The lower level of the central section of the Prison (nos. 20–24), the last area one visits, has undergone more changes than any other space, but Park promotions, commerce, and entrepreneurship have been abiding elements. Along

with the recreated warden's office, this section was the location of the preview center and, for a time, of the Park's most expensive gift shop.

29. The events leading to her incarceration suggest extenuating circumstances. She and her husband were involved in a shoot-out with a party of seven men who waylaid them (Frye 1990:170). Her prison profile describes her as a housekeeper (that is, a homemaker) and a woman of "fair education" who displayed good behavior while in prison. In the roster of women presented at the WTP she seems to fit somewhere between the society matrons and Calamity Jane. That working class women and women of color are entirely absent from the WTP interpretive program is notable. Minnie is probably the most recognizably middle class woman to have served time at the Prison.

30. The current Wyoming State Penitentiary is located in Rawlins, farther west along I-80. The old prison building there has also been opened as a museum, though in this case the structure has largely been left as it was when in use. The effect is far more disturbing than anything at the WTP.

31. Here again, Lee Clark Mitchell's argument concerning Wister's anxiety over these historical developments is apposite (1996:113–19, and see above, Chapter 4, n. 11).

Chapter 7

1. In an essay on special effects in science fiction films, Scott Bukatman refers to Spielberg's "typically slack-jawed observers" (1995:272), and to the fact that his films are much concerned with spectatorship. The image of characters "staring upwards" is a common Spielberg motif (272, n. 34). This interesting essay is of general relevance to the issues addressed in the present study.

2. Robert Torry has offered a subtle Lacanian reading of Spielberg's film, connecting the desire seemingly implanted from heaven with the mechanism of modern consumption (Torry 1991:191–92).

3. There is much more to be said about this film's postcolonial implications. For one thing, Spielberg has acknowledged the influence of John Ford's classic western film *The Searchers*, where the Indian (Scar) is a hostile, alien Other who has spirited away a white child. The theme of compulsion to confront an alien force, in this case for revenge, drives the plot of Ford's film. In *Close Encounters* Spielberg plays a complex game of liberal reinscription and displacement that bears examination in terms of postcolonial containment.

4. The origin of the name Devils Tower is something of a mystery and no doubt involves multiple factors. One of these is certainly the nineteenth-century penchant for perceiving elements of the western landscape in either paradisiacal or infernal terms.

5. The original of this image is a painting that hangs above the fireplace in the visitor center. It has been reproduced in poster format and as a postcard.

6. William Henry Jackson's photographs of Devils Tower were displayed in the Wyoming exhibit at the Exposition. It was in this form that the Tower first became known to the general American public (Gunderson 1988:107).

7. These are National Park Service estimates based on registration cards submitted by climbers. The nature of this registration system may lead to some exaggeration of actual climber numbers (Hanson and Moore 1993:64).

8. Perhaps the inaugural date of these developments should be pushed back to 1981. Like several other sacred sites in the Black Hills, Devils Tower was "occu-

pied" in that year by members of the American Indian Movement (AIM), who maintained a camp for several months on the grounds of the National Monument. The encampment was subjected to a number of acts of harassment. Since 1984 the Sundance has been performed with the permission and cooperation of the National Park Service, under the mandate of the American Indian Religious Freedom Act (AIRFA) of 1978. Currently, Lakota groups from the Pine Ridge Reservation appear to be the most active religious practitioners at Devils Tower/Bear Lodge (Hanson and Moore 1993:8–10). It is quite possible that Native American religious observances have been continuous at this site, though performed secretly until 1984.

9. Ethnographic information on current religious practices at Bear Lodge indicate that the performance of ceremonies do not depend upon having the geological formation itself in view. I should perhaps add the obvious point that of course Native American visionary spirituality has been appropriated in many ways by the processes of commodification, and it is by no means only Euro-Americans who participate in this process. And by the same token rock climbing is fully caught up in the elaborate webs of advanced consumer recreation. Nevertheless, at their cores as visual experience, neither Native American spiritual practice nor the physical activity of rock climbing are easily subsumed under the discourse of commodity optics.

10. A first effort at cultural programming occurred in 1995. It included an eclectic range of presentations and performances: a living history depiction of Theodore Roosevelt, an American Indian flutist, Indian dancing and crafts, cowboy poetry, an explanation of sweat lodges, and a classical guitar performance. An estimated nine hundred visitors attended these programs (*Casper-Star Tribune* Dec. 17, 1995).

11. The determination of a range of "management" alternatives, ostensibly based on input from public forums, professional experts, implementers of the policy, etc., is a crucial step in the management process. It sets the parameters of the final decision and usually pre-inscribes the middle range of alternatives as the set of desirable outcomes.

12. As an example of the last of these, a contentious panel discussion regarding the Devils Tower controversy occurred at a fall 1997 symposium on concepts of space and place in American culture (American Heritage Center, University of Wyoming). This was something of a small media event in itself.

13. I hope it is obvious that I have not been talking about conscious management policies and strategies, but rather something that operates at an entirely different level of discourse. Most site managers themselves certainly operate from a good faith belief in the need for and possibility of resolution through rational, democratic procedures.

14. I would suggest as well that through its conceptual framing Devils Tower has also been rendered a rather pure embodiment of the basic semiotic principle of binary difference, a metaphor for abstract verticality against the horizontal plane.

Works Cited

Alter, Robert
    1981   *The Art of Biblical Narrative.* New York: Basic Books.
Banner Associates, Inc.
    1988   "The Wyoming Territorial Penitentiary: Historic Structure Report." Report to Wyoming State Archives, Museums, and Historical Department. n.p.
Berger, John
    1972   *Ways of Seeing.* London: British Broadcasting Company; Hamondsworth: Penguin.
Berkhofer, Robert. F., Jr.
    1978   *The White Man's Indian: Images of the American Indian from Columbus to the Present.* New York: Vintage Books.
Boime, Albert
    1991   *The Magisterial Gaze: Manifest Destiny and American Landscape Painting, c. 1830–1865.* Washington, D.C.: Smithsonian Institution Press.
Bold, Christine
    1987   *Selling the Wild West: Popular Western Fiction, 1860–1960.* Bloomington: Indiana University Press.
Brunvand, Jan Harold
    1986   *The Mexican Pet: More "New" Urgan Legends and Some Old Favorites.* New York: W.W. Norton.
Bryson, Norman
    1988   "The Gaze in the Expanded Field." In Foster, ed., pp. 87–108.
Bryson, Norman, Michael Ann Holly, and Keith Moxley, eds.
    1994   *Visual Culture: Images of Interpretation.* Hanover, N.H.: Wesleyan University Press.
Buck-Morss, Susan
    1989   *The Dialectics of Seeing: Walter Benjamin and the Arcades Project.* Cambridge, Mass.: MIT Press.
Bukatman, Scott
    1995   "The Artifactual Infinite: Special Effects and the Sublime." In Cooke and Wollen, eds., pp. 255–89.
Clay, Grady
    1973   *Close-Up: How to Read the American City.* Chicago: University of Chicago Press.

Cooke, Lynne and Peter Wollen, eds.
1995   *Visual Display: Culture Beyond Appearances.* Seattle: Bay Press.
Crary, Jonathan
1990   *Techniques of the Observer: On Vision and Modernity in the Nineteenth Century.* Cambridge, Mass.: MIT Press.
Cutrer, Emily Fourmy
1993   "A Pragmatics of Seeing: James, Howells, and the Politics of Vision." In *American Iconology: New Approaches to Nineteenth-Century Art and Literature,* ed. David C. Miller, pp. 259–75. New Haven, Conn.: Yale University Press.
Debord, Guy
1983 [1967] *Society of the Spectacle.* Detroit: Black and Red.
Dorst, John D.
1989   *The Written Suburb: An American Site, An Ethnographic Dilemma.* Philadelphia: University of Pennsylvania Press.
FCMP/FONSI
1995   "Final Climbing Management Plan/Finding of No Significant Impact, Devils Tower National Monument." U.S. Department of the Interior, Rocky Mountain Region.
Foster, Hal, ed.
1988   *Vision and Visuality.* Seattle: Bay Press.
Foucault, Michel
1977[1975] *Discipline and Punish: The Birth of the Prison.* New York: Vintage Books.
Friedberg, Anne
1993   *Window Shopping: Cinema and the Postmodern.* Berkeley: University of California Press.
Frye, Elnora
1990   *Atlas of Wyoming Outlaws at the Territorial Penitentiary.* Laramie, Wyo.: Jelm Mountain Publications.
Gamman, Lorraine and Margaret Marshment, eds.
1989   *The Female Gaze: Women as Viewers of Popular Culture.* Seattle: The Real Comet Press.
Gardner, Mark L.
1985   "The Western Photographs of Owen Wister." M.A. thesis, University of Wyoming.
Glassie, Henry
1972   "Folk Art." In *Folklore and Folklife: An Introduction,* ed. Richard M. Dorson, pp. 253–93. Chicago: University of Chicago Press.
Goetzmann, William H.
1966   *Exploration and Empire: The Explorer and the Scientist in the Winning of the American West.* New York: W.W. Norton.
Goetzmann, William H. and William N. Goetzmann
1986   *The West of the Imagination.* New York: W.W. Norton.
Goodyear, Frank
1996   "The Narratives of Sitting Bull's Surrender: Bailey, Dix & Mead's Photographic Western." In *Dressing in Feathers: The Construction of the Indian in American Popular Culture,* ed. S. Elizabeth Bird, pp. 29–43. Boulder, Colo.: Westview Press.

Greenfield, Verni
    1986   *Making Do or Making Art: A Study of American Recycling.* Ann Arbor: University of Michigan Press.

Gunderson, Mary Alice
    1988   *Devils Tower: Stories in Stone.* Glendo,Wyo.: High Plains Press.

Hales, Peter B.
    1988   *William Henry Jackson and the Transformation of the American Landscape.* Philadelphia: Temple University Press.

Handler, Richard and Eric Gable
    1997   *The New History in an Old Museum: Creating the Past and Colonial Williamsburg.* Durham, N.C.: Duke University Press.

Hanson, Jeffery R. and David Moore
    1993   "Ritual and Recreational Perception and Use at Devils Tower National Monument, an Applied Ethnographic Study." Unpublished study for the National Park Service, Rocky Mountain Region.

Hanson, Jeffrey R. and Sally Chirinos
    1991   "Ethnographic Overview and Assessment of Devils Tower National Monument." Unpublished study for the National Park Service, Rocky Mountain Region.

Hartigan, Linda Roscoe
    1990   *Made with Passion: The Hemphill Folk Art Collection in the National Museum of American Art.* Washington, D.C.: Smithsonian Institution.

Hooper-Greenhill, Eilean
    1992   *Museums and the Shaping of Knowledge.* New York: Routledge.
    1989   "The Museum in Disciplinary Society." In Pearce, ed., pp. 61–72.

Hufford, Mary, Marjorie Hunt, and Steven Zeitlin
    1987   *The Grand Generation: Memory, Mastery, Legacy.* Seattle and Washington, D.C.: University of Washington Press and the Smithsonian Institution.

Hyde, Anne Farrar
    1990   *An American Vision: Far Western Landscape and National Culture, 1820–1920.* New York: New York University Press.

Jackson, Zig
    1995   "Social Identity: A View from Within." *Aperature* 139: 34–38.

Jay, Martin
    1993   *Downcast Eyes: The Denigration of Vision in Twentieth-Century French Thought.* Berkeley: University of California Press.
    1988   "Scopic Regimes of Modernity." In Foster, ed., pp. 3–23.

Jenks, Chris, ed.
    1995   *Visual Culture.* London: Routledge.

Jones, Michael Owen
    1989   *Craftsman of the Cumberlands: Tradition and Creativity.* Lexington: University Press of Kentucky.

Karp, Ivan and Steven D. Lavine, eds.
    1991   *Exhibiting Cultures: The Poetics and Politics of Museum Display.* Washington, D.C.: Smithsonian Institution Press.

Karp, Ivan, Christine Mullen Kreamer, and Steven D. Lavine, eds.
    1992   *Musuems and Communities: The Politics of Public Culture.* Washington, D.C.: Smithsonian Institution Press.

Kirshenblatt-Gimblett, Barbara
1991   "Objects of Ethnography." In Karp and Lavine, eds., pp. 386–
            443.
Krauss, Rosalind E.
1993.   *The Optical Unconscious.* Cambridge, Mass.: MIT Press.
Lacan, Jacques
1981 [1973] *The Four Fundamental Concepts of Psycho-Analysis.* Ann Arbor: Uni-
            versity of Michigan Press.
Lawrence, Amy
1995   "From Fox Hounds to Farming: The History of the Douglas-
            Willen, Sartoris Ranch, and the Wyoming Central Land and Im-
            provement Company." M.A. thesis, University of Wyoming.
Levin, David Micheal, ed.
1993   *Modernity and the Hegemony of Vision.* Berkeley: University of Cali-
            fornia Press.
Lutz, Catherine A. and Jane L. Collins
1993   *Reading National Geographic.* Chicago: University of Chicago Press.
Lyotard, Jean-François
1977   *Les TRANSformateurs DUchamp.* Paris: Galilée. Trans. as *Duchamp's
            Transformers,* trans. Ian McLeod. Venice, Calif.: Lapis Press, 1990.
MacCannell, Dean
1989 [1976] *The Tourist: A New Theory of the Leisure Class.* New York: Schocken
            Books.
McMurtry, Larry
1995   *Dead Man's Walk.* New York: Simon and Schuster.
1990   *Buffalo Girls.* New York: Simon and Schuster.
1985   *Lonesome Dove.* New York: Simon and Schuster.
Martin, Jean-Hubert
1995   "The *Musée Sentimental* of Daniel Spoerri." In Cooke and Wollen,
            eds., pp. 54–67.
Mattison, Ray H.
1973   "Devils Tower National Monument, a History." Devils Tower Natu-
            ral History Association pamphlet, n.p.
Melville, Stephen and Bill Readings, eds.
1995   *Vision and Textuality.* Durham, N.C.: Duke University Press.
Metz, Christian
1982   *The Imaginary Signifier: Psychoanalysis and the Cinema.* Trans. Celia
            Britton, et al. Bloomington: Indiana University Press.
Mitchell, Lee Clark
1996   *Westerns: Making the Man in Fiction and Film.* Chicago: University
            of Chicago Press.
Mitchell, Timothy
1988   *Colonising Egypt.* Cambridge: Cambridge University Press.
Moore, John Hartwell
1974   "A Study in Religious Symbolism Among the Cheyenne Indians."
            Doctoral dissertation, New York University.
Mowitt, John
1992   *Text: The Genealogy of an Antidisciplinary Object.* Durham, N.C.:
            Duke University Press.
Mulvey, Laura
1989   *Visual and Other Pleasures.* Bloomington: Indiana University Press.

Munn, Debra
    1989   *Ghosts on the Range: Eerie True Tales of Wyoming.* Boulder, Colo.: Pruett Publishing Co.

Payne, Darwin
    1985   *Owen Wister: Chronicler of the West, Gentleman of the East.* Dallas: Southern Methodist University Press.

Pearce, Susan M., ed.
    1989   *Musuem Studies in Material Culture.* Leicester: Leicester University Press.

Pomeroy, Earl Spencer
    1957   *In Search of the Golden West: The Tourist in Western America.* New York: Alfred A. Knopf.

Raban, Jonathan
    1996   *Bad Land: An American Romance.* New York: Vintage Books.

Riebsame, William E. and James Robb, eds.
    1997   *Atlas of the New West: Portrait of a Changing Region.* New York: W.W. Norton.

Ringe, Donald A.
    1971   *The Pictorial Mode: Space and Time in the Art of Bryant, Irving, and Cooper.* Lexington: University of Kentucky Press.

Roberts, Phil, David L. Roberts, and Steven L. Roberts
    1994   *Wyoming Almanac.* Laramie,Wyo.: Skyline West Press.

Robinson, Charles S.
    n.d.   "Geology of Devils Tower National Monument." U. S. Department of the Interior pamphlet.

Rugoff, Ralph
    1995   "Beyond Belief: The Museum as Metaphor." In Cooke and Wollen, eds., pp. 68–81.

Sandweiss, Martha A.
    1993   "Views and Reviews: Western Art and Western History." In *Under an Open Sky: Rethinking America's Western Past,* ed. William Cronon, George Miles, and Jay Gitlin, pp. 185–202. New York: W.W. Norton.

Schivelbusch, Wolfgang
    1986[1977] *The Railway Journey: The Industrialization of Time and Space in the 19th Century.* Berkeley: University of California Press.

Schlereth, Thomas
    1990   *Cultural History and Material Culture: Everyday Life, Landscape, Musuems.* Ann Arbor, Mich.: UMI Research Press.

Sears, John F.
    1989   *Sacred Places: American Tourist Attractions in the Nineteenth Century.* New York: Oxford University Press.

Seelye, John
    1988   "Introduction" and "Explanatory Notes." In Wister, *The Virginian,* pp. vii–xxxiii, 431–50.

Sherman, Daniel J. and Irit Rogoff, eds.
    1994   *Musuem Culture: Histories, Discourses, Spectacles.* Minneapolis: University of Minnesota Press.

Silverman, Kaja
    1996   *The Threshold of the Visible World.* New York: Routledge.

Slotkin, Richard
1992   *Gunfighter Nation: The Myth of the Frontier in Twentieth Century America.* New York: Atheneum.
1985   *Fatal Environment: The Myth of the Frontier in the Age of Industrialization.* New York: HarperCollins.
Stacey, Jackie
1994   *Star Gazing: Hollywood Cinema and Female Spectatorship.* London: Routledge.
Starr, Eileen F.
1992   *Architecture in the Cowboy State, 1849–1940.* Glendo,Wyo.: High Plains Press.
Stewart, Susan
1984   *On Longing: Narratives of the Miniature, the Gigantic, the Souvenir, the Collection.* Baltimore: Johns Hopkins University Press.
Toelken, Barre
1979   *The Dynamics of Folklore.* Boston: Houghton Mifflin.
Tompkins, Jane
1992   *West of Everything: The Inner Life of Westerns.* New York: Oxford University Press.
Torgovnik, Marianna
1990   *Gone Primitive: Savage Intellects, Modern Lives.* Chicago: University of Chicago Press.
Torry, Robert
1991   "Politics and Parousia in *Close Encounters of the Third Kind.*" *American Literature and Film* 19: 188–96.
Twain, Mark
1985[1872] *Roughing It.* New York: Penguin Classics.
Urry, John
1990   *The Tourist Gaze: Leisure and Travel in Contemporary Society.* London: Sage Publications.
Walker, John A. and Sarah Chaplin
1997   *Visual Culture: An Introduction.* Manchester: Manchester University Press.
Wiencek, Henry
1987   *The World of Lego Toys.* New York: Harry N. Abrams, Inc.
Williams, Raymond
1977   *Marxism and Literature.* Oxford: Oxford Unversity Press.
Wilson, David Scofield
1987   "The Rattlesnake." In *American Wildlife in Symbol and Story,* ed. Angus K. Gilllespie and Jay Mechling, pp. 41–72. Knoxville: University of Tennessee Press.
Wister, Owen
1988 [1902] *The Virginian, a Horseman of the Plains.* New York: Penguin.
1987 [1895] "The Evolution of the Cow-Puncher." In *Owen Wister's West: Selected Articles,* ed. Robert Murray Davis, pp. 33–53. Albuquerque: University of New Mexico Press.
1979 [1936] "Old Yellowstone Days." In *Old Yellowstone Days,* ed. Paul Schullery, pp. 67–83. Niwot: University Press of Colorado.
1958   *Owen Wister Out West: His Letters and Journals,* ed. Fanny Kemble Wister. Chicago: University of Chicago Press.
1928   "Bad Medicine." In *When West Was West.* The Writings of Owen Wister, vol. 6. New York: Macmillan.

Index

Acknowledgments

A book that has been as long in preparation as this one inevitably garners assistance from many quarters. I want to acknowledge with much gratitude the help I have gotten from the numerous friends and colleagues who provided material and insights. Paul Fees, Paul Flesher, Rebecca Menlove, Bruce Richardson, Robert Torry, and Donald Warder all in one way or another made contributions, for which I am grateful. My thanks as well to my colleagues in American Studies at the University of Wyoming. Along with creating an atmosphere conducive to scholarly work, program director Eric Sandeen made it possible for me to shuffle my teaching schedule as I was completing the manuscript. Although just arrived on our faculty, Frieda Knobloch was generously willing to read some of the text in its late stages. Terri Given provided every kind of administrative support, and always with good cheer. Perhaps most important, I owe a great deal to our American Studies graduate students. Through seminar discussions and individual conversations many of them have shaped the ideas and arguments presented here.

Some more remote colleagues and friends also deserve mention. Patricia Smith, my editor at University of Pennsylvania Press, has stayed with this project over quite a few years now. Her patience and encouragement have been invaluable. Thanks as well to Alison Anderson and the other members of the Penn Press staff who assisted in the publication process. Michael Ann Williams improved Chapter 3 with many helpful comments. Barbara Kirshenblatt-Gimblett offered perceptive suggestions during a walk-through of the prison museum discussed in Chapter 6. Paul Stoller's observations about the manuscript as a whole gave me a general direction for revisions. Most especially I want to thank Christine Bold, who made detailed comments about all aspects of this work. She has saved me from both infelicities of wording and inconsistencies of argument, and the final product is considerably improved through her good offices. Needless to say, whatever shortcomings remain in this text are all my own doing.

I also want to offer a special word of thanks to Mrs. Edna Young and Mr. and Mrs. Jake Dellos, my main informants for the material in Chapter 5. In my opinion Mrs. Young and Mr. Dellos are artists of a high order, although I doubt they think of themselves in that way. I hope this book brings at least a bit of attention to their work. It certainly deserves it.

The staff of the American Heritage Center at the University of Wyoming provided able assistance in my work on Owen Wister's journals. Thanks are particularly due to Rick Ewig in this regard. Rick Walters, also on staff at the AHC, provided his expertise in producing the final prints of the illustrations that appear here. He has done a remarkable job of turning my feeble photographic efforts into legible images and I am much obliged. The University of Wyoming Photo Services also contributed to production of the illustrations. I am especially grateful to the American Studies Program for funding this part of my work. The Buffalo Bill Historical Center of Cody, Wyoming provided the photograph of Buffalo Bill and Sitting Bull that appears in Chapter 1 and on the cover.

I have no doubt left out some who have contributed to this project as it has moved along its meandering way, and to them I apologize. Last but far from least, my loving thanks to Holly, Jesse, and Emma, who have put up with me through this process, and done so in much better humor than I had any right to expect. The dedication is small recompense.

*   *   *

An earlier version of Chapter 7 appears in *Postcolonial America*, ed. C. Richard King (Urbana: University of Illinois Press).